The Bumper Book of Football

First published in Great Britain in 2007 by

Quercus
21 Bloomsbury Square
London
WC1A 2NS

A CIP catalogue record for this book is available from the British Library

ISBN 1 84724 137 9
ISBN-13 978 1 84724 137 5

Printed and bound in Portugal

Designed by Two Associates

10 9 8 7 6 5 4 3 2 1

The
Bumper
Book
of
Football

HUNTER DAVIES

Quercus

CONTENTS

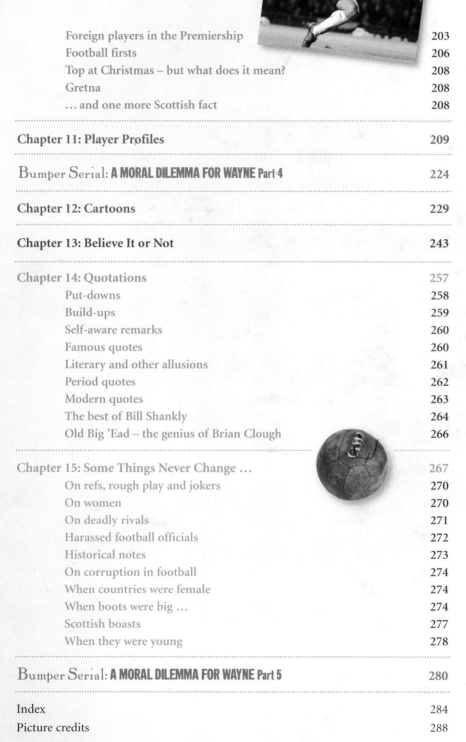

INTRODUCTION

This book is not an exercise in nostalgia. Certainly not. Even though it includes a lot about the history of the game, past events and great players, it is also bang up to date, about football being played now, covering our current stars and leading clubs, as relevant and topical as any other book about football has ever been. It's just that its format harks back to an earlier age.

When I was a lad, tra la, we had loads of football annuals which covered a vast array of topics – great players of yesterday, interviews with present stars, down memory lane stories, jokes and cartoons, facts and figures. There was so much to READ in these books, hours of fun and knowledge and amusement for healthy boys and girls.

There were also magazines like *Charlie Buchan's Football Monthly*, which first came out in 1951. They were absolutely crammed with excellent stuff, proper articles, well-researched features, good interviews, plus fun.

Now, when I look at present-day footer publications, say like *Match*, which is very successful and obviously appeals to many young football fans of today, brought up on computers and TV and text messaging, my first reaction is always the same – what is there to READ? It seems to be all captions, often just word bubbles slapped onto a glossy photo of a superstar, as if they fear the concentration level of their readers is 30 seconds. It does have some stats, match facts, which take a bit longer to pore over, but essentially it's one-dimensional, a quick disposal fix for the modern footer fan.

Pretty thin gruel, it seems to me, with no richness or depth or roughage. Modern football programmes also tend to be photographic and glossy, and heavily dependent on keeping in with sponsors, merchandizing and commercial interests. There is little context, football is set only in the present. There's no past, no explanation of what came before, how it all developed. Football is considered as transient as a computer game.

So I thought I'd offer today's football fans, old and young, the sort of publication I used to enjoy many years ago. It should bring back memories for older fans of bygone heroes and amusements, but also help younger football fans to understand where it's all come from, that they are part of a great tradition of football following, which now goes back some 150 years. It's meant to be informative and fun, classic and contemporary, old as well as modern, as the old Bumper books tried to be.

These publications, from the 1950s and 1960s, and even more so from the 1930s, could be naïve and optimistic, didn't rubbish our stars, accuse them of being money-grabbing mercenaries, nor were they cynical about our great game. And I've decided not to go down that road either. So sex romps, bungs and wags do not feature in this book.

One of the many attractions of football is that it links all ages, all nationalities, men and women, boys and girls, old and young, all levels of brains and education. It has an equalizing effect. Our opinions, feelings, memories are as valid as any other football fan's. This book is for all of us, all fans, everywhere ...

Hunter Davies

London, July 2007

1. How to be
a footballer

Making it in football

It's a pretty natural desire, for any healthy boy or girl, to want to play football. Not just because these days you can end up very wealthy, get seen on television, get asked for your autograph, but because actually, it's jolly good fun, playing football.

You don't have to have any specific physique. You can be tall or small, plumpish or weedy. There's no need for much gear or equipment, or even space and facilities. Or even other people. Have ball, find wall, away you go. (Perhaps not in your bedroom, though, unless you have a soft ball, or an even softer mum and dad.)

That's been one of the joys of playing football these last 150 years or so, since football as we know it got itself organized – anyone can have a go. And it's one reason why football is now the most popular game in the whole world. The other reason is that football, played properly, combines artistry, skill and technique, wonderful to take part in, beautiful to behold. When played properly.

In theory, it couldn't be easier to be a footballer than it is today, despite the fact that many school sports fields have closed and not every school has a proper football team, the way they all used to. But the actual teaching of football is much better than it has ever been, whether you want to play for fun or you have a serious desire to become a professional.

If all you want is to improve your football and get some sort of proper coaching, there are now hundreds of coaching courses available, many of them held in the school holidays. You will have to pay for them, of course, but many are attached to real, professional clubs, so the standard is high.

It's hard to work out total numbers, but counting all types of soccer schools and courses, by professional clubs and other bodies, there are probably around one million boys and girls every year in Britain who are receiving some sort of football coaching. (So why is England rubbish at World Cups? Ah, if only we knew.)

If, however, you hope to take it up professionally, rather than just have fun and improve your skills, then in England and Wales you have to join an Academy or a Centre of Excellence attached to one of the professional league clubs. (In Scotland and Ireland, there are similar systems, but not as many.) Don't worry. Just wait. They will come to you – if by the age of seven or eight you have shown amazing, exceptional skills and promise. In fact, they will be banging on your front door. The scouting systems of our major clubs are now enormous. You have, of course, to be playing in some sort of team. They'll find it hard to know about your incredible talents if all you've been doing is kicking a rubber ball around your own bedroom.

Almost all school teams and youth club teams, pub teams and local district teams will have some sort of semi-professional representative watching their games, looking out for talent. He or she will tip off a professional club, should they think they have spotted a star of the future.

Opposite **Footballers come in all shapes and sizes – strong or weedy, thin or plump, small or (in the case of Peter Crouch) really quite tall ...**

At seven or eight, you might then be invited by a professional club to be a pre-Academy member, which is an unofficial way of the club giving you some after-school training without any forms being signed. Then, at nine, if all goes well, you will be signed on and become an official member of their Academy or Centre of Excellence.

The top Premier League and Football League Clubs – usually the best known and wealthiest – have Academies, which have the best facilities, while elsewhere they are called Centres of Excellence. But the object is much the same – to scout out any likely local boys from the age of nine, put them in a football 'school', which they attend after ordinary school or at weekends, teaching them how to be a footballer.

Each year they progress upwards to the next year, just as in an ordinary school. Or so they hope. Unlike an ordinary school, a good proportion gets chucked out each year. At 17, they are eligible to sign on and become a professional footballer.

There are around 9,000 boys at any one time attending such Academies and Centres attached to professional clubs in England. All of them have hopes of making it into the first team, or at least becoming a professional.

However, only around 10–15% of them will come through the system and be offered professional forms at the age of 17. So, even if you're one of the fortunate 9,000, your chance of becoming a pro is still very slim.

As for coming through and making it as a regular in the first team, that is even harder, especially in the Premiership. Over half of all the 17-year-olds who do get given professional forms drift down to non-leagues or out of football. By 21, only 25% are still professionals.

In the Premiership, on average only one or at most two make it as a first team regular every year. In the Premier League in 2005–06 there were 2,651 boys in their Academies. They get whittled down as they get older, so if you reckon

Above For any boy born a Brit, getting into Arsenal's first team (pictured here, the 2006-07 squad) can be a bit hard. For the last few seasons, it's often been totally filled by foreigners. Why not try Boro?

Opposite Apprentices in the old days knew their place, which was cleaning the first team's boots. Now they dream of cleaning their new motors…

on just 40 making it in the end, it means that only 2% of those fortunate enough to join a Premiership Academy will become a Premiership player.

If your fantasy is to play for Arsenal or Chelsea, who these days always have a high proportion of foreign or bought players on their books, it is almost certain that it will remain a fantasy. However, if you sign up with Middlesborough's Academy, you might have a better chance. On the last game of the 2005–06 season, against Fulham, the 11 Boro players on the pitch, when the final whistle blew, had all come through Boro's Academy.

When the World Cup comes around in 2022, there will be 23 English boys in England's World Cup squad, none of whom any of us have heard of today. So why shouldn't one of them be you? After all, they have to come from somewhere. So, get out of your bedroom and join a team at once …

Apprentices

The term 'apprentice' is no longer used in football, not since the advent of Academies in 1997. Traditionally, from the beginning of professional football, most clubs had some informal way of finding and training young boys to become professionals, but it was a fairly haphazard and disorganized process and didn't start until they were 14 or 15 years old.

Before the Second World War, in the 1930s, likely looking boys, aged 15 or 16, would be hired as 'ground staff boys'. They would spend two years full-time with the club, were put into club digs with an experienced landlady and paid £2 a week.

Bill Nicholson, the famous manager of Spurs, joined that club as a ground staff boy in 1935. He remembered very little training, apart from Tuesday and Thursday afternoons, but a great deal of hard work. 'In the summer, from eight to five each day, I worked on painting the girders under the stands.'

In the 1960s and 1970s, by which time the term 'apprentice' was being used and the system was more structured, boys taken on at 15, or later 16 when the school-leaving age went up, were still expected to do some manual work, mainly around the dressing room of the first team, cleaning their boots or sweeping the floors.

The advent of Academies in 1997 has meant that boys are being associated with clubs at a much younger age – and without having to do any manual work, not even cleaning boots.

You can even join a club informally from the age of six and receive some training. 'When I was working at Southampton's Academy,' says Huw Jennings, who is Academies' Manager for the Premier League, 'I was once rung up by a father who wanted his son to be given a trial. It turned out he was aged three. We had to say no …'

Going professional: Academies and Centres of Excellence

The main difference between them is that Academies have stricter conditions, better facilities, more coaches and are normally associated with bigger, more affluent clubs.

In the 2006–07 season, 18 out of the 20 Premier League clubs had Academies, the exceptions being Portsmouth and Wigan, who had Centres of Excellence. Altogether there were 40 Academies, mostly in the top two divisions but also including Huddersfield Town and MK Dons in the Second Division.

At the same time, there were 47 Centres of Excellence – the only five members of the Football League without one were Accrington, Barnet, Hereford, Yeovil and Notts County.

The total number of boys, aged 9 to 18, in both Academies and Centres of Excellence in the Premiership and Football League in 2006 came to 8,700.

How Wayne Rooney did it

Wayne Rooney came through the Everton Academy, which he joined at the age of nine in 1995 when it was called a Centre of Excellence. He'd been spotted playing for a boys' team run by a local pub. Both Liverpool and Everton scouts offered him a trial. He went to Liverpool first, who then told him to come back for a second trial. Then he went to Everton – who were his boyhood team – and they immediately offered him a place at their Centre of Excellence.

He went for training three nights a week, on Monday, Wednesday and Friday after school from 5.00 p.m. to 6.30 p.m. There were around 15 other boys in his year – 140

in the Centre in all – who trained together, at Bellefield, Everton's training ground. On Saturdays, they would routinely play a game against a team of their age from another Academy in the North West.

(Football Association rules state that boys up to the age of 14 in these Academies must live within one hour's travelling time of the ground. Over 14, it can be one and a half hours. This is to save young boys, and their parents, from having to travel huge distances and also to prevent the big clubs from poaching all the best boys from all over the country.)

Wayne received reports at the end of each year, where his control, passing, stamina, strength, speed, positional sense and attitude were assessed and marked. In the early years, there were two or three other boys he thought were better than him,

Above **Wayne Rooney came through the Academy system at Everton, which he joined aged nine, and went on to win the Carling Cup in 2006 with Manchester United.**

FOOTBALL CLUB

(54)

RH/JMF

GOODISON PARK
LIVERPOOL L4 4EL
Tel. (Administration)
0151 330 2200
Fax 0151 523 9666
Tel. (Box Office)
0151 330 2300
Fax 0151 524 0550

March 1996

Wayne Rooney
28 Armill Road
Croxteth
L11 4TR
Liverpool

Dear Wayne,

Everton Football Club: Centre of Excellence

On behalf of Everton Football Club I am very pleased to be able to offer you a place at our Centre of Excellence for Season 1996/7.

The coaching staff have been very happy with your progress since joining us. As a consequence you will now form an important part of our special group of Centre of Excellence players and to this end you will need to set and maintain excellent examples to your fellow pupils at school and clubs. If you or your parents would at any time like to discuss your progress please contact me whenever it is convenient on 0151 228 3174.

May I request your assistance in completing the Centre of Excellence Registration Form enclosed and forward it by return of post in the enclosed stamped addressed envelope.

Yours sincerely,

RAY HALL
Youth Development Officer

Secretary
M.J. DUNFORD
Manager
J. ROYLE

Registered Number
36624, England

Main Sponsors

but as he progressed up through the years, some of them began to fall away, did not develop at the same rate as he did, or show the same discipline and dedication.

Around the age of 14, Wayne did have a difficult spell when he fell out with one coach and also developed pains in his knees, resulting in fluid on the knee, which had to be constantly drained. It turned out to be Osgood-Schlatters Disease, commonly known as growing pains, which can happen to teenage boys during a growth spurt. So, beware…

It wasn't until the age of 16 that Wayne began to realize he might be a special player. This was when, in his last term at school, Everton sought leave from the school for him to have more time at Everton. Until then, he had hopes of making it, but was still by no means certain he would.

Up to the age of 16, Academy and Centres boys cannot be paid, but their parents may get travelling expenses, depending on their situation. They also usually get several free tickets a year to watch the first team. There are always rumours of other,

Opposite **Wayne Rooney's letter from Everton's Centre of Excellence (later their Academy) when he was aged ten, letting him know how pleased they were with his progress.**

IF YOU WANT TO BE A FOOTBALLER, WHICH IS THE BEST MONTH TO BE BORN IN?

The list shows the number of Premiership first-team squad players born in each month of the year, and a player with a birthday that month.

1	October	Wayne Rooney (24th)	54
2	March	Didier Drogba (11th)	53
3=	August	Thierry Henry (17th)	52
3=	September	Sol Campbell (18th)	52
5	December	Michael Owen (14th)	51
6	February	Gary Neville (18th)	49
7	January	Jamie Carragher (28th)	42
8	May	Steven Gerrard (30th)	38
9	November	Joe Cole (8th)	34
10	July	Craig Bellamy (13th)	33
11	April	Aaron Lennon (16th)	31
12	June	Frank Lampard (20th)	29

hidden inducements, such as their parents receiving a car, holidays abroad or even a house, but of course these are always denied.

Wayne did indeed turn out to be exceptional and was playing for Everton's first team at 16 – while still technically a member of their Academy – before making his England debut at 17.

Wayne was the only one of his year at Everton to make it into the first team. Two others at 16 were upgraded to professionals, but didn't make the first team and are now playing for lower-league teams. (Wayne was, of course, exceptional – but the system is there to train all boys who show promise in the basic skills.)

How to be spotted

Obviously, scoring 23 goals in your school's 24–0 win over your deadly rivals, and doing it week after week, is likely to get you noticed.

But if you feel you have been overlooked, and yet you have tremendous hidden talents, and perhaps you live in an isolated part of the country with no proper teams to play for, you can request a trial with your local club. It's best to get a school teacher or some figure in authority to write on your behalf. Or even a parent or relation.

It probably won't work with Chelsea or Man Utd, approaching them out of the blue, but for clubs much lower down the leagues, if your letter is persuasive enough, they might invite you for a trial on one of their open days. Good luck, chums.

How to get ahead – get a name

It's noticeable how often football runs in families, how famous footballers often have fathers who were professional players, such as Frank Lampard (whose father, also called Frank, played for West Ham and England), Jamie Redknapp (son of former West Ham player and current Portsmouth manager Harry Redknapp) and Michael Owen (whose father played for Chester).

Nigel Clough, now a manager, who used to play for Nottingham Forest and Liverpool, is the son of the famous manager, Brian Clough. Sir Alex Ferguson's son Darren, now a manager, used to play for Manchester United and Wolves.

So, being born the son of a famous player will do nothing to harm your chances of making it in the world of football.

Failing that, it's a good idea to have a brother who's a footballer. The chances are you will be spotted earlier, and given a trial, even if it turns out you are not as good, or as committed, as your brother.

Football for fun: coaching courses during school holidays

If you are invited to join an Academy or a Centre of Excellence, it means you are considered amongst the very best young footballers of your age. You will then be training two to three nights a week after school, plus playing on Saturday.

But most professional clubs also offer short-term coaching courses, open to anyone, regardless of their skill or potential, which take place during school holidays.

Opposite Frank Lampard of England and Chelsea, whose father, also called Frank, played for West Ham and England. Frank junior is also the nephew of Harry Redknapp.

Other bodies also offer holiday and weekend courses, such as schools, youth clubs and commercial soccer schools. The vital thing to look for is the phrase 'FA Charter Standard' which indicates that the courses, and the coaches and tutors, have met certain standards of coaching and child security laid down by the FA.

● Newcastle United is one of the big professional clubs that have run coaching courses for many years. They are organized by their Football in the Community department, which is separate from their Academy, although it can happen that

FOOTBALLING BROTHERS

● At the present time in the Premiership, there are two very successful sets of brothers. Rio Ferdinand plays for Man Utd and England, while his younger brother Anton is at West Ham. Then there are the Nevilles — Gary of Man Utd and England and Phil of Everton and England.

● The most successful English brothers were the Charltons, Bobby and Jack, who each played in the 1960s at the very top — for Man Utd and Leeds respectively — but also both played for England in their famous World Cup win. Their uncles, the Milburns, also played professionally.

● In the 1970s, there were three Allen brothers and cousins — notably Clive Allen of Spurs and England — who all played professional football. Today a third generation, Oliver Allen, son of Clive, plays for Barnet. The Gray family — notably Eddie Gray of Leeds and Scotland — included several brothers and cousins who became professionals.

● The first brothers to play for England in the same game were Frank and Hubert Heron of the Wanderers, who turned out for

England in the international game against Scotland in 1874.

● The first time three brothers played in the same League game was in August 1953, when Jack, Alan and Herbert Keen played for Barrow in a Third Division (North) game against Port Vale.

● The first time *two* pairs of brothers appeared on the same side was in November 1955, when Wales fielded the Charles brothers, John and Mel, and the Allchurch brothers, Ivor and Len.

● The first father and son to become full England internationals were the George Easthams in 1963 when George Jnr of Arsenal first played for England. He went on to gain 19 England caps. His father, also called George, had got one cap in 1935.

Anton Ferdinand (left) of West Ham and his brother Rio of Man Utd.

● Five members of the Clarke family all played League football between 1968 and 1982. Allan (Leicester City, Leeds Utd and Barnsley), Derek (Oxford Utd), Frank (QPR, Ipswich Town and Carlisle Utd), Kelvin (Walsall) and Wayne (Wolves).

boys spotted on their holiday courses can be recommended for a trail at the Academy.

● The courses are open to boys and girls aged 5–14 and they take place at half-terms, Easter and summer holidays. They usually run for four days, from ten in the morning until three, and take place mainly on school playing fields, but also public football pitches or stadiums. The cost in 2007 for four days was around £44.

● Over the year, Newcastle United holds these courses at over 50 different schools in the North East and also in Cumbria, and employ 35 coaches and staff. The aim is to improve the ball skills and techniques of young players, their passing, heading and shooting. They also have specialised courses for goalkeepers and strikers. Every participant receives a certificate to say they have attended and there's also a chance to win medals and trophies.

For more information, contact Newcastle United Football in the Community, St James' Park, Newcastle-upon-Tyne, NE1 4ST. Telephone: 0191 263 6585 or email Julie.Oxley@nufc.co.uk.

Above A 2006 leaflet from Newcastle United, advertising some jolly exciting coaching courses for healthy boys and girls.

Soccer camps

● In the USA, residential soccer camps, held each summer in the school holidays, are big business, but there are not as yet very many in the UK.

● The two best known in England are named after well-known footballers – though Bobby Charlton is no longer connected with the one named after him. They are both commercially run organizations, not connected with any individual clubs or the FA, but do have qualified coaches.

Bobby Charlton Soccer and Sports Academy

● Began operating 30 years ago. David Beckham was an early student. A more recent student, Freddy Eastwood, scored the winning goal for Southend in 2006 that knocked Manchester United, the cup holders, out of the Carling Cup.

● Their residential courses take place at Myerscough College, set in 600 hectares near Preston in Lancashire, during the school summer holidays. Open to boys and girls aged 11–18, there are normally 250 boys and girls at a time. On average there is one coach to 16 pupils. The fee for five days in 2007 was £375. Telephone: 01565 632 555 or visit the website www.bcssa.co.uk.

The David Beckham Academy

● A relatively new soccer school, open during most school holidays at East Parkside on the Greenwich Peninsula, London. It offers coaching to boys and girls

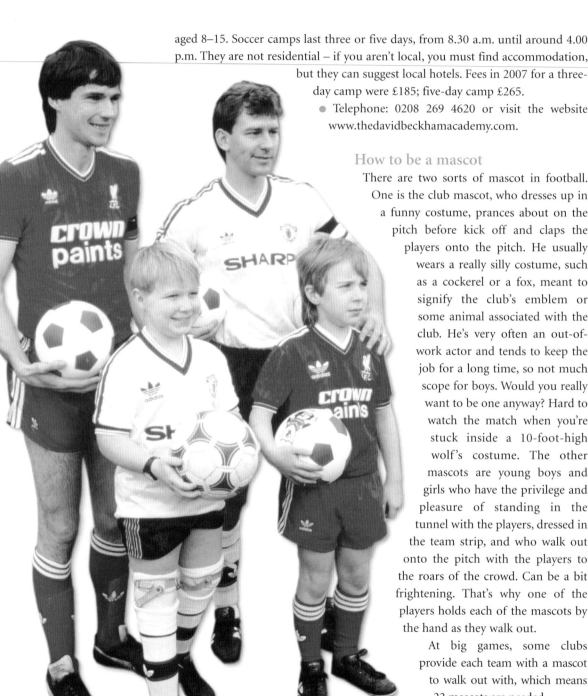

aged 8–15. Soccer camps last three or five days, from 8.30 a.m. until around 4.00 p.m. They are not residential – if you aren't local, you must find accommodation, but they can suggest local hotels. Fees in 2007 for a three-day camp were £185; five-day camp £265.

● Telephone: 0208 269 4620 or visit the website www.thedavidbeckhamacademy.com.

How to be a mascot

There are two sorts of mascot in football. One is the club mascot, who dresses up in a funny costume, prances about on the pitch before kick off and claps the players onto the pitch. He usually wears a really silly costume, such as a cockerel or a fox, meant to signify the club's emblem or some animal associated with the club. He's very often an out-of-work actor and tends to keep the job for a long time, so not much scope for boys. Would you really want to be one anyway? Hard to watch the match when you're stuck inside a 10-foot-high wolf's costume. The other mascots are young boys and girls who have the privilege and pleasure of standing in the tunnel with the players, dressed in the team strip, and who walk out onto the pitch with the players to the roars of the crowd. Can be a bit frightening. That's why one of the players holds each of the mascots by the hand as they walk out.

At big games, some clubs provide each team with a mascot to walk out with, which means 22 mascots are needed.

Most Premiership clubs these days charge for the privilege, which is a bit unfair, and the prices can range from £60 to £250, depending on what is on offer. A 'mascot package' can include several match tickets, a pre-game meal, a replica strip, signed ball and a visit to the changing room. Sometimes mascots are part of a sponsorship deal.

At some clubs, there is a combination of some mascots paying while others are 'deserving' children from local hospitals and institutions who are not charged. Manchester United, Arsenal and Liverpool were amongst a handful of top clubs who in 2007 were not charging mascots (or their parents) any sort of fee. Contact your local club to find out details.

There is no charge for being an England mascot, walking out with the players at an England game – but you have to be a member of the England Fans' Club and then enter various competitions. Contact the FA for details.

How to be a ball boy

These are the boys – though girls sometimes get a chance – who sit beside the edge of the pitch, ready to collect and return the ball when it goes out of play. You have to be quick, attentive, know the rules of football and be able to throw a ball back quickly and efficiently. You are not supposed to kick it. Wayne Rooney did, when he was an Everton ball boy, and was quickly told off.

It's an enviable job, as you see the game for free, close up, but in almost all cases the ball boys are drawn from the members of the club's Academy or Centre of Excellence. Sometimes, though, they also use boys from local schools. So enquire at your local club, just in case.

Top faves

In 2007, a random nationwide survey was conducted of 1,777 boys and girls aged 5–16 by a market research firm called Childwise. They were asked which football club they supported, if any.

The most popular club by far turned out, not surprisingly, to be Manchester United. The top eight, in percentages, were:

Manchester United	22%
Newcastle United	17%
Liverpool	13%
Arsenal	9%
Chelsea	8%
Spurs	2%
West Ham	2%
Aston Villa	2%

Opposite Being a match-day mascot means having to stand properly, but you also get to meet the team captains, in this case Alan Hansen of Liverpool and Bryan Robson of Man Utd, pictured in 1987.

Below Kids want to be associated with successful teams, so little wonder that Man Utd is supported all over the country.

The popularity of the Premiership was clearly demonstrated by the fact that 70% supported a Premiership team. Just 2% named a club in Leagues One or Two. This could be seen as a worrying sign for football as a whole, suggesting not many children are growing up to follow their local team, preferring the big and famous ones. On the other hand, the fact that only 13% of the random sample said they didn't have a favourite team shows the all-pervasive influence of football in the life of young people today.

Starting late

It is still possible, even in these days of worldwide scouting systems and million-pound Academies, for talented young players to slip through the net. For instance, they might happen to play badly on the day a scout is watching. Or they might be late developers. Or at a certain stage in their life they may just lose interest, preferring trivial pursuits such as music, pubs, girls. Or it could be they choose to concentrate on their school-work. Or they just like playing for fun.

It can also happen that Premiership Academies make mistakes, because they have become so selective, with so many to choose from, and so may let promising players go too quickly.

So there are still the occasional examples of players arriving at the top relatively late in life which, in football, means 19 or 20. Until then, they have been playing in some lower league, perhaps even part-time football.

Reading, for example, took a chance when they signed Kevin Doyle aged 19 from Cork City for the piddling sum of £79,000. The club's gamble paid off handsomely; in the 2006–07 season Doyle was one of the most successful strikers in the Premiership.

Kevin Keegan, who played 63 times for England, was also a slow starter. When young, he was rejected by his local club Doncaster Rovers and told that he was 'too small to make it'. Undeterred, he 'made' himself into a footballer, so he always claimed, by sheer willpower and determination to improve himself. Aged 20, he was plucked from obscurity when playing for Scunthorpe by Bill Shankly and became one of Liverpool's greatest ever players. In the 1976–77 season, he was a key player in Liverpool's unprecedented achievement of the 'treble' – winning the League Championship, the FA Cup and the European Cup. During his three years with the leading German club Hamburger SV, from 1977–80, he was twice named European Player of the Year. He played for England 61 times, 31 of them as captain, and scored 21 goals. So much for being a late starter.

Didier Drogba, Chelsea star and Ivory Coast international, never went to an Academy or School of Excellence, playing for minor teams in France, not becoming a full-time professional until he was 19.

Henrik Larsson, a star at Celtic and also Man Utd and a leading Swedish international player, was rejected at the age of 12 as being too small. So, he worked part-time packing fruit and vegetables and didn't become a full-time professional until he was 22.

Opposite Kevin Keegan was told when young that he was too small to make it, but he eventually grew big enough – and good enough – to play for Hamburger SV, then one of the top teams in the German Bundesliga.

Some Advice from the Past

In December 1913, the most famous footballer of the day, Steve Bloomer, wrote an article for the magazine, telling young chaps how to succeed as a footballer. His jolly sensible advice could be followed to advantage by all boys and girls to this day.

There is no need to train as if your life depends on the early reduction of your weight; in fact, the one aim a youth should have is an improvement in the nerves, wind, and muscles. He doesn't want to take off any weight unless he is clogged with fat; and, as for the idea of starving himself, there is not the slightest reason for him to make any change in his diet, unless, of course, he has been in the habit of over-feeding, or drinking intoxicants. Mind you, I am not saying that knocking off food for a bit is not good for one, because I know it is one of the best things in the world, but I do maintain that a youth who wants to put on muscle wants plenty of food and exercise combined. But not only must the exercise be very regular, the meals must be regular as well. Pure water is by far the healthiest of all drinks…

…However, all the exercise in the world will not have the beneficial effect that it should unless your heart and lungs are right. Neither will the muscles, nerves, wind and sight be improved if some of your little vices are continued. For instance, I know of no worse habit, which is really doing incalcula-ble harm to would-be footballers than that of cigarette smoking, a vice which injures and stops the growth of all football's attrib-utes. Now I am well aware that some of you senior readers occasionally smoke cigarettes. I have seen some of you indulging and looking as if you thoroughly enjoyed it; a result, probably, of endeavouring to appear manly.

Before you can start your training prop-erly, and before you can make any serious effort to become a first-class player, you must knock off cigarettes, or any other form of smoking, and I can promise you that not only will you benefit in appearance and in nerve, but you will experience a really delightful feeling of freshness and buoyancy which will add years to your life…

…Some of you will perhaps say that this article was supposed to be dealing with the right way to train and will wonder why I

How the novice feels when he first "heads" the ball!

don't get on with it. My dear boys, this is the right way to train, and I maintain that in looking after the food department properly, knocking off intoxicants and smoke, and being particularly careful about getting to bed at a respectable hour, you are doing more to keep fit than you would with all the exercises in the world.

I have noticed during the past few years a steady growth of places where cheap evening entertainment can be obtained, and quite one quarter of the audience at the perform-ances consists of youths who would be better at home. I refer, of course, to picture palaces and other places that have sprung up in nearly every town. Not that an occasional evening spent in this form of amusement is harmful; but the young fellow who makes it a habit to attend these places two or three times a week, and loses his "beauty sleep" by so doing, is pretty certain never to attain a high position in the world of athletics.

Now let us suppose that we have conquered all the petty vices which appeal to most young people, and that we are going to take up some form of exercise in order to harden the muscles and improve our bodies generally. First of all, I would suggest the frequent use of the skipping-rope as it is not only of wonderful benefit but is quite easy to indulge in, seeing that rope is cheap and can be used in the back garden. Then I think the next best thing to improve the muscles is the dumb-bell.

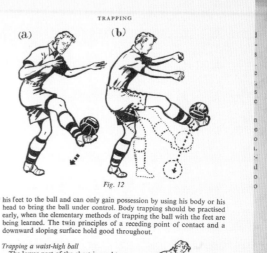

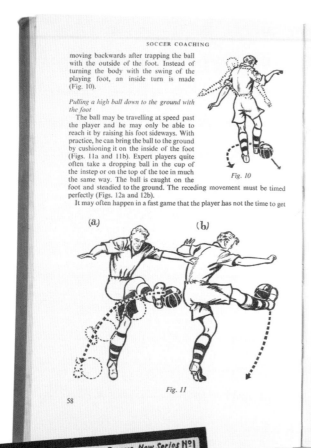

SOCCER COACHING

moving backwards after trapping the ball with the outside of the foot. Instead of turning the body with the swing of the playing foot, an inside turn is made (Fig. 10).

Pulling a high ball down to the ground with the foot

The ball may be travelling at speed past the player and he may only be able to reach it by raising his foot sideways. With practice, he can bring the ball to the ground by cushioning it on the inside of the foot (Figs. 11a and 11b). Expert players quite often take a dropping ball in the cup of the instep or on the top of the toe in much the same way. The ball is caught on the foot and steadied to the ground. The receding movement must be timed perfectly (Figs. 12a and 12b).

It may often happen in a fast game that the player has not the time to get

Fig. 10

Fig. 11

58

TRAPPING

(a)   (b)

Fig. 12

his feet to the ball and can only gain possession by using his body or his head to bring the ball under control. Body trapping should be practised early, when the elementary methods of trapping the ball with the feet are being learned. The twin principles of a receding point of contact and a downward sloping surface hold good throughout.

Trapping a waist-high ball

The lower part of the chest is used to bring a high-bouncing ball – or any ball about waist height – down to the ground quickly. From there, it can be played immediately by the foot. The player moves into the ball and takes it just below his ribs. At the moment of contact, he arches his body, drawing in the abdominal muscles and bending the shoulders forwards. The impact of the ball is cushioned, and if this 'folding' movement is well timed the ball will drop lightly to the ground (Fig. 13). The temptation to use the arms to form a socket for the ball must be avoided. It

Fig. 13

59

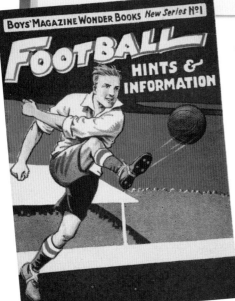

BOYS' MAGAZINE WONDER BOOKS *New Series No 1*

FOOTBALL

HINTS & INFORMATION

Ten top tips

So, you want to improve your game but for some reason a Premier League Academy is not rushing to sign you on. Don't fret – Uncle Hunter has a few tips and hints.

1. **Learn to use both feet.** As soon as possible, force yourself not to use your 'best' foot. Practise hitting a ball against a wall with your 'wrong' foot. With two or three friends, practise passing to each other with your 'wrong' foot. When you can take a dead-ball kick, like a corner or free kick, with either foot, then you'll know you've mastered it.

2. **Controlling the ball.** Traditionally, coaches used to advise trapping the ball under your foot as it landed, but these days the game is played at so fast a pace that you would soon be knocked off the ball. So you must learn to instantly control the ball by cushioning it. This means moving your foot away ever so slightly

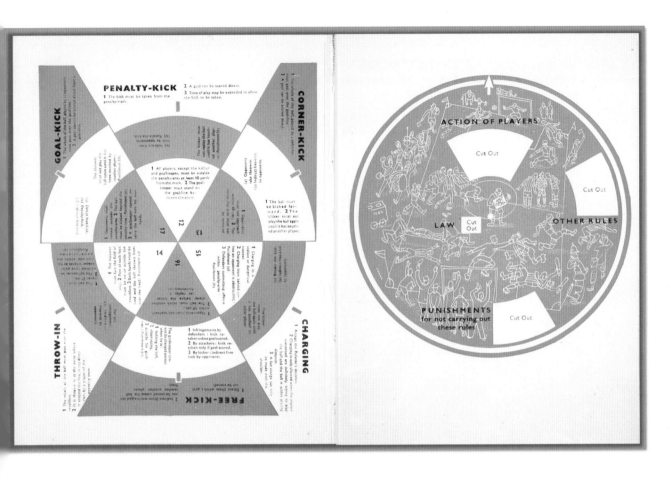

as the ball comes to you, so that it doesn't bounce off your foot, cushioning the ball on your instep. Easy to say, harder to do.

3. Chest and Thigh Control. You need, of course, to have a chest or a thigh. That helps. The principle is the same – move the chest or thigh back ever so slightly as the ball comes to you, then use your chest or thigh to cushion it.

4. Shooting. Mark a wall with numbered squares. Then get someone to shout out the numbers and try to hit them (the numbered squares, not your friend). If on your own, take five shots at each number. Keep trying to improve your score.

5. Dribbling. Practise by laying down a line of tin cans, cones or whatever, each about two yards apart, then dribble between them, using both feet, as fast as you can without actually falling over or scattering the cans.

6. Heading. The vital thing is to attack the ball. Do not wait for it to reach you, or let it just drop off you. Thrust your neck and body forward to give maximum power. Always head the ball with your forehead. Keep your eye on the ball till the second you head it. It won't hurt, honestly, if you do it properly.

Above and opposite Almost since football began, the experts have been kindly sharing their tips. Above, cut-out tactics diagrams from the FA *Book for Boys* and opposite, coaching hints from Walter Winterbottom, England's first manager (1946–62) and a 1930s boys' magazine.

HOW TO BE A FOOTBALLER

Opposite More helpful hints on play from the *Boys' Magazine Wonder Book.*

Below David Beckham opening his Academy in East London, which provides state-of-the-art training facilities for budding young footballers. Don't count on being coached by the star in person, though ...

7. Boxes. Professionals use this training technique, though the name of it differs. You need at least three other people to make it worthwhile. Mark out a box or circle, or you can just imagine it, though this can lead to arguments. One person stands in the middle while the others pass the ball across the box, back and forward, trying to avoid the one in the middle. When the one in the middle finally intercepts the ball, the one who has made the mistake goes in the middle instead. To make it harder, try it using one-touch football, so the ones passing are only allowed one touch.

8. Keepy-uppies. There's always some flash kid who can do loads of them, but they don't help much in a real game, though they are good fun to practise when you are on your own. Make the best use of your time by keeping the ball up with alternate feet, your best and then your wrong foot.

9. Keep your head up. Sounds obvious, but even in Premiership games you will see wingers dashing down the wings or dribbling round full backs with their heads down, unable to see where they are going or where other people are.

10. Er, that's it, really ... except to say that a really thorough reading of *The Bumper Book of Football* is a totally excellent way of improving your football skills and knowledge.

16 BOYS' MAGAZINE WONDER BOOK.   New Series No. 1

Improve Your Game

HINTS on PLAY

How the Experts Do It.

EVERY boy who plays football wants to be a success. Here are three good points which should help every young player to achieve that success of which all boys dream. First of all put your whole heart and soul into the game. Secondly, practise hard, for it is only from continual practice that you will correct your faults. Thirdly, take every opportunity to watch the stars playing, and do your best to emu-

late their various moves.

Now let us take a look at the various positions and see what we can learn about improving our game.

The goalie needs to be one of the coolest-headed fellows in the team, a chap with a keen sense of anticipation. In other words, he must think a move ahead of the other fellow and be in the right place at the right time. This anticipation comes from practice; without it a goalie is useless. The goalie must know when to stop "at home" and when to run out. If you're a 'keeper you must be firm and quick in your decisions. If you decide to run out and grab the ball from the forwards—do it. Don't get halfway out and then try to get back into your chicken-run again. That won't pay!

Always try to get your hands to the ball. Never fist away when you can safely gather the ball, and don't try and kick the ball clear, unless you're forced to; kicks often swerve into goal.

Much depends upon the full-backs in front of the goalie. They should both be level-headed, clear-thinking, and powerful-kicking players,

Headmaster: I hear your son is hoping to get in the school team. What position does he play?

Proud Mother: Well, I heard the sports teacher say he was one of the drawbacks.

Chelsea FC programme, 1907

. . . .

Wee Alec was rather underweight and was told by his doctor that he'd be a better footballer if he put on some weight. 'Try eating a plum, but swallow it whole,' he said. 'That way you'll gain a stone.'

It didn't work, so Wee Alec went back again.

'Okay, this time,' said the doc, 'I'll put you on a seafood diet.'

'How does that work?'

'See food – then you eat it.'

. . . .

Two friends meet in the street and start boasting about their sons and how well they are doing at football.

'My son has been accepted at Bobby Charlton's School of Excellence.'

'Oh, that's good,' says his friend. 'How's he doing?'

'Oh, very well indeed,' says the first dad. 'He's only 14 but he's bald already.'

. . . .

Coach:	Why are you late for training?
Young player:	I sprained my ankle.
Coach:	That's a lame excuse.

. . . .

Now on to the next exciting section…

2. Football history

What every boy and girl should know about the origins of our favourite game

Below **Football was already being played in 16th-century Germany, though not as we know it now.**

Like so many other things, it all began in Great Britain in the middle of the 19th century – that is, the rules and language of the 'beautiful game': Association Football as we know and love it today. There is no need to swank, however, as it is clear that football, of some sort, had been played all over the world for many hundreds, if not thousands, of years. It probably goes back to when we were all living in caves.

Below Football was already being played in 16th-century Germany, though not as we know it now.

Kicking or throwing a ball, or some round object which looks and feels like a ball, is a pretty natural thing to do. When one or more were gathered, there would then arise, as likely as not, the idea of competition: let's see who can kick or chuck it the furthest or the most accurately.

In 1848 at Cambridge University, a group of chaps who had gone to different public schools got together to try to thrash out a set of rules. They had played football back at their own schools, kicking and chucking a ball according to the rules in their own schools, but in each case the rules had been slightly different. This naturally made it a bit difficult when they all wanted to play together.

They argued about things like handling the ball. Could you run while holding the ball? And also about 'hacking'. Hacking was a violent form of tackling, then present in most variations of football, whereby you could assault any player on the other side and bring him down, whether he had the ball or not. (This still happens, but is not advisable. In fact, it is illegal, so please don't try it.)

Alas, we don't know the exact rules on which they agreed that day in 1848. If they were ever written down, they soon disappeared.

The vital meeting, which sorted out and codified the rules once and for all, took place in 1862 at the Freemasons' Tavern near Lincoln's Inn in London. Over the centuries, football fans have rarely been far from a tavern.

At this meeting were several football clubs from the London area made up of ex-public-schoolboys, Oxbridge graduates, plus some hearty young clerics. They managed to establish a set of rules on which they could all agree and organized themselves into an association which they called the Football Association.

In the North of England, in Sheffield, there already existed the Sheffield Club, established in 1857, which had created its own rules. In 1870, it agreed to abide by the FA's version.

In Scotland, Queen's Park, established in 1867, also had its own rules, but then the Scottish FA was formed and they, like the football associations in Wales and Ireland, soon agreed to recognize and stick to the rules formulated by the English FA. Until about 1900, these rules were regularly modified, with the introduction of crossbars, corner kicks, throw ins, as well as changes to the offside rule, which was always a complicated subject. But by the beginning of the 20th century, the basic rules of football had been established, give or take further changes in the offside rule.

If a boy who was alive in 1900 came back today and went to a Premiership match, if of course he could wangle a ticket, he might well find our football boots and shirts a bit weird, but he would, more or less, understand what was happening on the pitch. He would be able to appreciate and enjoy the game just as much as we all do today.

Above The Football Association, as well as giving us the rules, has also given us a fair few footer books over the years.

Below Queen's Park, founded in 1867, is Scotland's oldest club.

HISTORY OF THE ENGLISH LEAGUE SYSTEM

Year	Division	Clubs
1888	Division 1	12
1892	Division 1	16
	Division 2	12
		= 28 clubs in all
1898	Division 1	18
	Division 2	18
		= 36 clubs in all
1905	Division 1	20
	Division 2	20
		= 40 clubs in all
1920	Division 1	22
	Division 2	22
	Division 3	22
		= 66 clubs in all
1921	Division 1	22
	Division 2	22
	Division 3: South	22
	Division 3: North	20 (to 22 in 1923)
		= 86 (88) clubs in all
1958	Division 1	22
	Division 2	22
	Division 3	24
	Division 4	24
		= 92 clubs in all

Year	Division	Clubs
1992	Premiership	22
	Division 1	24
	Division 2	24
	Division 3	22
		= 92 clubs in all
1995	Premiership	20
	Division 1	24
	Division 2	24
	Division 3	24
		= 92 clubs in all
2004	Premiership	20
	Championship	24
	Division 1	24
	Division 2	24
		= 92 clubs in all

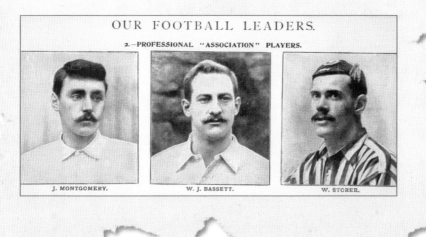

OUR FOOTBALL LEADERS.

2.—PROFESSIONAL "ASSOCIATION" PLAYERS.

J. MONTGOMERY.   W. J. BASSETT.   W. STORER.

Left One of the problems about comparing football today with the past is that not only are the players different, but the League system has changed many times since 1888.

There were two notable people, players who went on to become officials, who will always be remembered in the early history of football.

Charles Alcock's father was a wealthy shipping magnate from Sunderland who had sent his son to Harrow School where he was a very keen and energetic footballer. He started writing about football and produced one of the earliest football books and edited the first football annual. He played cricket and rugby as well and was involved in shaping the first county cricket championships. Clearly, an all-round good egg.

From 1870 to 1895, Alcock was Secretary of the FA – and for most of that period he was unpaid. In 1870, he arranged a game in London between England and Scotland. The English and the Scots were mainly drawn from the London area, so it wasn't quite a representative game. Alcock captained the winning English side. Two years later, in November 1872, Alcock and the FA organized the world's first official international, between England and Scotland. It was held in Glasgow and ended 0–0.

As Secretary of the FA, Alcock also came up with the idea of the FA Cup challenge cup. He based it on what had happened at his old school, Harrow, where the different houses had competed to be cock house.

The first FA Cup was held in 1872. In the final, Wanderers beat Engineers 1–0. The captain of the winning team was C.W. Alcock. Yes, the chap who had first thought up the competition.

Opposite Lord Kinnaird, early football superstar, later President of the Football Association.

Below Public school boys had a big hand in the early days of football … A ripping yarn from the 1906 *Boys' Herald*.

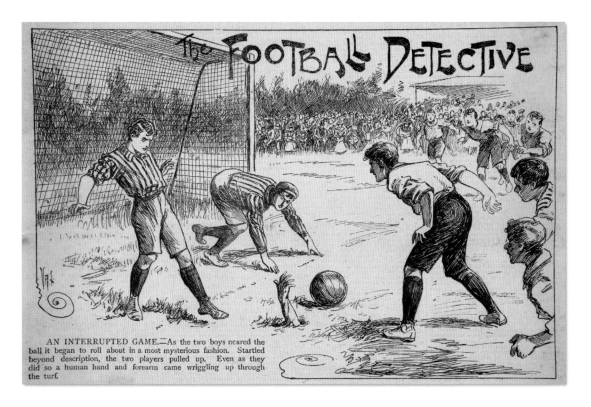

AN INTERRUPTED GAME.—As the two boys neared the ball it began to roll about in a most mysterious fashion. Startled beyond description, the two players pulled up. Even as they did so a human hand and forearm came wriggling up through the turf.

The Hon. Arthur Kinnaird, later Lord Kinnaird when he inherited a large estate in Perthshire, had also learned to play football at his public school, Eton. He played for Old Etonians in several of the early FA Cup finals.

Kinnaird was a huge, red-bearded man who was loved by the fans. On one occasion, arriving for a game in his own carriage, the fans took the horses away and pulled the coach themselves up to the players' entrance.

On the pitch, he was a fierce competitor, not to say jolly violent. He got stuck in – as we say today: he took no prisoners.

His mother, Lady Kinnaird, was always worried that one day he might arrive home with a broken leg. 'Don't worry, my Lady,' said a fellow competitor. 'It won't be his own.' This story, or variations of it, has been told now for almost 150 years.

Kinnaird played in nine Cup finals and when he retired became an FA official, serving for 33 years as President of the FA.

In the early decades of organized football in England, the players were all amateurs, playing for love not money, which was easy enough, as so many had private means and access to lush playing fields. But by the 1880s, football was taking hold in the industrial North. Factory workers or church groups had set up their own football clubs.

Ordinary men could not afford to take time off to play football, and the clubs needed money to hire pitches, pay for travelling to away games, so an official system of 'expenses' sprang up. Players began finding pound notes had mysteriously appeared in their boots after a game. Inducements were offered to star players at rival clubs. The FA banned all these illegal payments, or 'shamateurism', as it was called, but in 1885 they bowed to the inevitable. They declared that professional football was now legal.

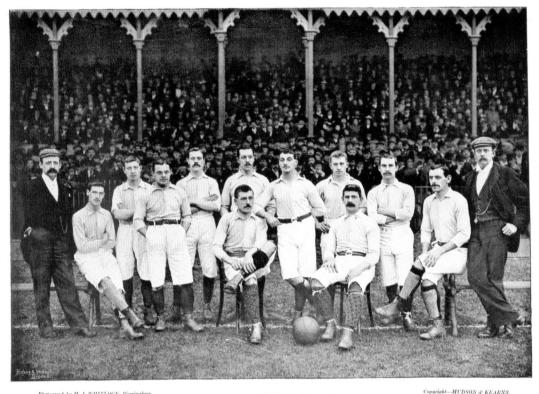

Photograph by H. J. WHITLOCK, Birmingham.   Copyright—HUDSON & KEARNS.

BLACKBURN ROVERS.

Mr. E. H. DODD, (Linesman).   J. HARGREAVES.   H. CHIPPENDALE.   G. ANDERSON, (Captain).   T. CLEGHORN.   J. HUNTER, (Trainer).
J. HAYDOCK.   J. WHITEHEAD.   G. DEWAR.   P. TURNBULL.   J. MURRAY.
T. BRANDON   A. OGILVIE.

Above Blackburn Rovers, now in the Premiership, were one of the founder members of the Football League in 1888. Pictured here are the 1895 team.

Until 1888, both the professional and amateur clubs played endless friendlies or competed in the FA Cup and other knock-out competitions. It seems so obvious to us now, yet no one had come up with the idea of a league – clubs grouping together to play each other for points.

This was first suggested by William McGregor, a Scotsman connected with the Aston Villa football club in Birmingham. He contacted various clubs with his new idea but not all that many were interested.

The world's first football league kicked off on 8 September 1888, with only 12 clubs, each promising to field their best teams. Two points were awarded for a win.

They were a few weeks into the season before they decided that a draw would earn one point.

Preston North End won that first league, going unbeaten for the whole season and giving rise to their nickname of 'The Invincibles'.

EARLY FOOTBALL MILESTONES

1863   FA formed

1870   First international, Scotland 0 England 0

1872   First FA Cup final, held at the Oval; 2000 attended

1873   Corner kicks introduced

1874   Shinguards introduced

1875   Crossbars replaced a tape between goal posts

1878   Referees acquired whistles

1885   Professionalism made legal

1888   Formation of the Football League

1891   Penalty kicks introduced; also goal nets

1892   Second Division of the Football League created

1901   FA Cup final at Crystal Palace, watched by 110,820

1904   FIFA founded

Below Spurs and Sheffield United battle it out at the 1901 Cup final at Crystal Palace.

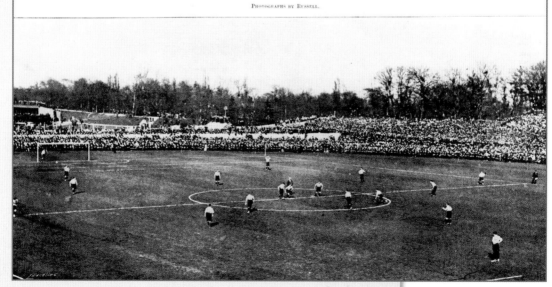

THE FOOTBALL ASSOCIATION CUP FINAL TIE AT THE CRYSTAL PALACE, APRIL 20.

PHOTOGRAPHS BY RUSSELL.

Now let's consider those first 12 members of the Football League. In alphabetical order, they were: Accrington, Aston Villa, Blackburn Rovers, Bolton Wanderers, Burnley, Derby County, Everton, Notts County, Preston North End, Stoke City, West Bromwich Albion and Wolverhampton Wanderers.

Football historians and general clever-clogs often try to catch each other out by asking for the names of these first 12, so it is worth trying to memorize them. Notice first of all that there were no London or Southern clubs. They came equally, six in each, from either Lancashire or the Midlands. Three begin with a B, two with an A, two with a W. That's a handy way of remembering them.

Some 120 seasons later, all these 12 clubs are still with us, and still in the Premier or the Football League, although Accrington Stanley – which took over from the plain old Accrington – did for some years suffer the humiliation of disbandment. They then had a rebirth and crawled up through the lower reaches of what we now call Non-League, till in 2006 they returned to the Football League. Well done, Accrington.

Below AC Milan, the famous Italian club (and Champions' League winners 2007) calls itself Milan, not Milano, betraying its English origins.

Football abroad

Once the rules and organizational structure of football had been established, the game was exported remarkably quickly.

Gentlemen of the officer class who found themselves in some far-flung part of the world set up their own football clubs, regardless of the heat and the local conditions.

At about the same time, railway workers sent out on jobs aboard, or sailors and soldiers fetched up on foreign soil, started kick-arounds once they had landed, if only to amuse themselves.

France's first football club, Le Havre, was formed in 1872 after a game organized by visiting British sailors. Around the same time, and for similar reasons, football clubs were taking root in Denmark, Holland and Switzerland.

In Italy, British residents keen on both summer and winter sports began the Genoa Cricket and Football Club in 1892 while, in 1899, the Milan Cricket and Football Club was formed, later called AC Milan. This is its name to the

FOOTBALL

SELECTED ALMERIA GRAPES

RTO FERRER
ENTE·VALENCIA

DALÍAS

TELEGR. FERRER
TELEF. Nº 8 - R.E. Nº 904

Above Football has always been big in Spain, and a useful way of advertising local grapes for export …

THE FIRST FOOTBALL LEAGUE TABLE, 1888–89

Two points for a win, one for a draw

		P	W	D	L	F	A	Pts
1	Preston	22	18	4	0	74	15	40
2	Aston Villa	22	12	5	5	61	43	29
3	Wolves	22	12	4	6	50	37	28
4	Blackburn	22	10	6	6	66	45	26
5	Bolton	22	10	2	10	63	59	22
6	WBA	22	10	2	10	40	46	22
7	Accrington	22	6	8	8	48	48	20
8	Everton	22	9	2	11	35	46	20
9	Burnley	22	7	3	12	42	62	17
10	Derby	22	7	2	13	41	60	16
11	Notts County	22	5	2	15	39	73	12
12	Stoke	22	4	4	14	26	51	12

Preston North End, winners of the first League championship.

PREMIERSHIP TABLE, 2006–07

Three points for a win, one for a draw

		P	W	D	L	F	A	Pts
1	Man Utd	38	28	5	5	83	27	89
2	Chelsea	38	24	11	3	64	24	83
3	Liverpool	38	20	8	10	57	27	30
4	Arsenal	38	19	11	8	63	35	68
5	Spurs	38	17	9	12	57	54	60
6	Everton	38	15	13	10	52	36	58
7	Bolton	38	16	8	14	47	52	56
8	Reading	38	16	7	15	52	47	55
9	Portsmouth	38	14	12	12	45	42	54
10	Blackburn	38	15	7	16	52	54	52
11	Aston Villa	38	11	17	10	43	41	50
12	Middlesboro	38	12	10	16	44	49	46
13	Newcastle	38	11	10	17	38	47	43
14	Man City	38	11	9	18	29	44	42
15	West Ham	38	12	5	21	35	59	41
16	Fulham	38	8	15	15	38	60	39
17	Wigan	38	10	8	20	37	59	38
18	Sheff Utd	38	10	8	20	32	55	38 (R)
19	Charlton	38	8	10	20	34	60	34 (R)
20	Watford	38	5	13	20	29	59	28 (R)

present day. Note that it is still spelled 'Milan' in the English manner, as opposed to the Italian name for the city where it is located – 'Milano'.

In Germany, following a huge growth in the popularity of the game and in the number of clubs being established from the 1880s onwards, the umbrella organization of the German Football Association (Deutscher Fußball Bund, or DFB for short) was founded on 28 January, 1900 in Leipzig. Representatives from 86 clubs took part in this inaugural meeting. A number of German clubs still commemorate the year of their foundation in their names, such as Hannover 96 and FC Schalke 04, from the former mining town of Gelsenkirchen in the industrial Ruhr region. Another club with a (surprisingly early) date is TSV München 1860, from the Bavarian capital Munich; however, this refers to the foundation of the broader sports and gymnastics club, into which a football team was later incorporated at the end of the 19th century.

National football associations soon grew up once the individual clubs were thriving and, in 1904, FIFA was created, forming a world body for football. Seven countries took part: France, Belgium, Denmark, Holland, Spain, Sweden and Switzerland.

Where was England? Good question. England, along with Scotland, Wales and Ireland, the so-called 'Home Countries', refused to take part.

It would seem they felt just a little bit superior. They considered that football was their game. They had begun it, so who were these foreigners trying to take it over, teaching us about the rules, telling us how to play it … ?

Right Football is played with a passion in Germany, the most successful European footballing nation. Here, amateur players in 1965 enjoy a game in the grimy surroundings of Gelsenkirchen, home of the great club FC Schalke 04.

What's next? Hurry on to Section Three to find out …

3. Great clubs

Basic facts you need to know about some of our most famous English and Scottish clubs

If your particular favourite is not here, sorry chums, but then you probably know everything about them anyway …

ABERDEEN

Formed: 1903
Ground: Pittodrie Stadium
Colours: red shirts, shorts; formerly black and gold
Nickname: The Dons
Best Achievement: Winning the European Cup Winners' Cup in 1983 and the Scottish Premier League three times in the 1980s, temporarily breaking into the Old Firm dominance.

Fascinating Facts: Where Alex Ferguson (manager 1980–86) honed his 'hairdrying' techniques. That 1983 Euro win was a good 'un – against Real Madrid.

ACCRINGTON STANLEY

Formed: Origins go back to 1886 when Accrington FC began. Accrington Stanley took over from 1891.
Ground: Fraser Eagle Stadium
Colours: red shirts, white socks
Nickname: very boring – The Old Reds
Best Achievement: Coming back from the dead after the club closed in 1963 to the Football League in 2006.
Fascinating Facts: Founder member of the Football League in 1888. The Stanley bit comes from the Stanley Arms in Stanley Street, where they used to meet. In the 1950s, they once fielded a team full of Scotsmen.

ARSENAL

Founded: 1886 by workers at the Royal Arsenal, Woolwich. Known as Dial Square, then Royal Arsenal, Woolwich Arsenal and finally, in 1914, as Arsenal. Moved from Woolwich to North London in 1913.
Ground: Emirates Stadium, previously at Highbury (1913–2006)
Colours: red shirts, white sleeves, white shorts
Nickname: Gunners or Gooners
Best Achievement: So many. Division 1 champs five times in the 1930s; Double of League and Cup three times (1971, 1998, 2002).

Fascinating Facts: Their original red shirts came from Nottingham Forest who provided a full set of shirts as Arsenal couldn't afford their own. Arsenal tube station was named after the club and not the other way round. The main stand at Highbury is now a listed building and can't be knocked down.

ASTON VILLA

Founded: 1874 by some cricketers, members of a Wesleyan chapel who wanted a winter pastime

Ground: Villa Park since 1997

Colours: claret shirts with blue sleeves

Nickname: The Villans

Best Achievement: In recent times, Division 1 champs in 1981, European Cup Winners in 1982.

Fascinating Facts: Villa was transformed by the arrival from Glasgow of George Ramsey in 1897 who managed the club for 42 years and won six FA cups; their most capped player is Steve Staunton, who won 64 caps for the Republic of Ireland.

BARNSLEY

Founded: 1887, by a church group

Ground: Oakwell Stadium

Colours: red shirts, white shorts

Nickname: The Tykes, the Colliers or just Reds

Best Achievement: Promotion to Premier League, 1998.

Fascinating Facts: Known as Barnsley St Peter until 1897 after Rev Preedy of St Peter's, their founder. 'Just like watching Brazil,' chanted their fans when they got into the Premier League – for one season.

BIRMINGHAM CITY

Founded: 1875 by some cricketers at a local church, known originally as Small Heath Alliance

Ground: St Andrews since 1906

Colours: royal blue with white trim

Nickname: The Blues

Achievements: Not many really, considering they entered the Football League in 1892; beating Walsall Town Swifts 12–0 in 1892 – they still talk about that; returning to the Premiership in 2007 after just one season in the Championship.

Fascinating Facts: Trevor Francis made his debut for them in 1970 aged 16 years and seven months, becoming the UK's first million-pound player when sold to Notts Forest in 1979; Karren Brady, aged 23 when appointed managing director in 1992, became the youngest and most powerful woman in football.

BLACKBURN ROVERS

Founded: 1875 by two old boys of Blackburn Grammar School

Ground: Ewood Park since 1890; bought in 1893 for £2,500

Colours: blue-and-white halved shirts

Nicknames: Blue and Whites

Achievements: In recent years, winning the Prem in 1994–95, helped by millionaire steel magnate Jack Walker; in ye olden days, winning the FA Cup six times, the last in 1928.

Fascinating Facts: A. Wainwright, the great Lakeland walker, helped begin their supporters' club in 1939.

BOLTON WANDERERS

Founded: 1874 as a Sunday School team

Ground: Reebok since 1997, previously Burnden Park

Colours: white shirts, white shorts

Nickname: The Trotters

Achievements: Beating Sheffield Utd 13–0 in 1890; won the FA Cup three times in the 1920s.

Fascinating Facts: Called Wanderers because they didn't have a permanent home until they landed at Burnden Park in 1895, the ground that features in L. S. Lowry's famous painting *Going to the Match*.

BURNLEY

Founded: 1881 by some rugby players

Ground: Turf Moor

Colours: claret and blue shirts

Nickname: The Clarets

Achievements: Won top league twice: 1921 and 1960, but not a lot since. In 1980s dropped from First to Fourth Div.

Fascinating Facts: In 1975, while in the First Div, suffered the humiliation of being knocked out of the FA Cup by a non-league club, Wimbledon.

CARDIFF CITY

Founded: 1899 by some cricketers
Ground: Ninian Park
Colours: royal blue shirts and shorts
Nickname: Bluebirds
Achievements: Won FA Cup in 1927 – the only time it's been won by a non-English club, so far.
Fascinating Facts: In that Cup-winning side were four Irish, three Scots, three Welsh – and only one English player.

CARLISLE UNITED

Founded: 1903
Ground: Brunton Park
Colours: blue shirts, white shorts
Nickname: The Cumbrians
Achievements: Getting to the First Div in 1974 – top after three games, then, in 2004, demoted to the Conference. Don't talk about it.
Fascinating Facts: Home town of Hunter Davies, hence its inclusion.

CELTIC

Founded: 1888 by a group of Irishmen to help the local poor
Ground: Celtic Park
Colours: green and white hoops
Nickname: The Bhoys
Achievements: First British club to win the European Cup in 1967; Scottish Cup and League wins – too numerous to list.
Fascinating Facts: Jimmy McGrory scored 297 goals between 1922 and 1938, the highest number at any British club.

CHARLTON ATHLETIC

Founded: 1905
Ground: The Valley
Colours: red shirts, white shorts
Nickname: The Addicks, The Robins
Achievements: FA Cup winners 1947; returning to The Valley in 1992 after seven years, during which time it was left overgrown.
Fascinating Facts: Their famous goalie Sam Battram turned out for them 582 times between 1934 and 1956.

CHELSEA

Founded: 1905
Ground: Stamford Bridge
Colours: blue shirts and shorts
Nickname: The Blues
Achievements: Getting Mr Roman Abramovitch, the rather well-off Russian tycoon, to buy them in 2005; winning the Premiership in 2005 and 2006.
Fascinating Facts: Might never have existed if Fulham FC had agreed to take over Stamford Bridge when offered it in 1905 – instead, the Stamford Bridge owners formed their own football club.

COVENTRY CITY

Founded: 1894 by workers at Singers cycle factory
Ground: Ricoh Arena, previously Highfield Road
Colours: all sky blue
Nickname: Sky Blues
Achievements: FA Cup winners in 1987.
Fascinating Facts: The ground was hit by three German bombs in November 1940 but they all missed the grandstands, landing in the middle of the pitch; Jimmy Hill, manager in the 1960s, was a pioneer of football publicity and marketing,

introducing a new sky-blue strip, sky-blue programme, sky-blue shop, sky-blue radio station. He insisted they should be called The Sky Blues – previous nicknames included The Bantams and the Peeping Toms.

DERBY COUNTY

Founded: 1884 by a cricket club wanting to increase income
Ground: Pride Park. From 1895 to 1997 they were at the Baseball Ground, where baseball was once played.
Colours: white and black
Nickname: The Rams
Achievements: FA Cup winners in 1946. Div 1 winners in 1972, under Brian Clough, and then in 1975 under Dave Mackay. Return to Prem in 2007.
Fascinating Facts: Steve Bloomer, star player of the 1890s, scored 352 League goals for Derby.

Glory days: The Rams lift the first post-war FA Cup, in 1946.

DUNDEE

Founded: 1893
Ground: Dens Park
Colours: navy shirt with white and red flashes
Nickname: The Dark Blues, or the Dee
Achievements: Scottish Div 1 champs 1962.

Fascinating Facts: They have won the Scottish Cup – but, hmmm, back in 1910.

DUNDEE UNITED

Founded: 1909
Ground: Tannadice Park
Colours: tangerine shirts, shorts
Nickname: The Terrors
Achievements: Scottish Premier League winners, 1983; European Cup semi finals 1984.
Fascinating Facts: Originally called Dundee Hibernian, changed to United in 1923. Stuffed Nithsdale Wanderers 14–0 in the Scottish Cup, 1931.

EVERTON

Founded 1878 by St Domingo's church Sunday School
Ground: Goodison Park

A joint Everton–Liverpool match programme from 1910; the clubs even shared Anfield until 1892.

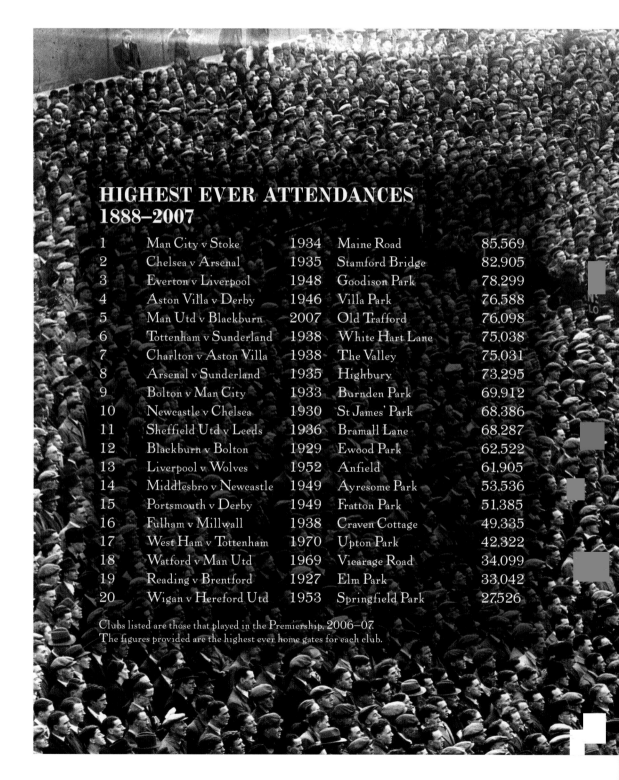

HIGHEST EVER ATTENDANCES
1888–2007

#	Match	Year	Ground	Attendance
1	Man City v Stoke	1934	Maine Road	85,569
2	Chelsea v Arsenal	1935	Stamford Bridge	82,905
3	Everton v Liverpool	1948	Goodison Park	78,299
4	Aston Villa v Derby	1946	Villa Park	76,588
5	Man Utd v Blackburn	2007	Old Trafford	76,098
6	Tottenham v Sunderland	1938	White Hart Lane	75,038
7	Charlton v Aston Villa	1938	The Valley	75,031
8	Arsenal v Sunderland	1935	Highbury	73,295
9	Bolton v Man City	1933	Burnden Park	69,912
10	Newcastle v Chelsea	1930	St James' Park	68,386
11	Sheffield Utd v Leeds	1936	Bramall Lane	68,287
12	Blackburn v Bolton	1929	Ewood Park	62,522
13	Liverpool v Wolves	1952	Anfield	61,905
14	Middlesbro v Newcastle	1949	Ayresome Park	53,536
15	Portsmouth v Derby	1949	Fratton Park	51,385
16	Fulham v Millwall	1938	Craven Cottage	49,335
17	West Ham v Tottenham	1970	Upton Park	42,322
18	Watford v Man Utd	1969	Vicarage Road	34,099
19	Reading v Brentford	1927	Elm Park	33,042
20	Wigan v Hereford Utd	1953	Springfield Park	27,526

Clubs listed are those that played in the Premiership, 2006–07.
The figures provided are the highest ever home gates for each club.

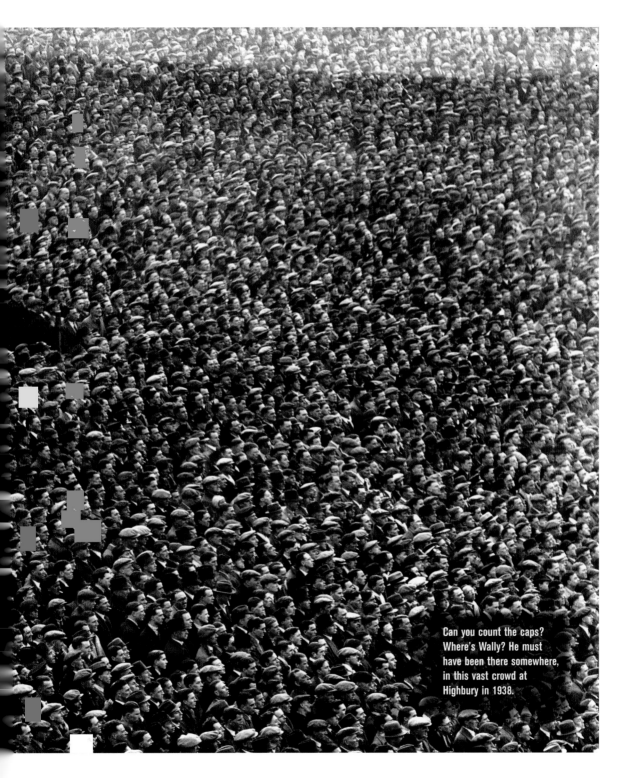

Can you count the caps? Where's Wally? He must have been there somewhere, in this vast crowd at Highbury in 1938.

Colours: blue shirts, white shorts

Nickname: The Toffees, after 'Ye Ancient Everton Toffee House', which was next door

Achievements: Div 1 winners nine times, FA Cup winners five times, European Cup Winners' Cup 1985.

Fascinating Facts: Dixie Dean, still the club's best ever scorer, scored 60 League goals in one season, 1927–28, and most overall: 349 between 1925 and 1937.

FULHAM

Founded: 1879 as a church Sunday school team

Ground: Craven Cottage since 1896. Before that they had 10 different grounds.

Colours: white shirts, black shorts

Nickname: The Cottagers

Achievements: Not many, pot wise, but when the maximum wage was abolished in 1961, they made Johnny Haynes the first £100-per-week player in the UK.

Fascinating Facts: Johnny Haynes played 594 games between 1952 and 1970 and 56 times for England; Fulham is the only UK club to have been managed by a father and son with the same name, Bill Dodgin Snr (1949–53) and Bill Dodgin Jnr (1969–72).

HEART OF MIDLOTHIAN

Founded: 1874

Ground: Tynecastle Stadium, Edinburgh

Colours: maroon shirts

Nickname: Jambos (from 'Jockney' rhyming slang, 'Queen of Hearts' = 'Jam Tarts')

Achievements: Four Div 1 championships, but a long time ago.

Fascinating Facts: Supposedly named after a local dance-hall. In an 1876 team photo, you can clearly see that they are wearing white shirts – with a red heart on the left breast. Very pretty.

Tense moment during a Hearts v Celtic Scottish Premiership match in 2006.

HIBERNIAN

Founded: 1875

Ground: Easter Road Stadium, Edinburgh

Colours: green shirts with white sleeves

Nickname: Hibees

Achievements: Like deadly rivals Hearts, also got four Div 1 wins, but a long time ago.

Fascinating Facts: Founded by Irishmen living in Edinburgh, hence the green.

HUDDERSFIELD TOWN

Founded: 1908

Ground: Galpharm Stadium, previously McAlpine

Colours: blue and white stripes

Nickname: The Terriers

Achievements: Three Div 1 championships in the 1920s plus one FA Cup final win 1922.

Fascinating Facts: Prime Minister Harold Wilson, Huddersfield's most famous native son, carried a photo of the 1920s winning team in his wallet; their youngest player was Denis Law, 16 years and 303 days old when he first turned out on 24 December 1956.

HULL CITY

Founded: 1904

Ground: Kingston Communications stadium

Colours: black and amber stripes

Nickname: The Tigers

Achievements: Beat Carlisle United 11–1 in 1939 in Third Div North – obviously dead jammy.

Fascinating Facts: The biggest city in the UK – population 320,000 – never to have had a team in the top division.

IPSWICH TOWN

Founded: 1878 but didn't make the Football League (Div 3 South) until 1938

Ground: Portman Road

Colours: blue and white

Nickname: Tractor Boys

Achievements: Div 1 winners in 1962 (under Alf Ramsey); FA Cup winners in 1978 (under Bobby Robson).

Fascinating Facts: John Wark scored a hat trick of penalties in a UEFA Cup match against Aris Salonika in 1981.

LEEDS UNITED

Founded: 1919

Ground: Elland Road

Colours: white shirts, white shorts

Nickname: The Whites

Achievements: Div 1 champs in 1969 and 1974 (under Don Revie) and in 1992; semi-final of Euro Champs League 2001 under David O'Leary.

Fascinating Facts: They began as Leeds City in 1904 but got wound up by the FA in 1919 for illegal payments to players, immediately reforming as Leeds United. A rather tricky club ever since.

Jack Charlton parading the FA Cup for Leeds Utd in 1972. In the mid-2000s, this once-great team has fallen on hard times, being relegated to Div 1, while the club went into receivership.

Photograph by A. PICKERING,   Leicester.

LEICESTER FOSSE TEAM.

Mr. LEE, (Sec.)   BAIRD.   ATHERTON.   W. A. THOMPSON.   STRACHAN.   LORD.   WALKER.   BAILEY.   NEWTON, (Trainer).
HOGAN.   MANSON.   THRAVES.   DAVIES.   PICKARD.   GALLOCHER.   HENRYS.
McARTHUR.   TRAINER.   SKEA.   BROWN.

LEICESTER CITY
Founded: 1884 as Leicester Fosse. Became City in 1919
Ground: Walkers Stadium, previously Filbert Street
Colours: blue and white
Nickname: The Foxes
Achievements: Winning League Cup in 1964, 1997, 2000.
Fascinating Facts: Founded by a group of old boys of a school who lived near the old Roman road, the Fosse Way – hence the club's first name. They had a whip round to raise ninepence for a ball and another ninepence for a carpenter to make the goalposts.

LIVERPOOL
Founded: 1892
Ground: Anfield – right from the beginning – but due to move in 2010
Colours: red shirts, shorts, socks
Nickname: The Reds
Achievements: The most successful English team ever – 18 league titles, five FA Cups, five European Cups. Took the Champions League in 2005, after being 3–0 down to AC Milan. Eat your heart out, Chelsea.
Fascinating Facts: Originally Everton played at Anfield, but when they fell out with the ground's owners in 1892, Everton decamped to Goodison – and the owners started their own club, Liverpool.

Why was the manager shaking the office cat? He was trying to find some money in the transfer kitty.

PREMIERSHIP ATTENDANCES 2006–07

		2005–06	2006–07	Change (+/−)
1	Reading	15,029	24,015	+59.8%
2	Arsenal	38,020	59,981	+57.8%
3	Sheffield Utd	19,385	28,524	+47.1%
4	Watford	13,565	18,600	+37.1%
5	Aston Villa	32,320	35,994	+13.7%
6	Manchester Utd	67,849	75,457	+11.2%
7	Fulham	18,542	20,404	+10.0%
8	West Ham	32,315	34,847	+7.8%
9	Everton	37,168	38,766	+4.3%
10	Chelsea	41,863	41,745	−0.3%
11	Tottenham	35,874	35,755	−0.3%
12	Liverpool	44,688	44,016	−1.5%
13	Charlton	25,996	25,490	−1.9%
14	Portsmouth	19,771	19,379	−2.0%
15	Newcastle	52,052	50,680	−2.6%
16	Blackburn	20,194	19,419	−3.8%
17	Man City	42,381	39,872	−5.9%
18	Middlesbrough	28,730	26,330	−8.4%
19	Bolton	24,763	22,566	−8.9%
20	Wigan	20,399	15,498	−24.0%

★★★ MANCHESTER CITY

Founded: 1887 as Ardwick. Became Man City in 1894
Ground: City of Manchester Stadium – previously Maine Road since 1923
Colours: sky-blue shirts, white shorts
Nickname: Blues, The Citizens
Achievements: Two Div 1 titles (1937, 1968); four FA Cups (1904, 1934, 1956, 1969); Euro Cup Winners' Cup (1970).
Fascinating Facts: For 20 months, from February 1986 to October 1987, City managed 34 consecutive league matches without a win. Their youngest ever player is Glyn Pardoe: 15 years, 314 days on his first team appearance in 1962.

MANCHESTER UNITED

Founded: In 1878 as Newton Heath by a group of railway workers; became Man Utd in 1902
Ground: Old Trafford since 1910
Colours: red shirts, white shorts
Nickname: Red Devils
Achievements: Record for the greatest number of Premiership titles so far: nine; in past, won old Div 1 seven times; European Cup (1968 and 1999).
Fascinating Facts: Old Trafford cost £60,000 to build – a huge sum for 1910 – and is today the biggest club ground in the UK, holding over 76,000 (setting a Premiership attendance record in 2007). Sir Bobby Charlton is still the club's highest scorer: 199 League goals, the most capped player with 106 England caps and has made the most League appearances: 606 games.

MIDDLESBROUGH

Founded: 1876 by members of a cricket club
Ground: Riverside Stadium
Colours: red shirts, white band
Nickname: Boro
Achievements: Very few, unless you count winning the League Cup in 2004.
Fascinating Facts: Brian Clough scored five goals for Boro when they beat Brighton 9–0 in 1958.

NEWCASTLE UNITED

Founded: 1881 as Stanley; became Newcastle Utd in 1892
Ground: St James' Park since 1892
Colours: black and white stripes, black shorts
Nickname: Magpies
Achievements: All in the past, alas: four Div 1 titles, the last in 1927; six FA Cups, the last in 1955. Oh, and there was a European Fairs Cup in 1969. Probably England's leading under-achieving 'big' club.
Fascinating Facts: Tony Blair, as Prime Minister, used to say he was a Newcastle fan, but nobody believed him, especially when he remembered watching heroes like Jackie Milburn, long after he'd finished playing. The Real Madrid connection: in 2004 they sold Jonathan Woodgate to them for £13.5 million, then, in 2005, bought Michael Owen from them for £16 million.

NORWICH CITY

Founded: 1902
Ground: Carrow Road
Colours: yellow shirts, green shorts
Nickname: Canaries
Achievements: Finishing third in the Prem, 1993.
Fascinating Facts: In 1950–51 season, while in Div 3 (South), they fielded an unchanged side for 21 games. One of their current directors is the popular TV chef, Delia Smith.

NOTTINGHAM FOREST

Founded: 1865

Ground: City Ground since 1898

Colours: red shirts, white shorts

Nickname: Reds

Achievements: European Cup winners (1979, 1980) under Brian Clough, plus Div 1 champs (1978); plus two FA Cup wins and four League Cup wins.

Fascinating Facts: Arsenal play in red because Forest game them a set of their shirts when they started. The first Nottingham Forest player to score four goals in the FA Cup tie was Sam Widdowson in 1882, though he is better known now for having invented shin guards.

Forest fans salute the manager who 'walked on water'.

NOTTS COUNTY

Founded: 1862

Ground: Meadow Lane

Colours: black and white stripes

Nickname: Magpies

Achievements: FA Cup, but not many remember it as it was back in 1894.

Fascinating Facts: The world's oldest surviving football club.

PORTSMOUTH

Founded: 1898

Ground: Fratton Park since the club's formation, but due to move soon

Colours: blue shirts, white shorts

Nickname: Pompey

Achievements: Just before and after the Second World War, Pompey were all-conquering, winning the FA Cup in 1939, and Div 1 titles in 1949 and 1950. Then came a sad decline back down to Div 3. But by 2003, they had won promotion to the Prem.

Fascinating Facts: Jimmy Dickinson played 764 games for Pompey between 1946 and 1965. Current manager Harry Redknapp briefly joined deadly South Coast rivals Southampton in 2004–05, when they were relegated: a dastardly Pompey plan?

PRESTON NORTH END

Founded: 1881. Formerly, they had been a cricket and rugby club

Ground: Deepdale

Colours: white shirts, blue shorts

Nickname: Lillywhites or North End (in the old glory days, known as The Invincibles)

Achievements: First club to win the double of League and Cup in 1888–89, the first year of the League. They went 22 games unbeaten, hence the 'Invincibles'.

Fascinating Facts: In 1887 they beat Hyde 26–0 in the FA Cup first round, the biggest win in any English competition.

QUEENS PARK RANGERS

Founded: 1885
Ground: Loftus Road
Colours: blue and white hoops
Nickname: The Rs
Achievements: Nearly won Div 1 in 1976 but Liverpool pipped them at the post; League Cup winners in 1967.
Fascinating Facts: QPR have had 12 different home grounds: an English record; in 1963 they had identical twins playing on opposite wings, Roger and Ian Morgan.

RANGERS

Founded: 1873
Ground: Ibrox Stadium
Colours: royal blue shirts, white shorts
Nickname: Gers
Achievements: Winner of Scottish League title 51 times and 31 Cup wins; European Cup Winners' Cup 1972.
Fascinating Facts: Record attendance was 118,567 v Celtic on 2 January 1939; goalkeeper Chris Woods set a British clean sheet record – 1,196 minutes unbeaten between 26 November 1986 and 31 January 1987.

READING

Founded: 1871
Ground: Madejski Stadium
Colours: blue and white hoops
Nickname: The Royals; once known as the Biscuitmen
Achievements: Getting into the Prem in 2006 – and staying there, so far; before that, about the best was reaching the semi of the FA Cup in 1927.
Fascinating Facts: Oxford Utd chairman Robert Maxwell had a cunning plan to merge Reading with Oxford in 1983 but was thwarted.

SHEFFIELD UNITED

Founded: 1889
Ground: Bramall Lane since foundation
Colours: red and white stripes, black shorts
Nickname: The Blades
Achievements: Div 1 champs back in 1898. Four FA Cup wins (1899, 1902, 1915, 1925); getting into the Prem in 2006 – for one season.
Fascinating Facts: In the 1996 film *When Saturday Comes*, actor Sean Bean, a Sheffield Utd fan, got to play at Bramall Lane.

SHEFFIELD WEDNESDAY

Founded: 1867
Ground: Hillsborough
Colours: blue and white stripes, black shorts
Nickname: The Owls
Achievements: Div 1 champs (1903, 1904, 1929, 1930); FA Cup (1896, 1935); League Cup (1991).
Fascinating Facts: Only Brit team to take its name from a day of the week. They were originally a cricket club who met on Wednesday half days.

SOUTHAMPTON

Founded: 1885
Ground: St Mary's Stadium since 2001; formerly at the Dell
Colours: red and white stripes, black shorts
Nickname: The Saints
Achievements: FA Cup win in 1976, while in Div 2, beating Man Utd 1–0; staying in the top flight from 1979 to 2005, when they were relegated.
Fascinating Facts: Terry Paine played 713 games for the Saints between 1956 and 1974.

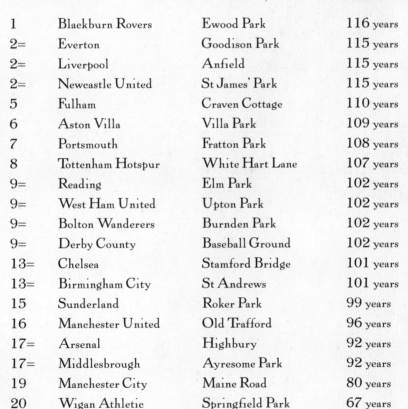

PREMIERSHIP CLUBS (2007–08) WHICH HAVE BEEN AT THEIR GROUNDS THE LONGEST (INCLUDING ONES THEY HAVE NOW LEFT)

1	Blackburn Rovers	Ewood Park	116 years
2=	Everton	Goodison Park	115 years
2=	Liverpool	Anfield	115 years
2=	Newcastle United	St James' Park	115 years
5	Fulham	Craven Cottage	110 years
6	Aston Villa	Villa Park	109 years
7	Portsmouth	Fratton Park	108 years
8	Tottenham Hotspur	White Hart Lane	107 years
9=	Reading	Elm Park	102 years
9=	West Ham United	Upton Park	102 years
9=	Bolton Wanderers	Burnden Park	102 years
9=	Derby County	Baseball Ground	102 years
13=	Chelsea	Stamford Bridge	101 years
13=	Birmingham City	St Andrews	101 years
15	Sunderland	Roker Park	99 years
16	Manchester United	Old Trafford	96 years
17=	Arsenal	Highbury	92 years
17=	Middlesbrough	Ayresome Park	92 years
19	Manchester City	Maine Road	80 years
20	Wigan Athletic	Springfield Park	67 years

STOKE CITY
Founded: 1863
Ground: Britannia Stadium
Colours: red and white stripes, white shorts
Nickname: The Potters
Achievements: League Cup 1972.
Fascinating Facts: Stanley Matthews played his last game for Stoke in February 1965, aged 50.

SUNDERLAND
Founded: 1879 as a team of teachers
Ground: Stadium of Light since 1997; before that Roker Park
Colours: red and white stripes, black shorts
Nickname: used to be The Rokermen, now their nickname as used by Newcastle supporters is too rude to repeat
Achievements: Div 1 champs six times, the last in 1936; winning the FA Cup in 1973 as a Div 2 team; winning the Championship in 2007.
Fascinating Facts: Sunderland were relegated from Div 1 in 1958 after a record 68 consecutive years in the top flight.

TOTTENHAM HOTSPUR
Founded: 1882
Ground: White Hart Lane since 1899
Colours: white shirts, navy shorts
Nickname: Spurs, Lillywhites
Achievements: In 1961, the first club to win the League and Cup double in the 20th century;

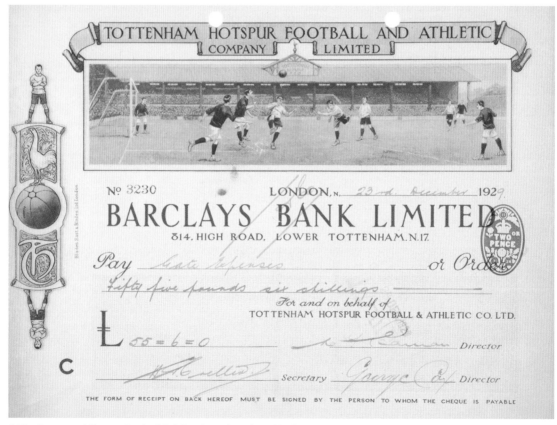

A big cheque – not the sum involved, but the sheer size – issued by Spurs in 1929.

CHEAPEST AND DEAREST SEATS IN THE PREMIERSHIP, 2006–07

		Cheapest	Dearest
1=	Sheffield United	£15	£34
1=	Blackburn Rovers	£15	£39
3=	Charlton Athletic	£20	£35
3=	Watford	£20	£35
5	Bolton Wanderers	£21	£39
6	Manchester City	£22	£38
7=	Manchester United	£23	£37
7=	Middlesbrough	£23	£40
7=	Newcastle United	£23	£53
10=	Aston Villa	£25	£35
10=	Fulham	£25	£46
10=	Wigan Athletic	£25	£35
13	Tottenham Hotspur	£27	£71
14=	Portsmouth	£28	£37
14=	Everton	£28	£38
14=	Reading	£28	£41
17	Liverpool	£30	£34
18=	West Ham United	£32	£57
18=	Arsenal	£32	£94
20	Chelsea	£45	£65

No problem filling grounds, at any price, for crunch matches against top clubs, but early-round cup ties against unglamorous sides are another matter entirely. A loyal Reading fan at the Madejski stadium.

WHAT HAPPENED TO SOME WELL-KNOWN GROUNDS WHEN THEY CLOSED ...

Arsenal: Highbury
Last game: 4–2 v Wigan, 7 May 2006
Now: Housing

Brighton: Goldstone Road
Last game: 1–0 v Doncaster, 24 June 1997
Now: Retail park

Coventry City: Highfield Road
Last game: 6–2 v Derby, 30 April 2005
Now: Housing

Darlington: Feethams
Last game: 2–2 v Leyton Orient, 3 May 2003
Now: Housing

Hull City: Boothferry Park
Last game: 0–1 v Darlington, 14 December 2002
Now: Housing

Leicester City: Filbert Street
Last game: 2–1 v Spurs, 11 May 2005
Now: Student accommodation

Millwall: The Den
Last game: 0–3 v Bristol Rovers, 8 May 1993
Now: Housing and industrial development

Northampton Town: County Ground
Last game: 0–1 v Mansfield, 12 October 1994
Now: Demolished

Oxford United: Manor Ground
Last game: 1–1 v Port Vale,
1 May 2001
Now: Hospital

Reading: Elm Park
Last game: 0–1 v Norwich,
3 May 1998
Now: Housing

Scunthorpe: Old Showground
Last game: 1–1 v Torquay,
18 May 1988
Now: Supermarket

Southampton: The Dell
Last game: 3–2 v Arsenal,
19 May 2001
Now: Housing

Stoke City: Victoria Ground
Last game: 2–1 v West Brom,
4 May 1997
Now: Planned offices, shops

Sunderland: Roker Park
Last game: 3–0 v Everton, 3 May 1997
Now: Housing

Swansea City: Vetch Field
Last game: 2–1 v Wrexham,
11 May 2005
Now: Planned housing

Walsall: Fellows Park
Last game: 1–1 v West Brom,
11 May 1990
Now: Supermarket

Wigan Athletic: Springfield Park
Last game: 1–1 v Man City,
15 May 1999
Now: Housing

Roker Park, former home of Sunderland, was a World Cup
venue in 1966; here, Italy play the USSR there.

FA Cup winners in 1901 as a non-league club, then in 1921, 1961, 1962, 1967, 1981, 1982 and 1991; UEFA Cup 1972, 1984.

Fascinating Facts: In the 1901 Cup final, none of the Spurs players came from London or even the Home Counties – five were Scots, two Welsh, one Irish and three Englishmen who came from Maryport, Grantham and the Potteries.

WATFORD
Founded: 1891
Ground: Vicarage Road
Colours: yellow shirts, black shorts
Nickname: Hornets
Achievements: Getting into the Prem again in 2006, but unfortunately went straight back down.
Fascinating Facts: Elton John became chairman in 1978 when they were struggling in the old 4th Div – by 1982, under manager Graham Taylor, they had made it to Div 1.

WEST BROMWICH ALBION
Founded: 1878
Ground: The Hawthorns
Colours: navy blue and white stripes, white shorts
Nickname: The Baggies
Achievements: Div 1 winners 1920; FA Cups 1886, 1892, 1931, 1954, 1968.
Fascinating Facts: Between 1975 and 1988, West Brom managers were called, in order, Johnny, Ronnie, Ron, Ronnie, Ron, Johnny, Ron, Ron – which could have made a great song.

WEST HAM UNITED
Founded: 1895 as Thames Iron Works; became West Ham Utd in 1900
Ground: Upton Park
Colours: claret shirts with blue sleeves, white shorts
Nickname: The Hammers, Irons

Achievements: FA Cup in 1964, 1975, 1980; European Cup Winners' Cup 1965.

Fascinating Facts: Played in first ever Wembley final in 1923 and got beaten 2–0 by Bolton Wanderers; West Ham provided three players for England's World Cup-winning side in 1966 (Bobby Moore, Martin Peters, Geoff Hurst) and all four England goals in the final were scored by West Ham players.

WIGAN ATHLETIC
Founded: 1932
Ground: JJB stadium
Colours: blue shirts, blue shorts
Nickname: The Latics
Achievements: Getting into the Prem in 2005.
Fascinating Facts: Didn't enter the Football League until 1978 when they got into Div 4.

WOLVERHAMPTON WANDERERS
Founded: 1877
Ground: Molineux
Colours: gold shirts, black shorts
Nickname: Wolves
Achievements: Div 1 champs 1954, 1958, 1959; FA Cup 1893, 1908, 1949, 1960.
Fascinating Facts: In the 1950s, led by England captain Billy Wright, they were called the 'best side in the world' after beating loads of not very brilliant foreign clubs in lots of friendlies.

So that's the clubs, now let's bring on the players...

4. Great players, past and present

Some past, present, and possibly future immortals in football's hall of fame

EARLY STARS

STEVE BLOOMER
Born: Cradley Heath, 1874. Died 1938.
Clubs: Derby County, Middlesbrough.
Caps: 23 for England, 28 goals.

The first truly great goal scorer, or striker as we would call him today, whose goal ratio for England shows just how prolific he was (28 in 23 games). In his league career, he scored 352 goals and was the leading scorer for five seasons. And yet he was a thin, weedy, delicate-looking player with a pale complexion – often known as Paleface – not one of those bullet-headed, burly strikers who were common in the early decades.

He was renowned for his quick thinking and first-time shooting. Technically, he was an inside right, not a centre forward, in the days when teams played with five up front (right winger, inside right, centre forward, inside left, outside left). Despite his great career he never actually won any major club honours, finishing on the losing side in two cup finals. He didn't smoke but enjoyed the odd pint or three of beer and was often up before the board of directors for his lack of sobriety – a pattern amongst gifted ball playing stars which has continued over the years, the obvious examples in modern times being Jimmy Greaves, George Best, Paul Gascoigne. When he retired from playing, he went abroad to coach. In 1914, at the beginning of the First World War, he was coaching in Berlin and found himself interned for the duration of the war.

BILLY MEREDITH
Born: Chirk, Wales, 1875. Died 1958.
Clubs: Manchester City, Manchester United.
Caps: 48 for Wales, 11 goals.

Meredith, the son of a Welsh miner, went down the pit aged 12. His extraordinary football skills brought him to the attention of English clubs and he played for 30 years in Manchester, from 1894 to 1924, having two spells with City and one with

Billy Meredith (left) in action for Man Utd in the first-ever FA Charity Shield match, on 28 August 1908, against QPR.

United. He was the first winger to be dubbed the 'Wizard of the Wing', a description that was bestowed on many later wingers, right up to George Best and Ryan Giggs.

In magazines, comics and programmes of the period you can tell it's a drawing of Billy Meredith because of the bit of wood sticking out of his mouth. He sucked a toothpick, even when playing, a habit which, he explained, went back to his years as a miner when he chewed tobacco. As a footballer, he felt the need to chew something and chose a toothpick. Fans would send him packets of tooth-picks, just as the Beatles used to be sent jelly babies by their fans in the 1960s.

Meredith was a rebel, and was often in trouble. In 1905, when the maximum wage was £4, he was suspended by the FA for offering a bribe to a rival player, which he claimed was a joke. He was also a reformer, working hard to establish a players' union, which collapsed but led the way for later improvements.

In 1920 he was still playing for Wales at the age of 45, helping them to their first ever victory over England. In 1924, with Man City, he appeared in the FA Cup aged 49. He neither smoked nor drank, at a time when most players did both. In 1926 he became the first British footballer to star in a full-length feature film, *Ball of Fortune*, in which he played the part of a football trainer.

STARS OF THE PRE-WAR ERA: THE 1920s & 1930s

DIXIE DEAN
Born: Birkenhead, 1907. Died 1980.
Clubs: Tranmere, Everton, Notts County.
Caps: 16 for England, 18 goals.

Britain's most prolific ever striker, whose record of 349 League goals is unlikely ever to be equalled. In the 1928–29 season, at Everton, he scored 60 goals in 39 games, another record that still stands.

His first name was William, which he preferred, but the foot-ball world always knew him as 'Dixie', a nickname that dated back to his early years at Tranmere. With his dark complexion and curly black hair, he was assumed to come from 'Dixie', the southeastern USA. After one game in 1938, a rival fan grabbed him and said 'We'll get you, you black bastard.' A policeman appeared and was about to apprehend the man, but Dixie said 'It's all right officer, I'll look after this.' Whereupon Dixie punched the man so hard he fell to the ground. 'That was a beauty,' said the policeman, 'but I never saw it.'

Dixie was a strong, bustling, traditional centre forward who won many trophies, notably two Division One titles, in 1928 and 1932, and the FA Cup in 1933.

Although he played at a time when players were still poorly paid, on a maximum of £9 per week, as a superstar, known throughout the land, he supplemented his income by advertising, especially cigarettes. He was known as the face of Carreras Club, 'the cigarettes with a kick in them'.

HUGHIE GALLACHER
Born: Bellshill, Scotland in 1903. Died 1957.
Clubs: Queen of the South, Airdrieonians, Newcastle United, Chelsea, Derby.
Caps: 19 for Scotland, 22 goals.

Scotland was rich in star footballers in the pre-war years, many of them small and tricky, such as Alex James (known as the 'Wee Wizard') and Alan Morton (the 'Wee Blue Devil'), and most of them spent their greatest years with English clubs.

Hughie Gallacher played for ten clubs in Scotland before he joined Newcastle United where

H. GALLACHER

his name will live on for ever. As captain, he helped deliver them the League title in his first season, in 1926–27, the last time Newcastle United won it. His transfer, for a massive £10,000, to Chelsea in 1930 prompted public protests on Tyneside.

Although only five feet five inches tall, he was stocky and strong and fearless, good at dribbling and tackling. In 1928 he was one of the legendary Scottish 'Wembley Wizards' who humbled England 5–1. He didn't actually score in that particular game, though his goal ratio for Scotland was exceptional.

He would have provided today's tabloids with endless copy as his private life was rather colourful, with court appearances and drunken behaviour. On one occasion, he was accused of being drunk on the pitch. He maintained he had only been drinking whisky and water as a mouthwash.

Alas, his later years ended in tragedy. He became an alcoholic and eventually took his own life by throwing himself in front of a train.

STANLEY MATTHEWS

Born: Stoke-on-Trent, 1915. Died 2000.
Clubs: Stoke City, Blackpool.
Caps: 54 for England, 11 goals.

A phenomenon of both the pre-war and also the post-war years, who set standards of behaviour and longevity which we'll probably never see again, and yet he never won a League title and only once won the FA Cup. This was the so-called Matthews Final of 1953, when the whole nation was willing Blackpool to win, for Matthews' sake, which they

did after coming back from being 1–3 down to beat Bolton Wanderers 4–3.

Matthews' nickname was pretty obvious: the 'Wizard of Dribble'. He was able to beat people at pace, bamboozle them with his body swerve while keeping the ball under complete control, before delivering perfectly weighted crosses for the centre forward.

He made his debut for Stoke aged 17 in 1932, and right from the beginning of his career he was obsessed by physical fitness and a healthy diet, which helps explain why his playing career lasted for so long. His final appearance in the first division, for Stoke against Fulham, came just five days after his 50th birthday.

He was probably the first English player to be known throughout the whole football world, at home and abroad, and in 1956 he was voted the first ever European Footballer of the Year. In 1965 he was the first footballer to be knighted. He remains the only player to be knighted while still playing. In a career lasting 35 years, he was never once booked.

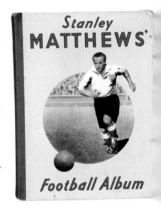

POST-WAR YEARS, THE 1950s & 1960s

BOBBY CHARLTON

Born: Ashington, Northumberland, 1937.
Clubs: Manchester United, Preston North End.
Caps: 106 for England, 49 goals.

Another much-loved, much-lauded English player with a spotless record, on and off the pitch, a hero for all boys to admire. He survived the Munich air crash of 1958 to become one of Man Utd's most successful ever players, helping them to win the European Cup in 1968. He is also remembered as a

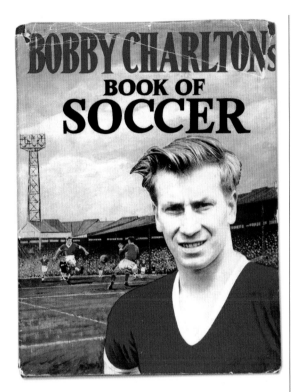

vital member of England's World Cup-winning team of 1966, along with his brother, Jack Charlton.

He never commanded the large transfer fees of some of his contemporaries, playing almost all of his career at the same club, Manchester United. He probably did not have the natural flair of George Best, but he more than made up for it through his application, intelligence, perfect passing and his thunderous shot.

He was knighted in 1994 and is still seen today as one of the best known and most admired ambassadors for football all over the world.

BOBBY MOORE

Born: Barking, Essex, 1941. Died 1993.
Clubs: West Ham, Fulham.
Caps: 108 for England, 2 goals

Moore was the golden boy of the Sixties, fair-haired and handsome, one of nature's officers, who had in many ways a golden career, with not too many disappointments along the way. He spent almost his entire career with his local club, West Ham, and once he got his first England cap in 1962, for the World Cup finals in Peru, he was a mainstay of the England team for the next 10 years, only missing 10 games.

He was the winning captain at Wembley three times in a row, lifting the FA Cup with West Ham in 1964, the European Cup Winners' Cup in 1965, then the World Cup with England in 1966.

As a right half – in modern terms roughly a central defender – he was a clever player, defending with his head as much as his feet, anticipating moves and passes, and rarely resorting to wild tackles or physical intimidation.

While 1966 was the climax of his career as far as trophies were concerned, his performance in the 1970 World Cup against Brazil and his duel with Pele were equally memorable. After his sudden death from cancer in 1993, Pele paid the following tribute to his old adversary: 'He was one of the world's finest defenders and a great sportsman.'

GEORGE BEST

Born: Belfast, Northern Ireland, 1946. Died 2005.
Clubs: Manchester United, Fulham, etc.
Caps: 37 for Northern Ireland, 9 goals.

George Best felt so homesick when he first arrived in Manchester from Belfast aged 15, that he ran away back home. After two weeks, his dad persuaded him to return. Until he was 19 he was a model player, hardly drank, was disciplined and obedient. But, by the time he was 21, winning the European Cup with United and voted European

Five days after George Best's death in November 2005, fans at Old Trafford hold up posters in a mass tribute to their fallen hero before Man Utd's game against West Bromwich Albion.

Player of the Year, he had adopted a playboy lifestyle, with his Beatles haircut, dating Miss Worlds, quaffing champagne, and skipping training sessions. In one of his most memorable quips, Best once remarked, 'I used to go missing a lot: Miss Canada, Miss England, Miss World.'

Best was the first modern superstar, who became a household name, and was followed everywhere by the paparazzi, with commercial companies constantly chasing after him for modelling and advertising contracts. Even so, in 1968, at the height of his career, his annual earnings – so he told me – were only £30,000, half of which came from football.

As a player, all those who saw him will never forget the beauty of his speed and movement, his outrageous skill and his deceptive strength. Unlike some naturally gifted wingers, he was rarely self-indulgent, avoiding the step-overs of a Cristiano Ronaldo. By the age of 27, he was as good as finished, having lost interest and fitness, although he played for a few more years for lower-league clubs. He died in 2005 after a kidney infection brought on by excessive drinking.

RECENT STARS, 1980s & 1990s

PAUL GASCOIGNE
Born: Gateshead, 1967.
Clubs: Newcastle United, Spurs, Lazio, Rangers, Everton.
Caps: 57 for England, 10 goals.

Gazza, as he was always known, was considered by many experts as the most naturally talented player of his generation, a creative midfielder with a strong upper body, an unexpected change of pace, an excellent shot, able to turn around a game with a moment of magic, such as the free kick for Spurs that beat Arsenal and England keeper Seaman in the 1991 FA Cup, and his cheeky goal against Scotland in Euro 1996. The public took him to their hearts after his tears in the 1990 World Cup.

Many believe that, like George Best, he wasted his talents. He was prone to reckless tackles on the pitch, leading to self-inflicted injuries, and excessive drinking off the pitch. But in fact he had a great career, playing in the Premiership until he was 36 and winning 57 caps for England. Barring injuries, he would surely have got many more.

Gazza's problems were mainly emotional rather than related to alcohol (which he said he never liked anyway). He was obsessive, and has struggled to overcome a tendency to depression most of his life.

DAVID BECKHAM

Born: Leytonstone, 1975.
Clubs: Manchester United, Real Madrid,
LA Galaxy.
Caps: 96 for England, 17 goals.

Beckham made his debut for Manchester United aged 17 and introduced himself to the general football public with a remarkable goal from the halfway line against Wimbledon.

In 1998, playing for England, he became a national hate figure after being sent off against Argentina in the World Cup and was subsequently booed at almost every away ground. By 2002, when his last-minute free kick against Greece won England a place at the World Cup finals, he was a hero again. His transformation was a triumph of determination and perseverance.

Beckham's speciality was his free kicks, bending the ball in from impossible-seeming angles and long distances, and his pinpoint crosses from the wing, which delighted the fans of Man Utd, England, and, for four seasons, Real Madrid.

For a long time he was a popular captain of England, until their poor showing in the World Cup of 2006 led to his demotion from the England team by the new England coach, Steve McLaren. However, in June 2007, following a run of bad results in qualifiers for Euro 2008, McLaren recalled Beckham to the squad for a vital match in Estonia, where he played a major part in a 3–0 win.

In the long run, his claim to immortality in the Halls of Football Fame might well rest on the phenomenon of Brand Beckham. His name, face and style made him a household name around the world, his every movement and change of hairstyle chronicled. It was estimated that, in 2007, his contract with LA Galaxy would earn him US$128 million, half from football and the other half from commercial activities. No other British footballer in history has achieved such high international recognition – for his style as much as his football.

PRESENT-DAY STARS

STEVEN GERRARD

Born: Liverpool, 1980.
Clubs: Liverpool.
Caps: 57 for England, 12 goals.

Liverpool have had some truly great players in recent decades, such as Ian Rush, Kenny Dalglish and Kevin Keegan, but few have been as influential as Steven Gerrard. He has been able to rally the team when all seemed lost, as in the 2005 European Cup final, when he inspired Liverpool to victory against Milan, who had gone 3–0 up by half-time.

Despite offers from Chelsea and most of the major clubs of Europe, Gerrard in 2007 was still playing for his boyhood team, and was still adored on Merseyside. Perhaps not the most naturally gifted of players, he made up for it by stamina, pace, and determination. He also had the ability to be both a hard-tackling, defensive midfielder and a creator, surging forward to lay on or score wonder goals.

His many appearances for England have not always been as remarkable, or as consistent, as his Liverpool performances, possibly because of the apparent difficulty of working alongside a similarly talented midfield player, Frank Lampard, but his magnificent 30-yard shot in England's legendary 5–1 win against Germany in Munich in 2001 was certainly one of the most memorable England goals of modern times.

WAYNE ROONEY

Born: Liverpool, 1985.
Clubs: Everton, Manchester United.
Caps: England 38, goals 12.

Since the age of 16, when he arrived in the Premiership with Everton, most experts have agreed Rooney is the most naturally gifted and exciting English player of the present day. In 2003, aged only 17 years and 111 days, he became England's youngest-ever international player and went on to be England's youngest scorer. His appearances for England in Euro 2004 in Portugal, still aged only 18, led to him being hailed as a world-class star. He announced his arrival at Manchester United in 2004 by scoring a hat-trick against the Turkish side Fenerbahce.

Over-exuberance on the pitch led to several red cards and suspensions, and a serious injury before the 2006 World Cup appeared to halt his progress, but he bounced back and, in the 2006–07 season, played a vital part in Manchester United's Premiership-winning season.

Who knows what lies ahead for him? Will he fade or continue to develop and fulfil his potential and have a long career? Is he a future captain of England? Or even one day World Player of the Year? All England football fans must keep their fingers well crossed.

GREAT FOREIGN PLAYERS

Some world-class foreign stars, legends still, known about by all true fans everywhere.

PELE
Born: Brazil, 1940.
Clubs: Santos (Brazil), New York Cosmos (USA).
Caps: 92 for Brazil, 77 goals.

The world's best-ever player? How can you prove that, or even truly believe it, unless you have somehow been watching every leading club and every country since 1888. In which case you are probably aged 150 and have an extraordinarily good memory. If we are considering post-war greats, then there are enough experts and fans still living who saw Pele in the flesh and are convinced that, yes, he was the best player they ever saw. He first played for Brazil when he was 16 and, a year later in 1958, he was at the World Cup finals

in Sweden. In the semi against France, he scored a hat-trick. In the final against Sweden, he got two more goals – and a World Cup winner's medal.

Injuries or foul play by rivals determined to hack him down ruined his next two World Cups, making him vow he'd never appear in a World Cup again but, in 1970 in Mexico, he returned and once again helped Brazil win the World Cup.

Pele had flair as well as technique, power as well as purpose, which made him almost impossible to stop without resorting to violence. He was calm and confident without being flash or ostentatious.

England fans remember him for the save that Gordon Banks made in the 1970 World Cup. Pele powered a header down inside the post which the whole world, including Pele, thought must go in, but Banks miraculously threw himself backwards, got a hand to it and flipped it up over the bar.

His real name is Edson Arantes di Nascimento but he was nicknamed Pele as a boy. When he retired from Brazilian fooball, Santos retired the number 10 shirt and have never given it to another player since.

FERENC PUSKÁS
Born: Budapest, 1927. Died 2006.
Clubs: Kispest, Honved (Hungary), Real Madrid.
Caps: 84 for Hungary, 83 goals.

As a boy, Puskás might have had trouble being taken on by a modern academy, being short and plump, useless in the air, not very fast and only using one foot – his left – to control and pass the ball. Ah, but what a magical left foot. It was as if he had glue on it, which stuck to every ball. At 18, his outrageous skills and shooting took him straight into the great Hungarian national side of the early 1950s, which was unbeaten for almost four years. They thumped England 6–3 at Wembley in 1953, then 7–1 in Budapest the following year. In the World Cup of 1954, Hungary got to the final against West Germany, but Puskás had been injured and they were beaten 3–2.

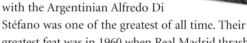

Puskás had a second career in Spain with Real Madrid. By this time some people believed he was too old, but he proved them wrong by becoming Spain's top scorer for four years. His partnership with the Argentinian Alfredo Di Stéfano was one of the greatest of all time. Their greatest feat was in 1960 when Real Madrid thrashed Eintracht Frankfurt 7–3 at Hampden Park in front of a crowd of 135,000 to win the European Champions Cup. Puskás got four of the goals.

In Hungary, he was known as the 'Galloping Major' from his early years playing with a Hungarian army club. He died in 2006, aged 79. His goal average for his country is still a world record – 83 goals in 84 games. Amazing.

JOHAN CRUYFF
Born: Amsterdam, Holland, 1947.
Clubs: Ajax, Barcelona.
Caps: 48 for Holland, 33 goals.

Mrs Cruyff was a cleaner at Ajax and persuaded them to give her son Johan a trial – but it's hard to believe he would not have been discovered anyway, as his natural talents were apparent to everyone from an early age. And his intelligence. This, and some very strong opinions, which often made him appear arrogant, led to quite a few bust-ups with his colleagues and authority during his playing and later management career. Like many of the very early footballers, he was also partial to a fag, which is practically unknown in football today.

Cruyff won the European Cup three times with Ajax and was three times European Footballer of the Year. As manager of Barcelona, he won four Spanish league titles and the European Cup.

He advocated 'total football', as practised by the Dutch team of the 1970s – the theory being that talented players should be able to move around the pitch and play in any position. When it worked, and all the other players were as good as Cruyff, it resulted in some of the best football ever seen.

One of Cruyff's legacies is a trick named after him – the Cruyff turn. This is a method of turning and dragging the ball back, which is often tried in tight spaces near the corner flag, to confound and get around a defender, but it doesn't always work with lesser mortals.

MARADONA

Born: Argentina, 1960.
Clubs: Boca Juniors, Barcelona, Napoli.
Caps: 91 for Argentina, 34 goals.

Unlike Pele, who played the best part of his career in his home country, Maradona moved early on to Europe, playing in Spain and Italy, being transferred for world record fees. His time with Barcelona was not a huge success, probably because he was still so young, but at Napoli he inspired them to their first ever 'Scudetto' (for winning Serie A, the Italian premier league).

He led Argentina in four World Cups, winning the title in 1986 when he was also voted World Footballer of the Year.

He was small and squat, with a tendency to tubbiness, even when still playing, but he had enormous strength, speed and skill, able to take control of a game and shape it to his will. British fans still moan about his 'Hand of God' goal when, in the 1986 World Cup quarter finals, he punched the ball past England's Peter Shilton, a goal which stood as the ref had not spotted it.

Maradona's weaknesses – for food, drink and drugs – which, alas, have shortened the careers of many players since football began, and probably will do so in the future, should not detract from the fact that, in football terms, he was a genius.

WHERE DO PLAYERS COME FROM?

Traditionally, we like to imagine that a team named after a town will mostly contain players born in that town, but this has rarely happened, even in the early days. Scotsmen in particular came down to Lancashire as early as the 1880s, attracted by the better pay. Then, as soon as clubs had a bit of money to spend, they went out looking for players, wherever they came from, from many parts of the UK and the Republic of Ireland. Rarely, though, did they venture abroad.

On the whole, though, until the last 20 years or so, a good percentage – between about a half and a third – of every League team's squad did come from the surrounding area. In 1972 the Football League Review did a survey of the 2,000 players then registered with the 92 teams and analysed their places of birth. They defined a local player as one born within 12 miles of their club or, in the case of a club in a rural area, such as Carlisle United or Plymouth Argyle, they widened 'local' to mean born in the county. They compiled a list of the clubs with the highest percentage of locally born players. Those clubs with over 50% home-grown players were as follows.

Percentage of players born locally, 1972–73

Club	%
Newport County	63%
Chesterfield	62%
Queens Park Rangers	58%
Tottenham Hotspur	57%
Oldham Athletic	56%
Everton	56%
Orient	56%
Liverpool	55%
Rotherham United	54%
Millwall	53%
Sunderland	53%
Manchester City	51%

West London boy Gerry Francis played for and managed QPR.

They also compiled an interesting list of the main towns and cities where British players had been born. Naturally, most professionals came from the largest city, London, but after that the North of England and Scotland had the most players.

Origins of players, 1972–73

	Population	Players
London	7,612,000	159
Liverpool	607,000	93
Glasgow	898,000	63
Manchester	541,000	63
Birmingham	1,013,000	44
Sheffield	520,000	40
Newcastle	222,000	40
Belfast	384,000	25
Bristol	425,000	25
Leicester	284,000	25
Stoke	265,000	20
Edinburgh	449,000	19
Leeds	495,000	19
Hull	285,000	14
Nottingham	300,000	14
Cardiff	278,000	13
Dublin	569,000	13
Bradford	294,000	11
Croydon	330,000	5
Coventry	335,000	4

The Premiership, with vast salaries and enormous scouting systems, now means that English clubs can hire players from any part of the world. When the Premiership began in 1992, there were just 37 foreign-born players. In 2006–07, this had risen to 252. Arsenal, for example, often play with a totally foreign-born team, even including subs on the bench, while Chelsea rarely field more than two or three British-born players.

A Middlesbrough lad born and bred, Stewart Downing of Boro and England.

Percentage of players born locally, 2006–07

1	Middlesbrough	11 out of 33 squad players	33.3%
2	West Ham United	9 out of 28	32%
3	Chelsea	9 out of 29	31%
4	Liverpool	10 out of 37	27%
5	Wigan Athletic	7 out of 28	25%
6	Watford	7 out of 32	21.8%
7	Charlton Athletic	8 out of 37	21.6%
8	Aston Villa	6 out of 28	21.4%
9	Tottenham Hotspur	6 out of 29	21%
10	Blackburn Rovers	5 out of 31	16.1%
11	Arsenal	6 out of 40	15%
12	Everton	4 out of 27	14.8%
13	Sheffield United	5 out of 34	14.7%
14	Manchester United	4 out of 28	14.3%
15	Bolton Wanderers	3 out of 25	12%
16	Fulham	4 out of 34	11.8%
17	Manchester City	3 out of 28	10.7%
18	Newcastle United	3 out of 30	10%
19	Reading	1 out of 30	3.3%
20	Portsmouth	1 out of 36	2.8%

PLAYERS' HEIGHTS AND WEIGHTS

Over the years, professional players have got taller, which is not surprising as the height of the average British person, male and female, has increased as well, with better diet, health, social conditions and medicine.

Before the Second World War, it was rare to find any player in any team who was six feet or more, except for the goalkeeper. And even then, many goalkeepers, even in the top division, were just five feet 10 or 11 inches. Today, the average height of all players in the majority of the Premiership teams is six feet.

Average height of Premiership teams, 2006–07

1	Man City	1.85m	6'1"
2=	Bolton	1.84m	6'0"
2=	Fulham	1.84m	6'0"
2=	Liverpool	1.84m	6'0"
2=	Middlesbro'	1.84m	6'0"
3=	Aston Villa	1.83m	6'0"
3=	Blackburn	1.83m	6'0"
3=	Sheffield Utd	1.83m	6'0"
3=	Watford	1.83m	6'0"
3=	Chelsea	1.83m	6'0"
4=	Arsenal	1.82m	6'0"
4=	Charlton	1.82m	6'0"
4=	Man Utd	1.82m	6'0"
4=	Portsmouth	1.82m	6'0"
4=	Tottenham	1.82m	6'0"
4=	Wigan	1.82m	6'0"
5=	Everton	1.81m	5'11"
6=	West Ham	1.80m	5'11"
6=	Reading	1.80m	5'11"
6=	Newcastle	1.80m	5'11"

HEIGHTS AND WEIGHTS IN THE PAST: 1923 CUP FINAL

Programmes, then as now, usually give a potted biography of each team's players. It is intriguing to look at the first ever Wembley Cup final programme of 1923 and see the heights and weights of the two teams, Bolton Wanderers and West Ham, and their careers.

WEST HAM

A. E. HUFTON (goal) has well earned the reputation of being one of the finest goalkeepers in the country. He is very quick to grasp a situation, and his long reach is of the utmost service in dealing with difficult shots. He stands 5 ft. 10 in. and weighs 12 stone. Previous club, Sheffield United.

W. M. HENDERSON (right back) is a young player who quickly made his mark, and probably the best of him has not yet been seen. A native of Whitburn, he was with Aberdare when West Ham signed him on. His height is 5 ft. 10½ in. and weight 12 stone 4 lbs.

J. YOUNG (left back) is another native of Whitburn. He played for Southend United at outside left, and went to Upton Park as a forward, but he displayed his aptitude as a defender, and well earned the position he now occupies. He is 5 ft. 9 in. in height and weighs 12 stone.

S. BISHOP (right half) also earned a reputation as a forward before he left the Ilford club to join the "Hammers." He has played in the front line occasionally, but can perform equally well in almost any position in the field. Height 5 ft. 11 in., weight 11 stone.

G. KAY (centre half), captain of the side, and a brilliant pivot. He was slightly indisposed

a few weeks ago, but is all right now and playing in splendid form. His judgment, both in tackling and feeding his forwards, is superb. Height 5 ft. 10 in., weight 12 stone 5 lbs. He was with Bolton Wanderers in pre-war days.

J. TRESADERN (left half) gained the highest honour that can be bestowed on a player when he was given his "cap" for the match with Scotland a fortnight back. Is only of medium build, but makes up for any lack of avoirdupois by his extraordinary cleverness and speed. He deserves all his honours. His height is 5 ft. 6 in. and weight 10 stone.

R. RICHARDS (outside right) came to Upton Park from Wolverhampton Wanderers as an extreme left winger, but after a time was transferred to the opposite side of the field. His merit was such that he represented Wales in international games during recent seasons, but he has never played better than at the present

The 1923 West Ham team, with manager Syd King (left).

time. Height 5 ft. 8 in., weight 11 stone 6 lb.

W. BROWN (inside right) did not get a permanent place in the team until the season was well advanced, but he has proved an exceptionally fine player and fits in beautifully with Richards and Victor Watson. His first time drives have done much towards building up the "Hammers'" excellent goal average. He stands 5 ft. 7½ in. and weighs 11 stone 6 lb.

V. WATSON (centre forward), a brilliant player whose skill is as great as his dash. A native of Cambridge, he has risen quickly to the top rung of the ladder, for he is now England's recognised leader of the attack. Height 5 ft. 8½ in., weight 11 stone.

W. MOORE (inside left) was famous in the Sunderland team before deciding to migrate to West Ham. Has delightful ball control, is quick and accurate in his passes, and shoots with judgment. He stands 5 ft. 7 in. and weighs 10 stone 6 lb.

J. RUFFELL (outside left), one of the cleverest wingers in the country, and many admirers expected him to be "capped." He possesses fine speed, is very smart in avoiding a tackle, and centres accurately. Height 5 ft. 6 in., weight 10 stone 3 lb. He is a local player.

BOLTON WANDERERS

RICHARD H. PYM (goalkeeper) is a fisherman from Topsham, and made his name with Exeter City in Southern League football. He cost

The 1923 Bolton Wanderers side, who ran out 2–0 winners in the first ever FA Cup Final played at Wembley.

the Wanderers over £3,000, and has been worth it. Height 6 ft., weight 12 stone 10 lb.

ROBERT HOWARTH (right back) hails from Atherton, and assisted the Atherton Club in Lancashire Combination before joining the Wanderers last season. A great tackler, but somewhat erratic. Height 5 ft. 8½ in., weight 11 stone 3 lb.

WALTER ROWLEY (right back or left half) belongs to neighbouring colliery village of Little Hulton, and went from his native club to Oldham Athletic, being transferred to Bolton eight years ago. Height 5 ft. 9½ in., weight 12 stone 2 lb.

ALEXANDER FINNEY (left back) and youngest player in team. Native of St. Helens, and last season played for New Brighton in Lancashire Combination. The find of the season, and shows remarkable judgment and ability. Height 5 ft. 8½ in., weight 11 stone 4 lb.

HENRY NUTTALL (right half back), born at Burnden Park when his father was grounds-man to the club. He joined Wanderers as a junior, and this season has proved a neat and effective middle-man, who knows how to assist his forwards. Height 5 ft. 9½ in., weight 11 stone 4 lb.

JAMES SNEDDON (centre half back), another Bolton man, who played with Hamilton Central in the West Lancashire League before Wanderers secured him. His great height and long reach make him a great defender, though his feeding is open to improvement. Height 6 ft. 1½ in., weight 12 stone 5 lb.

WILLIAM JENNINGS (left half back), a Welsh International and a real artist both in attack and defence. Came to Bolton from

Barry as a full back, but has made his name as left half. Height 5 ft. 9 in., weight 11 stone 9 lb.

WILLIAM BUTLER (outside right), like Howarth, comes from Atherton, and attracted Wanderers' attention whilst playing centre forward for Atherton Collieries in Lancashire Alliance. He got his chance when Donaldson joined Sunderland. Height 5 ft. 7 in., weight 10 stone 10 lb.

DAVID BONE NIGHTINGALE JACK (inside right), born at Bolton when his father played outside left for the Wanderers. Has scored six goals in as many cup-ties this season. Cost club transfer fee of £3,500 from Plymouth Argyle, where his father is manager. Height 5 ft. 10½ in., weight 12 stone 1 lb.

JOHN REID SMITH (centre forward), born at Glasgow. Helped his first professional club, Kilmarnock, to win the Scottish Cup in 1919–20, scoring in every round. Then assisted Cowdenbeath and Glasgow Rangers, who got over £3,000 for his transfer. Height 5 ft. 8 in., weight 12 stone 1 lb.

JOSEPH SMITH (inside left), native of Dudley, captain and veteran of the team – a rare general, and a dangerous shot with the left foot. Not so quick as of yore in snapping up chances, but a tireless worker. Went from a Sunday school team at Newcastle (Staffs) to Bolton. Height 5 ft. 7½ in., weight 12 stone 8 lb.

EDWARD T. VIZARD (outside left), another Welsh International, was with Cogan Old Boys, his native club, when the Wanderers invited him to play a month on trial. They signed him after his first game. A subtle drib-bler, who loves to get defences into a tangle. Height 5 ft. 9 in., weight 11 stone 6 lb.

ENGLAND 1966

Some 40 years later, and England players are still quite small. This was the England squad that played against the Irish league in September 1966, just after the World Cup win, as described in the match programme. Only 3 out of 23 are over 6 feet.

JOHN CONNELLY (Manchester United). Previous Club: Burnley. Height: 5 ft. 9 in. Weight: 11 st. Place of Birth: St. Helens. Age: 27 years. International Record and other honours: Full International Caps, 20 (First Full International game was against Wales in 1959); Under 23, 1. 6 Football League appearances. 2 First Division Championship medals. F.A. Cup Runners-up medal. Style of Play: Speedy Winger, able to perform on either flank.

JAMES CHRISTOPHER ARMFIELD (Blackpool). Height: 5 ft. 10 in. Weight: 12 st. 2 lbs Place of Birth: Denton (Manchester). Age: 30 years. International Record and other honours: Full International Caps, 43 (First Full International game was against Brazil in 1959); Under 23, 9. 12 Football League appearances. He was Young Footballer of the Year in 1959. Style of Play: Fast attacking Full Back.

ALAN JAMES BALL (Everton). Height: 5 ft 7 in. Weight: 10 st. 2 lbs. Place of Birth: Farnworth (near Bolton). Age: 20 years. International Record and other honours: Full International Caps, 14 (First Full International game was against Yugoslavia in 1965); Under 23, 8. 3 Football League appearances. Played for Farnworth and Worsley Schoolboys. Style of Play: Fast and fiery, ball-playing Inside Forward.

PETER BONETTI (Chelsea). Height: 5 ft 10½ in. Weight: 11 st. Place of Birth: Putney, London. Age: 24 years. International Record and other honours: Full International Caps, 1: Under 23, 12. Has played for Worthing Under 13 and Brighton Under 15. Also played for Sussex Youth. Has Football League Cup Winners Medal. Agile and fearless Goalkeeper.

NORMAN HUNTER (Leeds United). Height: 5 ft. 11¼ in. Weight: 11 st. 12 lbs. Place of Birth: Eighton Bank, Gateshead, Co. Durham. Age: 22 years. International Record and other honours: Full International Caps, 4 (First Full International game was against Spain in 1965); Under 23, 3. 4 Football League games. Has an F.A. Cup Runners-up Medal and a Second Division Championship Medal. Style of Play: Strong tackling attacking Half Back.

IAN CALLAGHAN (Liverpool F.C.). Height 5 ft. 7 in. Weight: 10 st. 10½ lbs. Place of Birth: Liverpool. Age: 23 years. International Record and other honours: Full International Caps, 4; Under 23, 4. 1 Football League appearance. Has First and Second Division Championship medals and Cup Winners medal. Played for

Liverpool Schoolboys and Liverpool County F.A. Style of Play: Tricky and direct Winger.

GEORGE REGINALD COHEN (Fulham). Height: 5 ft 10 in. Weight: 12 st. 5 lbs. Place of Birth: Fulham, London. Age: 26 years. International Record and other honours: Full International Caps, 30; Under 23, 8 (First Full Cap was against Uruguay in 1964). Has played three times for the Football League. Has played for West London and London Schoolboys and for Middlesex at Youth level. Style of Play: Fast attacking Full Back.

JAMES GREAVES (Tottenham Hotspur). Previous Clubs: Chelsea and A.C. Milan. Height: 5 ft. 8 in. Weight: 10 st. 6 lbs. Place of Birth: London. Age: 26 years. International Record and other honours: 54 Full International Caps, 12 Under 23 appearances and 8 Football League appearances. (First Full International Cap was against Peru in 1959.) Has an F.A. Cup Winners medal and European Cup Winners medal. Played for Essex and London Schoolboys and Middlesex and

Above **The full England squad pose for a group picture during training for the World Cup at the National Recreation Centre at Lilleshall in Shropshire on 10 June 1966.**

England at Youth level. Style of Play: Goalscoring Inside Forward, very fast with a good shot.

GORDON MILNE (Liverpool). Previous Club: Preston North End. Height: 5 ft. 7½ in. Weight: 11 st. Place of Birth: Preston, Lancs. Age: 28 years. International Record and other honours: 14 Full International Caps (First Full Cap was against Brazil in 1963). Has played twice for the Football League. Also played for Lancashire Schoolboys and Lancashire Youth. Has First and Second Division Championship medals. Style of Play: A precise and cultured, attacking Half Back.

RONALD FLOWERS (Wolverhampton Wanderers). Height: 5 ft. 11 in. Weight: 12 st. 12 lbs. Place of Birth: Edlington. Age: 31 years. International Record and other honours: 49 Full International Caps (First Full Cap was against France in 1955). 1 Under 23 game and 11 Football League appearances. Also played for Doncaster Boys and Yorkshire Schoolboys. As a youth played for Sheffield and Hallamshire. Also has three First Division Championship medals and 1 F.A. Cup Winners medal. Style of Play: Strong attacking Wing Half.

BOBBY MOORE (West Ham United). Height: 6 ft. Weight: 12 st. 12 lbs. Place of Birth: Essex. Age: 24 years. International Record and other honours: 47 Full International Caps (First Full Cap was against Peru in 1962). Has played in 8 Under 23 games and 4 Football League games. Also played for Essex, London, Leyton and Barking at schoolboy level and Essex, London and England at Youth level. Has an F.A. Cup Winners medal and European Cup Winners Cup medal. Style of Play: Defensive Half Back, strong tackler and Captains the team.

GEOFF HURST (West Ham United). Height: 5 ft. 11¼ in. Weight: 12 st. 10 lbs. Place of Birth: Ashton-under-Lyne. Age: 24 years. International Record and other

Below Possibly the most controversial goal of all time. Geoff Hurst unleashes a shot from the edge of the box to make the score 3–2 to England in the 1966 World Cup Final. But did the ball cross the line after rebounding from the underside of the bar?

honours: 8 Full International Caps against West Germany in 1966. Has made 4 Under 23 appearances and also has an F.A. Cup Winners medal and European Cup Winners Cup medal. Has played for Essex Boys and England Youth. Style of Play: Strong and fast goalscoring Inside Forward.

JOHN CHARLTON (Leeds United). Height: 6 ft. 1½ in. Weight: 12 st. 11 lbs. Place of Birth: Ashington, Northumberland. Age: 29 years. International Record and other honours: 22 Full International Caps (First Full Cap was against Scotland in 1965). Has made 4 Football League appearances and also has a Second Division Championship medal and F.A. Cup Runners-up medal. He played for East Northumberland at Schoolboy level. Style of Play: Tall, dominating Centre Half. Good in the air.

ROBERT CHARLTON (Manchester United). Height: 5 ft. 8½ in. Weight: 11 st. 7 lbs. Place of Birth: Ashington, Northumberland. Age: 28 years. International Record and other honours: 73 Full International Caps (First Full Cap was against Scotland in 1958). Has played 6 times for the Under 23 team and 7 times for the Football League. Also played as a Schoolboy for England and at Youth level. Has two First Division Championship medals and an F.A. Cup Winners medal. He played for the Rest of Europe v. Scandinavia in 1964. Style of Play: Fast and strong with a tremendous shot.

TERRY PAINE (Southampton). Height: 5 ft 7 in. Weight: 10 st. 4 lbs. Place of Birth: Winchester. Age: 27 years. International Record and other honours: 19 Full International Caps (First Full Cap was against Czechoslovakia in 1963). Has played 4 times in the Under 23 team and 4 times for the Football League. At Youth level he played for the National Association of Boys Club. Has a Third Division Championship medal. Style of Play: Fast and tricky Winger.

MARTIN PETERS (West Ham United). Height: 6 ft. Weight: 11 st. 10 lbs. Place of Birth: Plaistow. Age: 22 years. International Record and other honours: 8 Full International Caps. Has played 4 times at Under 23 level and once for the Football League. At Schoolboy level he played for Essex, London and England and at Youth level for London and England. Has a European Cup Winners Cup medal. Style of Play: Attacking Wing Half who can play in either defence or attack.

RONALD DERRICK SPRINGETT (Sheffield Wednesday). Previous Club: Queens Park Rangers. Height: 5 ft 10½ in. Weight: 12 st. 4 lbs. Place of Birth: Fulham, London. Age: 30 years. International Record and other honours: 33 Full International Caps (First Full Cap was against Ireland in 1959). Has played for the Football League on 9 occasions and has a Second Division Championship medal. Style of Play: Agile and fearless Goalkeeper.

RAY WILSON (Everton). Previous Club: Huddersfield Town. Height: 5 ft. 7½ in. Weight: 10 st. 10 lbs. Place of Birth: Shirebrook, near Mansfield. Age: 31 years. International Record and other honours: 51 Full International Caps (First Full Cap was against Scotland in 1960). Has played for the Football League on 8 occasions and played for the Rest of Europe v. Scandinavia in 1964. Style of Play: Determined, tenacious Full Back.

GORDON BANKS (Leicester City). Previous Club: Chesterfield. Height: 5 ft. 11 in. Weight: 13 st. Place of Birth: Sheffield. Age: 27 years. International Record and other honours: 33 Full International Caps (First Full Cap was against Scotland in 1963). Has played for the Under 23 team on 2 occasions and for the Football league on 4 occasions. Played for Sheffield Boys on 5 occasions and has a Football League Cup Winners medal and two F.A. Cup Runners-up medals. Style of Play: An agile and reliable Goalkeeper.

GEORGE EASTHAM (Stoke City). Previous Club: Newcastle United. Height: 5 ft. 7½ in. Weight: 10 st. Place of Birth: Blackpool. Age: 29 years. International Record and other honours: Has 19 Full International Caps (First Full Cap was against Brazil in 1963) and has played 6 times for the Under 23 team and twice for the Football League. Style of Play: Scheming Inside Forward.

ROGER HUNT (Liverpool). Height: 5 ft. 9 in. Weight: 11 st. 12 lbs. Place of Birth: Glazebury, near Warrington, Lancs. Age: 27 years. International Record and other honours: 19 Full International Caps (First Full Cap was against Austria in 1962). Has played for the Football League on 4 occasions. Also has an F.A. Cup Winners medal, 2 First Division Championship medals and one Second Division Championship medal. Style of Play: Striking Forward, frequent goalscorer and an opportunist.

GERRY BYRNE (Liverpool). Height: 5 ft. 10 in. Weight: 11 st. 10 lbs. Place of Birth: Liverpool. Age: 27 years. International Record and other honours: 2 Full International Caps against Scotland and Norway, and one Under 23 game. As a Schoolboy he played for Liverpool County. He has 2 First Division Championship medals, one Second Division Championship medal and an F.A. Cup Winners medal. Style of Play: Tough-tackling Full Back.

NORBERT STILES (Manchester United). Height: 5 ft. 6 in. Weight: 10 st. 7 lbs. Age: 23 years. International Record and other honours: 22 Full International Caps (First Full Cap was against Scotland in 1965). Has played 3 times for the Under 23 team and twice for the Football League. Played for England to Schoolboy and Youth level. Also has a First Division Championship medal. Style of Play: Tireless, tough-tackling Half Back.

PLAYERS WITH THE MOST INTERNATIONAL CAPS AT EACH CLUB (1886–2007)

Clubs all have a host of different international players, some with more experience than others. The table shows the player, his club, his nationality and the number of caps he won while with the club.

1	Bobby Moore	West Ham	England	108
2	Bobby Charlton	Man Utd	England	106
3	Neville Southall	Everton	Wales	92
4	Patrick Vieira	Arsenal	France	79
5	Pat Jennings	Tottenham	Northern Ireland	74
6	Shay Given	Newcastle	Republic of Ireland	68
7=	Marcel Desailly	Chelsea	France	67
7=	Ian Rush	Liverpool	Wales	67
9	Steve Staunton	Aston Villa	Republic of Ireland	64
10	Henning Berg	Blackburn	Norway	58
11	Johnny Haynes	Fulham	England	56
12=	Colin Bell	Man City	England	48
12=	Jimmy Dickinson	Portsmouth	England	48
14	Jonatan Johansson	Charlton	Finland	41
15	Mark Fish	Bolton	South Africa	34
16	John Barnes	Watford	England	31
17	Wilf Mannion	Middlesbrough	England	26
18	Billy Gillespie	Sheffield Utd	Ireland	25
19	Jimmy Quinn	Reading	Northern Ireland	17
20	Roy Carroll	Wigan	Northern Ireland	9

(Clubs listed are those that played in the Premiership, 2006–07.)

PLAYERS WITH THE MOST LEAGUE APPEARANCES AT EACH CLUB (1888–2007)

1	Jimmy Dickinson	Portsmouth	1946–65	764
2	Billy Bonds	West Ham	1967–88	663
3=	Ron Harris	Chelsea	1962–80	655
3=	Steve Perryman	Tottenham	1969–86	655
5	Ian Callaghan	Liverpool	1960–78	640
6	Joe Shaw	Sheffield Utd	1948–66	629
7	Bobby Charlton	Man Utd	1956–73	606
8	Derek Fazackerley	Blackburn	1970–82	596
9	Johnny Haynes	Fulham	1952–70	594
10	Sam Bartram	Charlton	1934–56	583
11	Neville Southall	Everton	1981–98	578
12	Alan Oakes	Man City	1959–76	565
13	Tim Williamson	Middlesbrough	1902–23	563
14	Charlie Aitken	Aston Villa	1961–76	561
15	David O'Leary	Arsenal	1975–93	558
16	Eddie Hopkinson	Bolton	1956–70	519
17	Martin Hicks	Reading	1978–91	500
18	Jim Lawrence	Newcastle	1904–22	432
19	Luther Blissett	Watford	1976–83; 84–88; 91–92	415
20	Kevin Langley	Wigan	1981–86; 90–94	317

(Clubs listed are those that played in the Premiership, 2006–07.)

Top Ron 'Chopper' Harris, long-serving stalwart of the Chelsea defence, taking on George Best.

EACH CLUB'S ALL-TIME TOP LEAGUE GOALSCORERS (1888–2007)

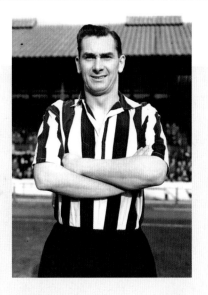

1	William 'Dixie' Dean	Everton	1925–37	349
2	George Mansell	Middlesbrough	1925–39	325
3	Vic Watson	West Ham	1920–35	298
4	Nat Lofthouse	Bolton	1946–61	255
5	Roger Hunt	Liverpool	1959–69	245
6	Jimmy Greaves	Tottenham	1961–70	220
7	Harry Hampton	Aston Villa	1904–15	215
8	Harry Johnson	Sheffield Utd	1919–30	205
9	Bobby Charlton	Man Utd	1956–73	199
10	Peter Harris	Portsmouth	1946–60	194
11	Jackie Milburn	Newcastle	1946–57	177
12	Simon Garner	Blackburn	1978–92	168
13	Thierry Henry	Arsenal	1999–2007	166
14	Bobby Tambling	Chelsea	1958–70	164
15	Gordon Davies	Fulham	1978–84; 86–91	159
16	Tommy Johnson	Man City	1919–30	158
17	Ronnie Blackman	Reading	1947–54	158
18	Stuart Leary	Charlton	1953–62	153
19	Luther Blissett	Watford	1976–92 (with breaks)	148
20	Andy Liddell	Wigan	1998–2004	70

(Clubs listed are those that played in the Premiership, 2006–07.)

Top **Newcastle United legend Jackie Milburn ('Wor Jackie').**

A MORAL DILEMMA FOR WAYNE

An exciting new story, written especially for
The Bumper Book of Football by Hunter Davies

Part One

Wayne Wright picked up the ball well into his own half. It was actually a poorly struck clearance by Darren, Brookpark School's goalkeeper, who was something of an ace at shot stopping, diving to his left and right, generally leaping about, but not so hot on goal kicks. Darren was quite small for a goalkeeper, rather weedy, not at all that strong, which was one reason why his clearances rarely made the halfway line.

This time the ball only just crept out of the penalty area, but Wayne had got onto it in a flash, sensing it wouldn't be going far, easily getting to it before Holloway Road Primary's giant but lumbering striker realised what had happened.

Once Wayne had the ball under control, he gave Darren the thumbs up, as if Darren had meant it as a pass rather than a rubbish clearance.

Darren could be rather temperamental. In an earlier round of the Camden Cup, Darren had clearly heard Rupert, Brookpark's left back, comment on Darren's 'useless clearances' and 'sh*t goal kicks'. Darren had promptly gone behind the nets and sat down, saying that he wasn't playing any more, that was it.

Wayne, as Brookpark's captain, had quickly sorted that out. He told the ref their goalie was just feeling a bit sick, sorry he'd left the field without permission, but he'd be okay in a minute. Wayne then whispered in Darren's ear that Rupert would be dropped for the next round, if they got through, no problem. Which they did – and Darren had played a blinder.

Now this was the semi-final, the first time Brookpark had ever got this far. They were just a small primary, with only 300 pupils, while Holloway Road was a huge

school with some very huge boys.

Wayne was still on the ball, heading for the halfway line. Holloway Road's midfield were backing off, marking space, waiting for Wayne to pass. Eventually two of them decided to tackle him, which was just what Wayne wanted. He did his Ronaldinho shuffle, moving the ball so quickly between his feet, from his left to his right and back again in an instant, that they were left floundering on the ground. Wayne dashed between them, heading straight towards their penalty area.

The score was 1–1, equally balanced in

chances and possession, with only five minutes to go, but Brookpark, being the younger, smaller team, had appeared to be tiring. Could they hold on? Would they get slaughtered if it went to extra time?

About 100 people were standing on the touchlines, cheering and encouraging. Almost all of them were parents or relations, plus a few strangers in raincoats, one of whom was clearly making notes. Wayne had spotted him at half time and wondered if he was a reporter from the Camden Journal. Brookpark had been in the paper twice already because of their excellent cup run.

Wayne was now almost inside Holloway Road's penalty area. Their defence was well organised, their two centre backs holding their arms out, indicating where everyone else should be marking.

'Lay it off!' Wayne could hear Mr Wilkins shouting. He was Brookpark's PE teacher and deputy head, known behind his back as Butch.

'Take him on,' Wayne could hear his father yelling.

It was surprising that he could identify any of the voices, with all the screaming and shouting. Some of the Holloway Road parents had been yelling non stop since the

game had begun. In fact, the ref had had to stop the game for a few moments in the first half when some parents had started fighting – either between themselves or with some Brookpark parents. Wayne hadn't been quite sure.

'Bloody lay it off!' yelled Mr Wilkins again, rushing down the touchline, desperate for Wayne to hear him. Wayne had never heard him swear before.

'Take them all on,' shouted Wayne's dad. 'You can do it, son.'

Wayne decided to do neither. From 30 yards, he let rip a cannonball of a shot. It took a wicked swerve and flew into the top right corner of the net. Their goalkeeper, still shouting at his defence, had not even moved.

All the Brookpark parents were going wild, jumping up and down, while the Brookpark players were mobbing Wayne, trying to jump on his back, but he managed to pull himself away.

Wayne ran back upfield towards Brookpark's goal mouth where Darren was waiting for him. They exchanged high fives. Or low fives, as they always called it, each being only a little over five feet.

'Thanks for the pass, Darren,' said Wayne. 'It goes down as an assist …'

Wayne was at home, playing a football game on his computer. He was waiting for his tea, then he would be going out into the Den to play football.

The Den was a sunken, five-a-side concrete pitch with a concrete wall at one end and very high railings around the rest. It was called a den because that's how it looked, where lions might be kept at the zoo. There were also some swings and a little adventure playground, all of them surrounded by high blocks of houses.

Wayne lived on the ninth floor of the

main block with his mum and dad and two little sisters, Karen and Kim, who were twins. Darren, his best friend, lived in the next block.

Wayne had spent the best part of his life so far playing football in the Den, often just on his own. He had taught himself to kick with both feet by hitting balls against the concrete wall, forcing himself to return the rebound with first his left and then his right.

Wayne couldn't wait to get into the Den. He hoped Darren would be there. Not much point in shouting 'that counts as in' if you are just playing on your own.

The intercom bell rang, just as Wayne's mum was serving the tea. It was pasta and chicken, Wayne's favourite. A year ago, when he was aged eight and had first got into Brookpark's school team, he had given up chips and burgers. For ever, so he said. Because that's what real footballers did. His mum was well pleased.

Wayne's dad groaned but went to pick up the intercom. Someone was at the front door of their block, wanting to be let in. Wayne's dad seemed rather brusque and irritated at first, but then appeared to soften his attitude.

'Okay, then,' replied Wayne's dad. 'I'll be down in about 10 minutes.'

Wayne ate his meal as fast as he could, which he should not have done. He jumped up from the table, saying he was off to the Den, as if they didn't know.

He went down in the lift and rushed through the front door, still in a hurry, almost knocking over a man in a long rain-coat who was waiting outside.

'Hi, Wayne,' said the man.

'Ugh,' grunted Wayne.

His mother was always telling him off for grunting but he was in a hurry to get to the Den and didn't want to stand around talking to some stranger.

Or was he a stranger? As he rushed past him, it struck Wayne that the man looked very like one of those who had been watching Brookpark's game. But Wayne wasn't bothered, or even interested. He just wanted to get to the Den and play football …

Hurry, hurry to page 138 for the next instalment of Wayne's story.

5. Great events

'If you can meet with triumph and disaster ...'

In football, there are many events which have become legendary, which you see references to, hear spoken about, but not always correctly, because legends can take on a life of their own. Here are some events, big and small, important and not quite so important, which all footer fans should know about, if only to correct other people, should they find themselves a bit wide of the mark ...

The beginning of the World Cup, 1930

FIFA (Fédération Internationale de Football Association) was formed in 1904 but it was not until 1930 that the first World Cup took place, after many years of discussions

and hopes. Football had been played at the Olympic Games in 1924 and 1928, and each time the gold medal was won by Uruguay. They were celebrating the centenary of their independence in 1930 and agreed to host the first World Cup and pay the expenses of visiting teams.

Only four European countries agreed to take part: France, Belgium, Yugoslavia and Romania. The King of Romania picked his country's team and managed to get each of them off work so they could travel abroad.

All four European teams travelled on the same boat, which took two weeks to reach South America. The players exercised on deck during the voyage to keep fit. On board was Jules Rimet, the French lawyer who was President of FIFA, carrying the World Cup trophy in his luggage.

Thirteen countries in all had entered, including the United States, who started well, getting to the semi-finals, and a rumour went around that their team was full of Scottish professionals. However, they got beaten in the semis 6–1 by Argentina, who went on to meet Uruguay in the final.

Before the final, they argued over the match ball. A compromise was reached by using an Argentine ball in the first half and a Uruguayan ball in the second. Uruguay won 4–2.

The 1934 World Cup was held in Italy, establishing the principle that the World Cup finals should alternate between South America and Europe, which continued until 2002, when they were held in Japan and South Korea.

Even though they were the Cup holders, Uruguay refused to take part in the 1934 tournament. They were still furious that so few European countries had come to the first World Cup.

For the 1934 World Cup there were qualifying matches beforehand, spread over the previous 12 months, in which 32 countries took part, leaving 16 teams to meet in the finals.

The Italian dictator Benito Mussolini had demanded that the Italian team should win, hinting at serious consequences for the players if they did not. Fortunately, they did, beating Czechoslovakia 2–1 in the final. Some 270 journalists from all over the world attended the final. The World Cup was established as a major world event, not just a footballing event, from then on.

Since 1930, there have been 18 World Cups, with Brazil having won five, followed by Italy with four. The next one will be in South Africa in 2010.

Christmas 1914

Some people still find it very hard to believe but, during the First World War, on Christmas Day 1914, German and British troops on the front line took a break from the war and climbed out of their trenches – to play a game of football.

The score has never been recorded but the event went into national folklore, both in Britain and Germany. Historians now know that it did happen as there is enough documentary evidence from eye witnesses.

Opposite The head of FIFA, Jules Rimet, presenting the trophy that bears his name to the president of the Uruguayan football association prior to the inaugural World Cup in 1930.

THE WORLD CUP 1930–2006

Year	Winners		Runners-up		Venue
1930	Uruguay	4	Argentina	2	Uruguay
1934	Italy*	2	Czechoslovakia	1	Italy
1938	Italy	4	Hungary	2	France
1950	Uruguay	2	Brazil	1	Brazil
1954	West Germany	3	Hungary	2	Switzerland
1956	Brazil	5	Sweden	2	Sweden
1962	Brazil	3	Czechoslovakia	1	Chile
1966	England*	4	West Germany	2	England
1970	Brazil	4	Italy	1	Mexico
1974	West Germany	2	Holland	1	West Germany
1978	Argentina*	3	Holland	1	Argentina
1982	Italy	3	West Germany	1	Spain
1986	Argentina	3	West Germany	2	Mexico
1990	West Germany	1	Argentina	0	Italy
1994	Brazil*	0	Italy	0	USA
	Brazil won 3–2 on penalties				
1998	France	3	Brazil	0	France
2002	Brazil	2	Germany	0	Japan/South Korea
2006	Italy	1	France	1	Germany
	Italy won 5–3 on penalties				
	*After extra time				

Top Brazil, the most successful nation in World Cup history, celebrating their 1994 win.

LEADING GOALSCORERS

Year	Player	Goals
1930	Guillermo Stábile (Argentina)	8
1934	Angelo Schiavio (Italy)	4
	Oldřich Nejedlý (Czechoslovakia)	4
	Edmund Conen (Germany)	4
1938	Leonidas da Silva (Brazil)	8
1950	Ademir (Brazil)	9
1954	Sándor Kocsis (Hungary)	11
1958	Just Fontaine (France)	13
1962	Valentin Ivanov (USSR)	4
	Leonel Sánchez (Chile)	4
	Garrincha and Vavá (both Brazil)	4
	Flórián Albert (Hungary)	4
	Dražen Jerković (Yugoslavia)	4
1966	Eusébio (Portugal)	9
1970	Gerd Müller (West Germany)	10
1974	Grzegorz Lato (Poland)	7
1978	Mario Kempes (Argentina)	6
1982	Paolo Rossi (Italy)	6
1986	Gary Lineker (England)	6
1990	Salvatore Schillaci (Italy)	6
1994	Oleg Salenko (Russia)	6
	Hristo Stoichkov (Bulgaria)	6
1998	Davor Suker (Croatia)	6
2002	Ronaldo (Brazil)	8
2006	Miroslav Klose (Germany)	6

Above **German striker Miroslav Klose, winner of the Golden Boot in 2006.**

In 2006, at Bonham's auction house in London, letters from an unnamed soldier, dated 25 December 1914, came up for sale. In them, the soldier describes hearing the Germans singing the carol 'Silent Night' ('Stille Nacht') and then the British troops joining in.

A football was brought out and both sides started playing a game. Later that day, when the unofficial truce was over, they returned to their guns and trenches and resumed the grisly task of killing each other.

Women's football and the story of the Dick, Kerr Ladies

Women's football is now one of the world's fastest growing sports, especially in the USA, China, Germany, France, Norway and Great Britain. Many schools have a girls' football team as well as a boys'. There's a Women's World Cup championship and also a European Championship that gets shown live on TV.

Many of our Premiership football clubs, such as Arsenal, have an equivalent women's team who play in similarly arranged leagues, but they don't quite, as yet, get the same press or TV coverage for ordinary league games.

Yet what many people don't realize is that women's football in Britain is not a recent phenomenon but has a long and rich history. The British Ladies' Football Club was formed in 1895 in London with Lady Florence Dixie, daughter of the Marquess of Queensberry, as President. Their first game, at Crouch End, North London, was between teams from the North and the South. As with the early years of the men's game, the players were mainly well-bred, upper- or middle-class girls.

In 1914, when the First World War broke out, around one million women went to work in munitions factories, replacing the men who had gone to fight at the front. In their breaks, the factory girls often had a kick-around with a ball, just as the men had done, with the young apprentices or older men. 'Huh, call yourself a footballer,' they'd say to the young boys. 'We could do better than that!'

This led to women's teams being formed to play women workers from other factories. Very soon, women's teams had sprung up all over the North of England and the Midlands, attracting large crowds.

THE LADY PLAYER

The fellows are anxious, it would seem,
To have a game with the ladies team.

One of the most successful was Dick, Kerr Ladies – made up of women who were employed in a munitions factory in Preston. (It was founded by two men, a Mr Dick and a Mr Kerr, owners of the factory, hence the comma in the team's name.)

On Christmas Day afternoon in 1917 Dick, Kerr Ladies hired Deepdale, the home of Preston North End. Over 10,000 turned up, most of them pretty merry after their Xmas pudding, to watch them play a game. The sum of £600 was then handed over to help wounded soldiers.

Dick, Kerr Ladies then began to travel all over the North of England, playing other teams, always for charity, and then to the South of England and even to France.

On 26 December 1920 they broke every possible record for a women's game in England – before or since – when 53,000 people turned up at Goodison Park, the home of Everton, to see them trounce St Helen's Ladies 4–0.

And then the rotten old, meany FA, who considered themselves the boss of all football played in England, came out against women playing football. In 1921 they declared that the game was medically unsuitable for women because of how they were built. They also suggested some fiddling was going on with the gate money, an

Above The formidable
Dick, Kerr Ladies' FC,
who swept all before
them in the early
1920s. The FA ban on
women's football,
imposed in 1921,
stayed in place for
fifty years.

accusation that was never proved, and, anyway, in the men's game, gate receipts had been fiddled from the beginning to pay 'expenses'.

The FA couldn't quite ban all women from playing football, so what they did was ban all the men's clubs affiliated to the FA from hiring out their grounds to women. Most women's clubs packed up, having nowhere to play, but Dick, Kerr Ladies managed to continue, hiring rugby grounds or playing abroad, until they finally disbanded in 1965.

In 1969 there was a revival, with the Women's FA being formed. In 1971 the FA relented and recognized women's football at last, having effectively banned it 50 years earlier. Today, the FA is responsible for the men's and the women's game in England.

So many women's teams and clubs now exist all over the world that FIFA estimates that, by 2010, there will be more women playing football than men worldwide.

The Wembley 'White Horse final', 1923

The final of the FA Cup, which began in 1872, was held at various venues in its early decades, such as Kennington Oval (the cricket ground), Crystal Palace, and also in Manchester and Liverpool.

In 1923 it was played for the first time at Wembley, which remained the home of the Cup final and many other important football matches until 2000, when it was knocked down and rebuilt.

The original Wembley Stadium, with its famous Twin Towers, was the focal point of the British Empire Exhibition of 1924–25 which was organized to show the wonders of the British Empire after a long, hard and debilitating war. There were many other pavilions, buildings, exhibition halls and attractions built especially for the Exhibition, but they were demolished afterwards or resold and carted away, apart from Wembley Stadium.

The Cup final programme of 23 April 1923, which ran to 28 pages, boasted that the Stadium was 'the greatest Arena in the World – the largest, most comfortable, best equipped, and holds more than 125,000'.

The first Wembley Cup final was between Bolton Wanderers and West Ham United – and at least twice the anticipated number of spectators turned up, hoping to get in. Many stormed the gates, or were let in by turnstile keepers, fearing casualties. It was estimated that 210,000 spectators did get in – still the unofficial record crowd for any football game played in Great Britain.

Kick-off was delayed because thousands and thousands of spectators had poured onto the pitch itself, scared that they were going to be crushed to death if they remained on the terraces.

A mounted policeman called PC George Scorey, on his white horse Billy, calmly but determinedly managed to persuade the crowds to move off the pitch so the game could commence. There were other mounted policemen on duty, of course, but Billy, the white horse, stood out, seen by most of the crowd and captured on photographs and early movie cameras, and he appeared in all the newspapers and newsreels of the day. Because of Billy the white horse, that first Wembley final became known as the 'White Horse final'. The game ended in a win for Bolton, 2–0.

Moscow Dynamo's 1945 visit to Britain

This was the first big exciting event for all football fans in Britain after the Second World War. Almost everything was still rationed, there was an atmosphere of austerity and drabness, the country felt cut off from the rest of the world.

The visit of Moscow Dynamo, the first Russian club ever to play in Britain, was seen as something of an exotic event. The whole country became fascinated by them, and not just football fans, because of the social and political implications of the tour. It was thought it would give people in Britain a glimpse into the mysterious communist world and the Soviet mentality.

Plenty of myths and rumours started circulating, claiming for example that their party was full of spies, and that the players were in fact soldiers recruited from all over Russia, not just from one club. Behind the scenes there were endless diplomatic rows and confusions.

The Russians arrived on 4 November 1945. Stanley Rous, Secretary of the FA, had gone with a party of dignitaries to meet them at Northolt aerodrome, not far from today's Heathrow, only to discover that they were landing at Croydon airport, miles away across London. A mad dash ensued to get there in time.

In amongst the vast, milling crowd that turned out to watch the first FA Cup final at Wembley Stadium in 1923, PC George Scorey and his white horse Billy valiantly keep order.

Moscow Dynamo brought their own chef and their own food, and insisted on eating it at the Russian embassy. This was seen as rather rude and insulting, but who can blame them, considering the awful food that British people were then living on? Today, of course, it is normal for clubs when travelling abroad to take their own chefs and provisions.

Their first game was against Chelsea at Stamford Bridge. On the pitch beforehand, the Russian team presented each of the Chelsea players with a bouquet of flowers. Again, this would hardly be worth commenting on nowadays but, in 1945, the sight of 11 tough, no-nonsense, stiff-upper-lip Englishmen holding bunches of flowers and looking totally embarrassed, amazed and amused the whole nation. Real men did not carry flowers in 1945. No more than they kissed or cuddled each other after scoring a goal.

The game ended in a 3–3 draw, perhaps a diplomatic draw, as the Russians were by far the more skilful, better drilled team.

In London, they also played Arsenal – but not at Highbury. During the war, Highbury had been taken over for military purposes, such as housing refugees and stationing anti-aircraft guns. So the game was played at White Hart Lane, the home of Arsenal's deadly North London rivals, Tottenham Hotspur.

Below Suits you, sir! The hard men of Chelsea appear distinctly ill at ease with their bouquets before the match with Moscow Dynamo.

NAMES AND POSITIONS OF PLAYERS.
Alterations in Teams will be shown on a Board carried around the Field.

Right—		CARDIFF CITY		—Left
		McLOUGHLIN		
	2 LEVER		3 RAYBOULD	
4 HOLLYMAN		5 STANSFIELD		6 LESTER
7 FOULKES	8 CARLESS	9 GIBSON	10 WOOD	11 CLARKE

REFEREE:
Mr. A. E. DAVIES
(Pontyclun).

PAGE STIBBS EVERYTHING ELECTRICAL

LINESMEN:
Mr. W. C. BUCKNALL (Cardiff).
Mr. C. O. HANCOCK (Pontlottyn).

SOLOVIEV, S. DEMENTIEV, N. BESKOV, K. KARTSEV, V. ARCHANGELSKY, E.		
SOLOVIEV, L.	SEMICHASTNY, M.	BLINKOV, S.
STANKEVICH, I.		RADIKORSKY, V.
	KROMICH, A.	
Left—	MOSCOW DYNAMO	—Right

There was a thick smog that day, as there very often was during winters in London until the 1960s, which made it impossible for the enormous crowds to see much of the game.

It was claimed later that the Russians had 12 players on the pitch for 20 minutes, without anyone realizing, which was why the Russians won 4–3. It probably did happen, but not for more than a minute while a substitute was coming on. The use of a substitute replacing an injured player was not allowed in British football at the time, but the Russians had brought their own refs and officials and insisted on some of their own rules, as the games were friendlies.

In the Arsenal team that day were Stanley Matthews – nominally of Stoke City – and Stan Mortensen of Blackpool. They had been drafted in at short notice, as so many of the Arsenal players were still in uniform, stationed elsewhere in Britain or serving overseas.

Moscow Dynamo also went to Wales and thumped Cardiff City 10–1, but Cardiff were then in the Second Division and some of the players were miners who had just come off shift work.

Above **The teams for the Cardiff City v Moscow Dynamo match, advertised in the Ninian Park programme. Cardiff were outclassed and suffered a drubbing, losing 10-1 to the Russians.**

Their tour finished in Glasgow where 90,000 turned out at Ibrox to watch them play Rangers in a 2–2 draw.

From a football point of view, the country was impressed by their close, short passing movements at a time when English football relied more on individual flair players, such as Stanley Matthews.

Before each game, the Russians came out onto the pitch and warmed up for about 20 minutes, before returning to the dressing room. This was considered bizarre behaviour by most British teams, but of course it is now standard practice. The Russians were also very keen on proper diets for footballers, again very much a joke subject in British footballing circles in 1945 – wasn't a big steak before a game what real footballers liked? They also used blackboards and diagrams in their pre-match meetings, which most British fans thought was pretty funny, not to say eccentric.

While most people in football were impressed by Russian methods and skills on the park, little was done afterwards to copy or learn from their methods. It was still felt that the old British ways were best.

It was not until the arrival of the Hungarians in 1953, when they walloped England 6–3 at Wembley, that the nation woke up to the fact that these funny foreigners actually had a lot to teach us about our own national game.

The visit of Moscow Dynamo to Britain in 1945 did at least make Stanley Rous of the FA realize that it was silly and petty for England to remain outside FIFA. So, in 1946, the FA finally decided to join, in time to take part in the World Cup for the first

MOSCOW DYNAMO'S BRITISH TOUR 1945

13 November v Chelsea at Stamford Bridge
Crowd: **85,000**   Score: Moscow 3 Chelsea 3

17 November v Cardiff at Ninian Park
Crowd: **40,000**   Score: Moscow 10 Cardiff 1

21 November v Arsenal at White Hart Lane
Crowd: **54,000**   Score: Moscow 4 Arsenal 3

28 November v Glasgow Rangers at Ibrox
Crowd: **90,000**   Score: Moscow 2 Rangers 2

time. This was held in Brazil in 1950. England suffered the ignominy of being beaten in the first round by the USA, 0–1, a country whose national game was not even football. Oh, shame!

Munich air crash, 1958

There have been many tragedies in football over the years, such as stadium disasters where stands have collapsed or caught fire, and spectators have been killed or injured. There have, fortunately, not been many air disasters involving footballers.

The worst such incident involving British players occurred on 6 February 1958 when a plane carrying the Manchester United team crashed and burst into flames just a few minutes after leaving Munich airport in a snowstorm.

On the plane were the so-called 'Busby Babes,' a team of young players destined for greatness, so everyone believed, who had been assembled by their manager Matt Busby. They had just drawn a game against Red Star Belgrade in a European Cup tie and were on their way home. The plane had tried to take off twice already. This was its third attempt. Slush on the runway meant that the plane failed to gain enough height.

Twenty-three of the 43 passengers and crew on board lost their lives, including eight players, seven of them under the age of 25. Among them was Duncan Edwards,

Above **As the young Manchester United team returned from a European Cup tie in Yugoslavia in 1958, their aircraft came to grief on a snow-bound runway at Munich airport. Twelve United players and officials were killed.**

who had been looked up to as the most outstanding player of his generation. At the age of 21, he had already played 18 times for England. Three members of the Man Utd staff also died, plus Frank Swift, who had been a famous England goalkeeper, along with seven sports journalists who had been covering the game. Bobby Charlton and Matt Busby were seriously injured but survived.

The programme for Man Utd's next game, against Sheffield Wednesday, contained blank spaces where players' names would normally have gone.

A memorial clock was erected at Old Trafford, with the date and the names of those killed. It is now a popular meeting place for fans.

The first major air crash involving a football club was in 1949 when the Torino team, which had just won Italy's Serie 'A' championship for the fourth season in succession, was entirely wiped out when their plane, returning from a testimonial game against Benfica in Lisbon, Portugal, plunged into the village of Superga on the outskirts of Turin. The death toll of 31 included 18 players, eight of whom were internationals.

England's World Cup win, 1966

Alf Ramsey, the England manager, said beforehand that England would win, but few people believed him, even though the finals were being played on English soil for the first time.

England started quietly, with a 0–0 draw against Uruguay. The major upset in the early rounds was Italy being knocked out by North Korea at Ayresome Park, which was then Middlesbrough's ground.

England got through their group stage and met Argentina in the quarter finals. There was great controversy as Ramsey brought in Geoff Hurst for his first game in a tournament in place of Jimmy Greaves, who had been England's star striker and a great hero to all England fans. Alan Ball was brought in instead of Ian Callaghan, Liverpool's winger. Ramsey's team was mocked as 'wingless wonders' by many of the back pages.

The game itself was even more controversial when the Argentinian captain Antonio Rattín was sent off. It was a violent, rather nasty affair which England won 1–0. After the match, Ramsey refused to let his players swap shirts with the Argentinians, whom he later described as 'animals'.

England met Portugal in the semi final. Portugal's star player was Eusébio. Many considered this was the best game of the whole competition. Bobby Charlton had probably his greatest game for England, who won 2–1, and afterwards received handshakes from the Portuguese players.

For the final against West Germany, Ramsey still refused to bring back Jimmy Greaves, and persevered with Hurst.

West Germany scored first. Hurst equalized. Martin Peters, also of West Ham, put England in front, 2–1. Towards the very end of the second half, when England appeared certain of victory, West Germany got a scrambled goal, making it 2–2. It therefore had to go to extra time.

Ramsey urged on his players to even greater efforts. 'You've won it once,' he said. 'Now go and win it again … look at them, they're finished.'

In the 100th minute, a Hurst shot hit the underside of the bar and went in – or did it? The Germans didn't think it was over the line. The Swiss referee appeared not quite sure but the Soviet linesman said yes, it had gone over, and the goal was given.

In the last minute, Hurst broke through again to score his third, the first ever hat trick in a World Cup final, making it England 4–1.

The BBC TV commentator that day, Kenneth Wolstenhome, also went down in English football history, for his final words. 'Some people are on the pitch. They think it's all over …' So he was saying as Hurst headed for the German goal.

'It is now!' he yelled, as the ball went in.

World Cup final, 1970

Best game ever? That's what many still believe. Very often cup finals, of any sort, are a let down, with better, more skilful, more exciting games taking place in earlier rounds.

Brazil, with Pele, Carlos Alberto, Gerson, Tostao and Rivelino, had come into the 1970 finals, held in Mexico, as the favourites. They saved their best game to the last when they met Italy, also one of the favourites, in the final.

Pele got the opening goal, but Italy equalized and so it was 1–1 up to the 65th minute. Then Brazil burst into life, sweeping Italy away with a glorious succession of passing movements, tricks, ball skills and shots.

Brazil ended the game 4–1 winners, with Pele laying on the final goal for Carlos Alberto. Brazil's third World Cup meant that they got to keep the Jules Rimet Trophy.

Munich, 2001 – Germany 1 England 5

The score is still hard to believe, even after six years, but it was equally remarkable at the time.

England appeared to be jinxed by Germany, having lost to them twice on penalties in vital semi-finals – in the World Cup of 1990 and the European Nations Cup of 1996. The previous year, England lost at home to Germany and had been booed off the pitch.

This game, on 1 September 2001, was an important game in the qualifying rounds for the World Cup of 2002. England's first ever foreign-born manager, Sven-Göran Eriksson, had only recently taken over from Kevin Keegan. There seemed a real possibility that England would fail to qualify.

The home side took the lead in the sixth minute after a mistake by Rio Ferdinand. Owen equalized, then Gerrard rifled in a stunning second goal to give England the lead at half time, slightly against the run of play.

In the second half, all England fans, at home watching on television or inside Munich's Olympic stadium, were soon pinching themselves in disbelief as England proceeded to totally trounce the Germans.

Everything they tried seemed to come off. Every shot on goal seemed to hit the target. Just three minutes after the re-start, Michael Owen made it 3–1. In the 66th minute, Owen got his hat-trick. Emile Heskey, then Owen's striking partner at Liverpool, added a fifth.

The final score line, 5–1, was England's best away result of all time. It proved the highlight of Eriksson's management. Under him, England never displayed such skills and magnificent teamwork again.

Above Read it and weep, Germany. Jubilant English fans celebrate a vintage performance from their side on that great night in Munich in 2001.

The new Wembley, 2007

Wembley Stadium officially re-opened on 19 May 2007 with the Cup final between Manchester United and Chelsea. It wasn't a vintage game of football by any means – Chelsea winning with a late goal in extra time from Didier Drogba – but it certainly was a great event.

It had taken seven years to knock down the old Wembley, with its famous twin towers, and build a completely new stadium at a cost of almost £800 million. (The original one, opened in 1923, had taken 300 days and cost £750,000.) Everyone on the day agreed that the new stadium was spectacular and will be a fitting home for English football for many decades to come.

Field of dreams: The spanking new Wembley hosts its first major match, the FA Cup final between Manchester United and Chelsea on 19 May 2007. Now all the national side has to do is to live up to this magnificent new arena …

So, here are some fascinating facts and figures about the new national stadium for you to keep at your fingertips:

- New Wembley has 90,000 seats and is the largest football stadium in the world with all the seats under cover.
- The stadium is twice the size of the Stade de France in Paris and three times the size of the Millennium Stadium in Cardiff.
- The Wembley Arch, arcing over the stadium like a rainbow, can be seen from 40 miles away. It reaches a height of 133 metres and is the longest single-span roof structure in the world. It ensures that all fans have views unobstructed by any pillar.
- There are 2,618 toilets. The old Wembley had 361.
- Players have to climb 107 steps to collect their trophies from the Royal Box, compared with 39 in old Wembley.
- The stadium roof covers 11 acres – four acres of which are movable, allowing sun and ventilation to reach the playing surface, but also keep out rain during bad weather.
- There are 30 escalators, 26 lifts and 688 food and drink units enabling 50,000 pints of beer to be poured every ten minutes.
- There are four main dining rooms, the biggest of which seats 2,000, making it London's largest banqueting hall.
- For a major event, 6,000 people are employed.
- New Wembley is spacious – with more legroom in each and every spectator's seat than there used to be for the royal legs and bottoms in the old Royal Box.

Section Seven awaits . . . but watch your P's and Q's.

6. Mind your language

Nutmegs and handbags: the strange world of soccerspeak

Football has always had a language of its own, not just the technical terms – like off side, penalty or corner – but the words and phrases that ordinary fans, and ordinary players, use to communicate with each other or to describe the beautiful game. Some of these words and phrases should not be used in polite company, certainly not, so naturally we will not do so. But there are terms and phrases that you ought to know about, their history and use, and understand what they mean, if anything.

OLD-FASHIONED FOOTBALL TERMS

Football is still played with 11 players, as it was in 1863, and yet, surprisingly, over the decades, almost every player on the pitch has been given a different name and sometimes a different function. You may still come across these terms in old books or programmes or from the mouths and pens of older fans.

Centre forward – now referred to as striker or main striker. Traditionally bustling, bullet-headed, with a cannonball shot.

Inside left, inside right – creative midfield players, usually nippy, crafty, with baggy shorts and educated feet.

Left winger, right winger – every team had one of each, numbered 11 and 7 so that you could quickly identify them. Usually thin and weedy, pale faced, but ever so tricky. Often got very cold as they stayed out on the wing, nobody passed to them and they never came back to defend. Today, if a team has a player who is good on the wing, and it's usually only one as they are often seen as a luxury, he is termed a wide midfielder and has to defend as much as attack.

Left half, right half – they played behind the five forwards (centre forward, left winger, right winger, inside left, inside right) and today they would be called midfielders.

Centre half – roughly today's centreback, but he stayed a bit more upfield. Always a giant, rugged, no nonsense.

Left **Spurs' attacking midfielder Aaron Lennon – in old football parlance, a right winger.**

Left back, right back – the terms have been retained but a modern fullback now has to overlap as well and go up the wing, especially if the team is playing without any recognized wing players. In the old days, a back stayed back.

Old-fashioned football terms no longer in use

Bladder – the blow–up rubber ball which went inside the leather outer case

Champion – a jolly good player, or a jolly good tackle, not necessarily a champion

Custodian of the nets – goalkeeper

Knickers – pre-war name for shorts, usually of the baggy variety

Leather – ball

Sphere – ditto

Old-fashioned football terms still heard, especially from old commentators and writers

Blinder – as in 'Giggs played a blinder'. Nothing to do with lack of eyesight or window blinds, but means he played very well.

Lads – regardless of their age, the other players in your team are always lads. 'The lads done good,' is footballspeak for played well.

Park – still in common use in Scotland, meaning pitch. But has been retained in England in phrases like 'freedom of the park'.

Pint-sized – despite the onward march of metrication, the Imperial measurement lives on in football, as in 'pint-sized Paul Dickov'.

Sixpence – A tiny coin long since defunct, worth six old pre-decimal pennies, but still a currency in football, as in 'Ronaldo can turn on a sixpence'.

Stinker – as in 'Ferdinand had a stinker'. Nothing to do with his smell. Means he played very badly.

Left The epitome of the 'pint-sized' player: Pat Nevin of Everton, pictured in 1989.

MODERN COINAGES

Words and phrases which have taken on a particular meaning when used in football:

Acquisition – a fancy way of saying 'signing'. Acquisitions can be 'astute', 'quality', or 'hurried' depending on how they turned out.

Unveil – new acquisitions are always unveiled, as if we didn't already know their name, having read it in yesterday's paper.

Wraps – before being unveiled, an acquisition is often 'kept under wraps', not to be confused with 'cotton wool' in which managers keep delicate, sensitive young players.

Kit – is what modern players wear. In the old days, they wore 'togs'. Then it became 'strips' which consisted of jerseys, knickers and stockings. Now their kit consists of tops, shorts, socks. Yet strip lingers on in the manager's request to a substitute: 'get stripped off'. He doesn't mean he has to go on the pitch naked, but wake up and take off his trackie bottom.

Into the Mix, or Mixer – derived from the idea of a concrete mixer. It's when a high ball is humped hopefully into a crowded penalty box for everyone to fight over.

Afters – nothing to do with pudding but a euphemism for retribution when a player is trying to get his own back on another player. 'A little bit of afters there between Savage and Rooney.'

History, or Previous – 'a bit of previous between them', used to explain why two players are trying to kill each other.

Legend – any player who has stayed at the same club for more than half an hour.

Servant – 'a good servant to the club' does not mean he has played for free, been treated like dirt and had no freedom. All it means is that he has been at the same club for at least two years.

Ask – a verb which has been turned into a noun. 'Watford staying in the Premiership is a big ask'; 'it's a big ask for Titus Bramble to score from this free kick.'

WAGs – Wives and girlfriends, especially of really famous footballers, who appear in the tabloids sporting new designer frocks or dancing on tables and drinking lots of cocktails while being photographed by the paparazzi … to support the lads, of course. A peculiarly English phenomenon, best witnessed at the World Cup 2006 in Germany.

Opposite **Afters, or previous?** England's Wayne Rooney goes head to head with Israel's Tal Ben Haim (then playing in the English Premiership for Bolton Wanderers) during a European Championship qualifier in Tel Aviv in March 2007.

Opposite **A BBC radio relay team broadcasts from a Corinthians v Newcastle match at Crystal Palace in 1927.**

Below **Sir Alex Ferguson turns on the Hairdryer, while an Assistant Referee pretends not to hear.**

DOMESTIC OBJECTS AND TERMS NOW COMMON IN FOOTBALL

Sheet – as in 'clean sheet,' meaning the goalie has not let in a goal.

Teacups – imagined but sometimes real teacups which miraculously 'fly' around in the dressing room at half time when the manager is really, really angry and his hairdryer isn't working.

Handbags – a non-fight, hissy fit, a girly squabble in which players square up to each other but don't actually do anything.

Early doors – nothing to do with household objects or their age but very early in a game. 'Dunne was sent off early doors.'

Overcooked – fashionable adjective for 'mis-hit'.

Hairdryer – which metaphorically gets taken out by the manager at half time when his team has played rubbish. He then gives them the 'hairdryer treatment', meaning he gets up close and shouts and swears at them. The term is particularly associated with Sir Alex Ferguson, as ex-Man Utd defender Garry Pallister explained in 1997: 'In the early days, we called him the Hairdryer, because he would come right up to your face and scream at you.'

. . . .

ORIGINS OF PHRASES

Back to square one. This is one of the many football phrases that have passed into the language. It goes back to the early 1930s, when the BBC first broadcast radio commentaries of live football games. To help listeners follow what was going on, the *Radio Times* helpfully printed a plan of a football pitch split up into eight boxes, marked one to eight. One commentator described the play while another, in the background, told you in which square the ball was. If it went back to square one, you knew it had reached the goalkeeper.

Derby match. A game between two deadly rivals, usually from the same town or locality, which has great significance to both sets of supporters, if not always to the rest of the country. The phrase did not originate in the town of Derby, which only has one team anyway, but the famous horse race, the Derby, founded by the Earl of Derby in 1780. It then became applied to any big, exciting sporting event. The best-known, fiercest derbies in England are traditionally between Spurs and Arsenal, Everton and Liverpool, Sunderland and Newcastle and, in Glasgow, between Celtic and Rangers. The term is also used abroad, as in Rome when Lazio and Roma meet.

Gutted. As in 'I was gutted' or 'I was well gutted'. A pretty concise, colourful image to convey a feeling of intense disappointment. Which, of course, you would feel if you happened to be a fish and had all your innards taken out. In use by footballers since the 1970s, then picked up by the next generation reading the back pages in their formative years, trotting it out when in turn they are asked that really hard question: 'How do you feel after being totally hammered?' 'Gutted.'

Below Kopites cheer on their team from Liverpool's famous stand. Despite losing some of its atmosphere when it was made all-seater in 1996, the Kop is still home to Anfield's most ardent fans.

Hat-trick. Three goals scored by the same player in one match, a phrase used in football since the 1870s, though in early decades it was applied to three consecutive goals. The phrase originated in cricket where a bowler taking three wickets in three balls was rewarded with a new hat. Today, footballers claim the match ball.

Hooliganism. A long-established word for anti-social behaviour, originating in South London in the 19th century after a family called Hoolihan terrorized the locality. The term 'football hooligans' became common in the 1960s. The same word has now been picked up by other football-playing nations, as a mark of respect for yet another English first.

Kop. Since 1906, the name for the most passionate, noisiest end of Liverpool's Anfield stadium. The origin lies in the Boer War and a hill called Spion Kop which was the scene of a bloody battle fought by British troops in 1900, many of them from Liverpool. Some other grounds later adopted the name to signify where their most loyal fans stood.

Mexican wave. First recorded at the World Cup in Mexico in 1986. Synchronized waving by a crowd, which goes around the whole ground, resembling a wave running through all the spectators. Usually takes place when a game has got a bit boring, so obviously very rarely happens in the Premiership …

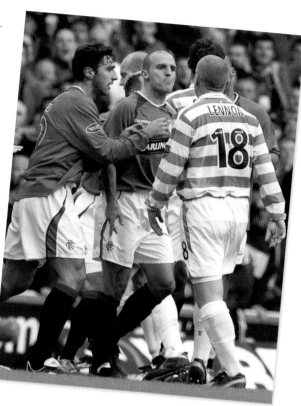

Above **No love lost between Alex Rae of Rangers and Neil Lennon of Celtic during an Old Firm derby at Ibrox Stadium in November 2004.**

Moon, as in **Over the Moon.** The opposite of being gutted. In 1972, Sir Alf Ramsey, after an England victory, said he felt like he 'could jump over the moon'. The phrase was already in use in football circles and presumably evolved from the nursery rhyme about the dish running away with the spoon and the cow jumping over the moon.

Nutmeg. To send the ball between an opponent's legs, then retrieve it on the other side. Very embarrassing when it happens to you. Two possible origins: it either dates back to a Victorian expression for a trick (derived from the nutmeg trade when a load of nutmeg would contain bits of ordinary wood to fool the purchaser). Or it could have been inspired by 'nuts', a slang term for testicles.

Old Firm. Refers to games between Rangers and Celtic, the two clubs who have dominated Scottish football since the beginning. The first Old Firm Cup final took place in 1894 (Rangers won 3–1). The term was used to suggest, rather cynically, that the same old firm will always be running things. Which has proved pretty accurate.

Sick as a parrot. Origins in doubt but it may date back to the 17th century, when the phrase 'melancholy as a sick parrot' was used in a West End drama. Probably made more popular in modern times by the famous Monty Python 'dead parrot' sketch of the 1970s.

We wuz robbed. Now a football cliché but originated in boxing after a world heavyweight fight in 1927 when Jack Dempsey said 'I was robbed of the championship'.

FOUL LANGUAGE

Fouls come in many forms and in degrees of seriousness, but whether fouls on the pitch are nasty and deliberate or purely accidental can depend on which side the person describing them supports. When a foul is blatant, nasty, ugly or cynical, the chances are it means one of the opposing players did it. When a foul is innocent, inadvertent, honest or professional, it was done by one of our players. There are many euphemisms for when a foul has been committed which can be applied to either side, usually as an ironic understatement: 'he left his calling card', 'he is putting it about', 'he was letting him know he was on the pitch', 'he let himself down'.

Below Play the man, not the ball: Bolton's Gary Speed commits a clear foul on David Bentley of Blackburn Rovers.

According to British fans and commentators, foreign teams, especially from South America or Southern Europe, tend to be moody, arrogant, cheating, shirt-pulling, diving and cynical. Our lads, however, are scrupulously honest, robust, enthusiastic, physical, competitive and whole-hearted. Which is usually another way of not admitting they too are dirty, rotten foulers.

FOOTBALL GRAMMAR

Football has its own grammatical rules and accepted usages, which should not necessarily be scoffed at by those clever boys who got top marks in English exams and understand about plurals and the correct parts of the verbs 'to be' or 'to do'.

When a manager says 'we wuz robbed', obviously he should have said 'we were robbed'. When he praises one of his players because 'the lad done good', he should of course have said 'the chap did jolly well'.

But these and other grammatical mistakes have become part of football. In a football context, they are common usage and have therefore every right to be seen as the accepted language of the game.

Some more examples to look out for. (You will, of course, be aware of the correct versions, but keep them to yourself, in your clever head.)

'The striker done his marker.'

'The boy Rooney done great.'

'We got done.'

'The ref never seen that incident.'

'He run past the defender.'

'We got beat 3–0.'

'I want one of them shirts.'

CLICHÉS

At the end of the day. The phrase has no known meaning, simply indicating a clearing of the throat, an emptying of the brain.

Let himself down. Said about a colleague who did something really stupid or appalling, but can't be criticized in public.

We're all up for this game. As indeed you should be, given that you're paid one million pounds a year and all you do is train all week, supposedly.

. . . .

Managers' clichés

He's got an attitude problem. The player is a total maniac who won't do a thing I tell him and/or is a lazy so-and-so just here for the money.

I was unsighted. Pleading ignorance, after one of his own players has been sent off for trying to kill someone.

I'll have to watch the replay. A semi-admission that, yes, he does have use of his sight but is not committing himself.

Our bench is much improved from last season. We've now got padded armchairs, heated armrests, oh, and two cheap Bulgarians and a Croatian no-one has heard of.

Below **Motty, doyen of commentators and proud possessor of a compendious knowledge of football stats and trivia.**

To be fair … The football manager's equivalent of the politician's 'With all due respect …' In other words, what I'm about to say will be unashamedly biased.

. . . .

Commentators' clichés

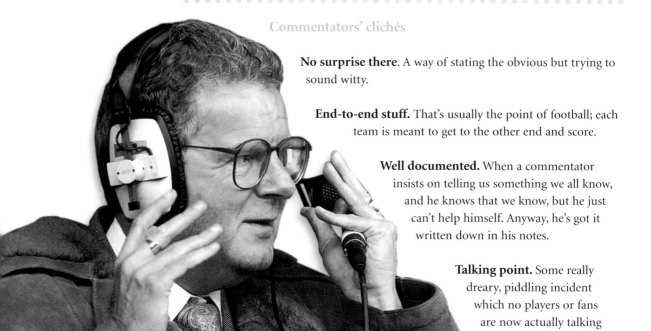

No surprise there. A way of stating the obvious but trying to sound witty.

End-to-end stuff. That's usually the point of football; each team is meant to get to the other end and score.

Well documented. When a commentator insists on telling us something we all know, and he knows that we know, but he just can't help himself. Anyway, he's got it written down in his notes.

Talking point. Some really dreary, piddling incident which no players or fans are now actually talking about.

A good time to score. As if there was a bad time to score.

The game needs a goal. Euphemism for 'Are you at home finding this match as stultifyingly boring as we are here in the commentary box ?'

Worth the admission fee. Said when the game is half-decent, and might get better, so don't switch off. Also meant to suggest the commentator had paid for his ticket. Fat chance.

Row Z. A mythical place, known only to commentators, where the ball goes after being hoofed by a lumpen defender.

He'll be disappointed by that. Said when a star player, whom the commentator or the player's manager does not wish to offend, has made a diabolical mistake or made a totally rubbish pass.

Welcome to the Premiership, [fill in any foreign player's name]! Attempted witticism when a newly signed, much-vaunted overseas player is poleaxed in his first game by some home-grown clogger's crunching tackle.

Above **Plenty of white (and hooped) shirts ... not in the penalty area this time, but on the washing line of a hard-pressed team captain's wife in the olden days.**

Above **Moving the goalposts, quite literally. In an infamous incident in 1977, the Tartan Army invades Wembley's hallowed turf after beating England 2–1.**

CONFUSING PHRASES AND TERMS

Lots of white shirts in the Bolton penalty area. Washday, is it?

Bodies in the box. No, it's not a mortuary.

Educated left foot. But the right one left school with no certificates at all.

Cultured midfielder. Does joined-up handwriting.

Reads the game well. Strolls around with the racing tips in his back pocket.

Shirts. As in 'Rooney has passed to a red shirt' or 'Now there are three red shirts upfield.' But what about the players? Where are they?

Giggs hit it with his wrong foot. Silly thing. He's picked up someone else's foot in the dressing room.

Bramble has put his body on the line. But where is he? Gone for a cup of tea?

Gerrard opened his body. Having an operation, was he?

Campbell is making his body big. Eating lots of hamburgers, blowing himself up with a pump?

Savage threw a leg at it. His own, we hope.

- -

FOOTBALL PHRASES THAT HAVE PASSED INTO THE LANGUAGE

Kick-off. This is used in business circles all over the English-speaking world, as in 'how shall we kick off the meeting?' or 'for a kick-off, let's discuss …'

Moving the goalposts. Another football image used in business.

Level playing field. Not necessarily from football, but a phrase taken from the need for all outdoor games to have a flat and equal playing surface. Mind you, the West Country side Yeovil Town used to play on a notoriously sloping pitch known as The Huish (now, inevitably, the site of a supermarket), which was the scene of several famous FA Cup giant-killing exploits.

In a different league, in a league of their own. Which, of course, has happened in football, almost from the very beginning, where there has been a variety of leagues at different levels.

Political football. This phrase was used in parliament as early as the 19th century to describe a topic that gets kicked around, battered and bashed, and very often ends up 'kicked into touch'.

He enjoys our full confidence. The kiss-of-death comment to the press by a club chairman on a manager who has failed to come up with the goods. It has made its way into the political arena; as with cabinet ministers, so with managers – once these dreaded words are spoken, you just know they're for the chop.

- -

TRUISMS

Non-football people also often scoff at what appear to be fatuous, pointless remarks made by players or commentators or fans, which on the face of it are not worth making as they appear so bleedin' obvious. But this is not always the case.

A game of two halves. Clearly, that's how the rules of the game ordained it, that we have 90 minutes divided equally in half, during which we change ends. As any fule know, to quote Molesworth. But, ah-ha, it can often happen that the two halves are not equal and bear no relation to each other. They can turn out to be shorter or longer depending on added time, incidents and injuries, or on players being sent off in the second half. A team which is all over the other in the first half, appearing to run away with victory, can completely collapse in the second half, for no apparent reason. Hence the notion of two halves, which turned out differently.

You can't score a goal if you haven't got the ball. Yes, we all agree with that, so why say it? Because it is emphasizing to players the need to keep hold of the ball, don't give it away. Technically, it isn't always true. When Ashley Cole, as he has done, thumps a wild clearance against one of his own defenders, and the ball rebounds into the net, then Chelsea have given away a goal – without the other side having the ball.

He knows where the goal is. No excuse for this one. Said of strikers who, well, … know how to strike. But on the face of it, it appears to damn a person with faint praise. Okay, no-one expects footballers to have brains the size of small planets, but surely the very least you can ask of the prima donna you've just paid a few million quid for is a basic sense of spatial awareness in his chosen profession.

So let's leave the language, and press on to some footballing foibles.

7. Superstitions

It's a funny old game: football rites and rituals

Players and managers have always been superstitious. So often a game does seem to go against you, or a ball bounces the wrong way, or your star player suffers a freak injury or a run of bad results sets in for no apparent reason, yet you are convinced you have been training and putting in just as much effort as normal. So what else can it be but sheer bad luck?

To bring good luck, players and managers will swear by signs and symbols, routines and objects, which were present when fortune seemed to be on their side.

In the early 1900s the Newcastle United team happened to pass a wedding on their way to a game – and they won easily. After that, the whole team became convinced that if they saw a wedding they would always win, whereas a funeral would bring them bad luck. So they went out of their way to spot a wedding party. It seemed to work for many years. Newcastle won the Division One title three times in the 1900s. Very little has gone their way since. So let's have some more weddings on Tyneside – Howay the lads!

In 1939 the Portsmouth manager Jack Tinn wore white spats (a pre-war fashion garment worn over the ankle and shoe to protect against splashes of mud) to bring good luck in the FA Cup. And he insisted they had to be fastened for him before each game by Pompey's winger, Fred Worrall. (He himself carried a lucky sixpence and a miniature horseshoe onto the pitch.)

Jack Tinn wore the same white spats all the way to the final, which Portsmouth won. Pompey have not won the FA Cup before or since.

In the 1953–54 season, Ipswich Town credited their run of victories to a four-leaf clover which an American had given them. They went on to win the Division 3 (South) title that season.

In the 1970s, Don Revie, manager of Leeds United, swore that wearing the same suit to the match brought the team good luck. George Graham, when manager of Arsenal from 1986 to 1995, was convinced that wearing the same red scarf helped his team to achieve success.

It usually has been an item of clothing which has been seen as a lucky totem, especially where players are concerned. Often it has depended on the order, such as putting on your shirt last, as with Rio Ferdinand of Man Utd or Paul Ince, formerly of Man Utd. Barry Venison, once of Liverpool, always put his right boot on first. 'And obviously my right sock.' Obviously, Barry.

Peter Schmeichel, Man Utd's famous goalkeeper, used to kick both goalposts before a game. This was not just a superstitious ritual but a warning to the opposition – declaring that his goal was now closed.

Opposite Portsmouth's outside-right Fred Worrall does up his manager Jack Tinn's spats, in a Fratton Park ritual that saw Pompey go all the way to FA Cup glory in 1939.

At the beginning of the 2006–07 season, Stuart Pearce, then manager of Man City, was given a little cuddly toy horse called Beanie by his seven-year-old daughter as a lucky charm. To the surprise of many fans, who remembered Pearce as a no-nonsense tough-guy player, formerly known as 'Psycho', he decided to keep it by his side in the dug-out during games. It seemed to work. They won two games and then drew the third. But the fourth game, away to Wigan, ended in a 4–1 drubbing. 'Stuart then decided to send the horse to the knacker's yard,' says Paul Tyrrell, Man City's head of communications.

Over the years, lucky food has also featured in superstitions, with players liking to have the same meal before a game. Jack Robinson, Derby County's goalkeeper of the 1890s, insisted he had to have rice pudding before every game. 'No pudding, no points,' he used to say.

Grounds, at home and more especially abroad, have often been thought to be cursed. This has continued until someone has lifted the curse, such as a local priest, gypsy or witch doctor.

Fans also have their lucky omens, very often wearing the same clothes to every game, going the same way, parking at the same place, eating the same food, drinking in the same pub. Until they lose. Then it all starts again with a different ritual.

A MORAL DILEMMA FOR WAYNE
Part Two

When Wayne got to the Den, Darren was already there, plus two other boys, so that was good. They could have a proper game of football, two a side.

The score was 32–16 when Wayne noticed that they were being watched by three men. Two were in jackets and ties, the other wore a black jumper. They were standing separately, not talking to each other. The one with the black jumper was using a small digital video camera.

Through the fence, while Wayne was taking a corner, one of the men in jacket and tie muttered, 'Wayne, could I have a word with you?'

'I'm busy,' replied Wayne.

When it was Wayne's turn to be goalie, the other jacket and tie positioned himself behind the goal and whispered, 'Wayne, which number do you live in?'

'Ugh?' replied Wayne. Not one of his usual grunts. More of a question as he wasn't sure what the man was referring to.

The man in the jumper had stopped filming and was standing at the little metal gate to the Den, the only way to get in or out.

Wayne and his friends were playing the first to 50. Wayne of course scored the winning goal. As he came off the pitch, the man in the jumper put his arm around Wayne.

'Congratulations, Wayne, great goal. Tell me, is your dad at home?'

'Yeh,' said Wayne, 'but someone's with him.'

'Oh sh*t,' said all three of the men at the same time.

Over breakfast next morning, before going off to school, Wayne asked his dad who all the strange men were.

'Scouts,' said his dad. 'From Chelsea, Spurs, Arsenal and United.'

'Scouts?' said Wayne's mother. 'Watching a nine-year-old?'

'Yes, they've left it late,' said Wayne's dad. 'These days they like to find them aged six. I don't know what kept them. It was that goal against Holloway what did it.'

'So what did the men want, dad?' asked Wayne.

'They want you to come for a trial after school next week.'

'Well, he can't,' said his mum, 'not during a school week. He'll be too tired.'

'I'll drive him there,' said his dad. 'If I can get the car started. We'll do two next week, and the next two the next. Got to shop around. We don't want to jump at the first offer, do we.'

'Offer?' said Wayne's mother, 'I think you're getting carried away. He hasn't had a trial yet …'

Before his first trial, which was at Chelsea's training ground, Wayne couldn't get off to sleep. When he eventually did, he was at Wembley, the new Wembley, so it must have been some time in the future. He was scoring the winning goal for England against Brazil. For some reason, Darren was Brazil's goalie. Perhaps that was why he let it in.

After school, his dad was there to pick him up, having taken the day off work, so he said, though most days his dad had no work anyway.

His mother had made sure that Wayne's football shirt, the one he always wore to school and for playing in, was clean. She'd stayed up late getting it off his back before he fell asleep then had it washed and ironed by morning.

For some reason, Wayne had imagined that he would be the only boy at Cobham, Chelsea's training pitch; that it would be a special trial arranged just for him. He even expected that the Chelsea manager José Mourinho and all the first team squad would be there, waiting to see him. After all, he was the star striker from Brookpark primary school, the one everybody was talking about, the one who had got Brookpark to the final.

There turned out to be 30 boys there, all of Wayne's age, though some a bit bigger, all standing around looking nervous. No sign of any of the famous players, least of all the Special One. Eventually two young and very bossy coaches appeared with clipboards.

One of them made a sarcastic remark about Wayne's shirt, which Wayne didn't quite catch.

They were quickly set to work, practising skills and techniques, passing to each other in little groups, two touches and then one touches, then passing with the left foot followed by the right foot, all easy peasy stuff to Wayne.

They finished with some five-a-side games in which Wayne immediately got barged over by two large boys whom he was convinced could not be aged nine, more like 19.

He managed to nutmeg one of them, who swore at Wayne, said he'd see him afterwards. Wayne ignored him. Mr Wilkins always said that it was a sign of weakness when players tried to intimidate you.

Afterwards, Wayne thought he had done pretty well. Not quite showed off all his skills, as the trial had been short and carefully controlled, but he was quite pleased.

One of the coaches called Wayne and his dad over when Wayne was in the dressing room. He was still carrying his clipboard. Could it contain a contract? Nah, that's silly, thought Wayne to himself. But, for a moment, it had gone through his mind.

'Okay, then, Wayne,' said the coach. 'We want you to come for another trial, this time next week.'

Then he was off, leaving Wayne to get dressed and go home.

Wayne's next two trials, at Spurs and then Arsenal, were much the same, with the same number of boys and similar exercises, each lasting about an hour.

Nothing was said after either of them, not even to come back next week.

'We'll be in touch,' was all he was told.

His third trial was at United's training ground, where he felt at home the moment he arrived. He was wearing his United shirt, which probably helped. This was the one he always wore and had led the coach at Chelsea to make the sarky comment.

Wayne had always followed United, thanks to his grandad who had followed them from the days of the Third Division (South), whatever that was.

London United had come up into the Premiership only very recently. They still didn't have the state-of-the-art training facilities of Chelsea, Spurs and Arsenal, but Wayne liked the atmosphere which was professional yet friendly and relaxed. He also liked the fact that most of the first team had come up through United's own academy.

Wayne's father, until recently, had not been much of a football fan. If anything, he favoured Chelsea, especially when they had suddenly become rich and glamorous. But Wayne had always loved United. His grandfather had given him a pile of old programmes and, as a little boy, he used to fall asleep with them nestling on his nose.

His mother maintained that it was thanks to United's programmes that Wayne had ever learned to read.

Immediately after his United trial, the director of their academy, Jock Docherty, came over to Wayne and his father.

'Well done, Wayne. You did good. We'll be offering you a place at our academy,' he said. 'You haven't signed up anywhere else, have you?'

'No,' said Wayne.

'Er,' said Wayne's dad. 'Not so far …'

On the way home in the car, Wayne asked his dad why he had said 'not so far'. As far as Wayne was concerned, United had always been his team, the one he'd dreamed about playing for. So what could possibly tempt him to join anyone else?

'We'll see,' said Wayne's dad, tapping his nose …

Want to know more about Wayne? Turn at once for the next exciting episode to page 188.

8. Fun and games

Game for a laugh …

Football fans have always had a sense of humour. Well, you have to if you follow Man City. (Old joke, and not a very good one.) Each season, only 10 or so out of England's 92 league clubs or Scotland's 42 can consider they have had a successful season, having won something. For most clubs it's usually been a case of grinning and bearing it. Success for them has been surviving. You just have to laugh, so most fans think, or you'll cry.

So right from the beginning, there have been comic postcards and cartoons, funny verses and bad jokes, which have appeared on the football pages or in programmes and then been repeated on the terraces as fans try to cheer themselves up.

Mocking the opposition, making jokes at their expense or rubbishing the referee or directors has been prevalent right from the outset.

One of the earliest wheezes was to print so-called 'Funeral Cards' when a club had just been kicked out of the FA Cup. The fans of the winning club could therefore gloat at the 'demise' of the team they had just defeated. These funeral cards were printed before the match with two versions, depending on who might win, which would then be sold to fans as they left the ground. And did they chortle! Here's one from 1893 which was sold to Wolves fans after they had beaten Everton 1–0 in the Cup final:

Above **Proving that refs have always been fair game, a Baines card from the early 20th century shows injured Runcorn players carting off a referee in a kit bag.**

IN MEMORIAM OF
EVERTON FOOTBALL TEAM
Who departed from the Cup Competition through a severe attack of Wolves.

And whose hopes were interred at the Football Cemetery, the same day.

They came in all their glory,
From that noted Toffy Town,
To fight the famous 'Wolves'
A team of English renown
The 'Toffy's' came on boldly,
Their victory for to seek;
But now they go home gravely
O'er their troubles for to weep,

Farewell, farewell dear old Everton,
No more for the Pot you
will dribble;
You have lost it to-day through
difficult play
And we'll shout farewell for ever
and ever.

Wanted!

A modern version of the same sort of joke announcement

On Thursday 24 October, the trophy room at Macclesfield Town FC was broken into and the contents stolen.

Police are looking for a man with a carpet, two spiders and some cobwebs.

If a member of the public sees this man, on no account should he be approached.

Just point and laugh.

GAMES AND QUIZZES

Fill in the blanks
The missing words are all names of football teams …

Once we got on board, the .... made us feel comfortable although the .... was riddled with holes. The cabin boy went to .... the fire and we all sat on deck .... our books. When we got to the island, we had a swim in a .... which made us feel very ....

On the island we were scared we might meet some .... but luckily there were some forest .... One of them said 'This path .... the way.' We came to an old house which had once been a fine .... or because of all the glass it might have been a .... We were then able to .... the treasure.

On the boat home we ate some .... which had been in the meat store and we all felt very sick.

FUN AND GAMES

This time, the missing words are the names of well-known modern footballers.

On the way to .... 's Cross, I met a very .... dog. He came at me at great .... but by great good .... he was only going to .... for a cat. Going over a .... , a man told me I would meet a .... in shining armour but this turned out to be .... information. I came to a nice little cottage, went inside and sat in the front .... Then clouds disappeared and the .... came out so I went outside into the .... and felt like a ....

Answers at bottom of page.

. . . .

Footer anagrams

Wayne Rooney	=	Eye on Norway	David Beckham =	Mad hived back
Paul Gascoigne	=	Cap goal genius	Dennis Bergkamp =	Pink German beds
Geoff Hurst	=	Fought refs	Shaun Wright-Philips =	Hit whiplash slurping
Michael Owen	=	I chew a lemon	Roman Abramovich =	Havoc. Iran a mob, Mr.
Frank Lampard	=	Park farmland		

. . . .

Football crossword

Clues Across

6   What every evening match needs
7   Part of Solano's first name
9   The ball may be shot like this
10 What no team wants to be
11 Look under your football boot
13 Black Cats

Clues Down

1   Chelsea's colour
2   What comes before Vale
3   Can be seen at Boundary Park
4   The sort of goals you don't want
5   What every good ref should be
8   A player needs permission from the ref before he does this
9   A free kick which often leads to a goal
10 Part of footballer Luther's surname
11 What poor clubs have to do
12 What half-time tea used to be served in

Answers on page 164

Answers: Gerrard, Savage, Speed, Fortune, Hunt, Bridge, Knight, Duff, Parlour, Sun, Park, King.

146   THE BUMPER BOOK OF FOOTBALL

Picture quiz (Answers at bottom of page)
Can you tell whose legs/arms/backs these are?

Ah, weren't they sweet ... Can you identify these stars when they were still playing for their school teams?

Famous managers – when they were not so famous players. Who are they?

FUN AND GAMES

A quiz for today (Answers at foot of page)

To test your knowledge of football now.

1. What is the name of Arsenal's new home?
2. Which club did Steve McLaren manage before managing England?
3. Name Rio's brother.
4. Name Wayne's fiancée.
5. Which country does José Mourinho come from?
6. Who plays at Brunton Park?
7. In what town is the National Football Museum?
8. What was the score in the World Cup 2006 final?
9. Who won the FA Cup in 2006–07?
10. Who scored most goals in the Premiership in 2006–07?

A quiz from yesteryear (Answers at foot of page)

To test your knowledge of the history of football and some of the great players and teams of past times.

1. Which year was the FA formed?
2. Which school did Lord Kinnaird go to?
3. Which famous player sucked a toothpick?
4. Who has scored most goals ever in an English league season?
5. Which is the only non-English club to win the FA Cup?
6. Name one of the clubs Stanley Matthews played for.
7. Which year was the Munich Air Disaster?
8. Who was England's 1966 World Cup-winning captain?
9. Which year was Glasgow Rangers formed: 1863, 1873 or 1883?
10. When was the first Premiership season?

FERGIE'S WORLD-CLASS PLAYERS

In December 2006, Sir Alex Ferguson said that in the 20 years he had been manager of Manchester United he had managed only five world-class players, plus one who could possibly be the sixth. Can you name his five definite – and one possible – world-class players? Here's a clue – David Beckham was not mentioned.

Answer: Peter Schmeichel, Eric Cantona, Ryan Giggs, Roy Keane and Wayne Rooney. He backed Cristiano Ronaldo to be his sixth.

Answers: 1. Emirates Stadium **2.** Middlesbrough **3.** Anton of West Ham **4.** Coleen McLoughlin **5.** Portugal **6.** Carlisle United **7.** Preston **8.** Italy 1 – France 1 at full time, then Italy won 5–3 on penalties **9.** Chelsea **10.** Didier Drogba (21)

Answers: 1. 1862 **2.** Eton **3.** Billy Meredith **4.** Dixie Dean, scored 60 goals for Everton, 1927–28 **5.** Cardiff City, 1927 **6.** Stoke City, Blackpool **7.** 1958 **8.** Bobby Moore **9.** 1873 **10.** 1992-93

Double identity (Answers at bottom of page)

Can you name the players and managers from the initial letters of their first and second names?

A... A...
- Manager of Carlisle United in 1974 when they were in the First Division

B... B...
- Combative Scot who captained Leeds United in the 1970s
- Manager of Northern Ireland in the World Cup finals of 1982 and 1986

C... C...
- Argentinian star of the 1994 World Cup, also played for Roma in Italy and Benfica of Portugal

D... D...
- Born Leicester 1969. Played for Norwich City, Cambridge United and Man United
- Captain of Ivory Coast, French footballer of the year, Chelsea star
- Everton's best-ever striker

J... J...
- Scottish jinker, star of Celtic's 1967 Euro triumph

K... K...
- Named Mighty Mouse when he moved from Liverpool to Hamburg

T... T...
- Man Utd centre forward, killed in the Munich air crash

W... W...
- Rangers' post-war star, later managed the club

Z... Z...
- Lost control of his head in the World Cup final of 2006

Above **CC** playing for Argentina in the 1994 World Cup.

Do you know the rules of football?

In 1949, the *Champion Annual for Boys* ran a 'Quiz for Footer Fans,' with drawings of incidents which might happen in a game, and asked readers to judge whether they would be allowed or not. **Can you answer the same questions today?**

(1) A forward shoots with the goalkeeper out of goal. A defender handles in an attempt to save, but the ball goes into the net. Is it a goal or a penalty-kick?

(2) If a footballer is injured during play, is the trainer allowed to run on to the field immediately and give him attention?

(3) A player takes a very long throw-in and the ball, without being touched by anyone else, enters the net. Is it a goal?

(4) If the ball hits a corner-flag post and rebounds on to the field, is it still in play?

(5) A corner-kick is taken. Is player "A" offside?

Answers on page 164

(7) A goalkeeper is clearing his lines when the ball strikes the referee and rebounds into the net. Is it a goal?

(6) This small forward heaved himself up on his team-mate's shoulders, so as to head the ball home. Should the ref award a goal, or give a foul against him?

(9) A penalty-kick rebounds from the cross-bar and the player shoots the ball into the net at his second attempt. Would the ref award a goal?

(8) Is a player allowed to remove a corner-flag post before taking a corner-kick?

(10) At the kick-off, is a player allowed to cross the half-way line as soon as the ref blows his whistle?

(11) Can a referee use a rattle instead of a whistle when he is controlling a game?

MASCOTS

Mascots are one of the modern methods of cheering up fans, or at least amusing the kiddies, but many of them do have long-established historical links with the club concerned.

The earliest known mascots were in existence at least 100 years ago. Manchester United in 1902 had a dog, The Major, as their club mascot, followed by a goat, both real live animals. In 1920, Barnsley FC used a donkey, which was ridden by a local character called Amos. In the 1920s, Millwall had a lion – this time a pretend one – while in the 1930s, Derby had a ram, Sunderland a black cat, and Leicester had a fox – all of them animals associated with those clubs.

The present-day trend, which began in the 1990s, is for someone to be inside a larger-than-life, cartoon-like costume, usually a furry animal which has some connection with the history or traditions of the club. They usually jump around on the pitch before the game, being very silly, take joke penalties or go round and shake hands with the crowds, then they clap the players as they come out on the pitch. Off the pitch, they often visit local hospitals and schools, do a bit of panto, sometimes becoming minor local celebrities.

(If you want to read more about the wonderful world of the mascots, there's a whole book about them: *Mascots – Football's Furry Friends* by Rick Minter, published by Tempus, 2004.)

Mascots of the major clubs

Aberdeen Angus the bull. Perfect symbol, as Aberdeen Angus bulls are known worldwide. 'He's as mad as a hatter,' said the announcer before one Aberdeen home game. 'It must be the BSE.'

Arsenal Gunnersaurus. A rather ugly, long-necked, green creature meant to have been hatched from a dinosaur egg, har har, in 1993. Likes to cuddle Arsenal's goalie before each game, if he can manage it.

Aston Villa Hercules and Bella. Two lions – a reference to the lion on Villa's badge, dating back to 1874.

Barnsley Toby Tyke. The real donkey has gone, now they have a joke dog called Toby who cocks his leg on the visitors' goalposts. Often accompanied by another dog, Tina.

Birmingham City Beau Brummie. Big, bear-like creature who runs across the pitch before the kick-off. Once almost finished off Ant and Dec when he fell on them while filming.

Blackburn Rovers Roar and Roarina. A lion and lioness dressed in Rovers strip.

Bolton Wanderers Lofty the Lion. Yet another lion. The reference here is to Nat Lofthouse, once known as the Lion of Vienna after a great England victory over Austria.

Celtic Hoopy the Hound, in green hoops of course. Has had a book written about him. Once had 61 scarves thrown at him when Celtic won the league, again.

Charlton Athletic Floyd and Harvey, a bulldog and a cat who take their names from two local streets beside the Valley: Floyd Road and Harvey Gardens.

Chelsea Stamford the Lion. Again a reference to the club's badge, but shouldn't an English lion now be replaced by a Russian bear?

Derby County Rammie the Ram. The local regiment had a ram as a mascot as early as 1858, a tradition continued by the football club.

Hartlepool United H'angus the Monkey. In 1800, a monkey got swept up on a local beach. Some fishermen thought it was a French spy in disguise so hanged it. People from Hartlepool then became known as 'Monkey Hangers'. Hence the origin of the club's unusual mascot. In 2004 something even more bizarre happened when Stuart Drummond, wearer of United's monkey costume, decided to stand for election as Mayor of Hartlepool. He stood as the monkey candidate – and got elected!

Hull City Roary the Tiger. Because of their amber and black colours, Hull got called the Tigers.

Leicester City Filbert Fox. Taken from their crest, and their address in Filbert Way.

Manchester City Moonchester and Moonbeam. Not animals, for a change. In fact, they are the only

Opposite **Bolton Wanderers mascot Lofty the Lion accompanies Japanese player Hidetoshi Nakata onto the pitch at the Reebok in 2005.**

Below **The bizarre Moonchester holds up a placard celebrating a legendary Man City comeback in 2004.**

known footer mascots to come from another world, i.e. the moon. Complicated joke on City's theme tune, 'Blue Moon'.

Manchester United Fred the Red, meant to look like a Red Devil, the nickname for the club since the 1970s, which also appears on their crest.

Middlesbrough Roary the Lion – yet another one, and also based on the club badge.

Plymouth Argyle Pilgrim Pete, one of the few mascots based on a human figure rather than an animal. He represents one of the Pilgrim Fathers who sailed to America from Plymouth in 1620. Look out for his big moustache.

Portsmouth Frogmore, a giant blue frog. The club ground is in Frogmore Road.

Below Cyril the Swan hugs Swansea manager John Hollins after a cup-tie win in 1999. This belligerent bird has found himself in a number of scrapes, including a fracas with Millwall's Zampa the Lion in 2001.

Reading Kingsley Royal, yet another lion, as on their badge. Sent off once for entering the field of play during a game while trying to stop a Reading ball going into touch. Naughty.

Sheffield United Captain Blade (after the famous Sheffield steel). Supposedly human, and carries a sword, so don't argue with him.

Sheffield Wednesday Ozzie the Owl. Usually joined by fellow owls, Ollie and Baz. The owl association is with Owlerton, a district of Sheffield.

Sunderland Samson and Delila, black cats, taken from the team's nickname.

Swansea City Cyril the Swan. Claims to be the UK's No. 1 mascot, or at least the most famous. Has been on TV, done a CD, had a book written about him and been up before the Welsh FA for bringing the game into disrepute, i.e. running onto the pitch. Gets mobbed on the streets of Swansea. Hard to miss as he's nine feet high.

Tottenham Hotspur Chirpy the Cockerel. A cockerel has been a symbol of Spurs for 100 years, supposedly because fighting cocks wore spurs.

Watford Harry the Hornet, taken from the club's nickname, despite the fact that, on their club badge, they have antler's horns.

West Ham United Herbie and Bubbles. Herbie is dressed as a hammer, for obvious reasons, while Bubbles is a bear, for reasons that are not so clear.

Wolverhampton Wanderers Wolfie and Wendy – wolves, of course.

Wigan Athletic JJ and B, male and female cartoon characters. The only mascots who are letters, taken from JJB, the club's main sponsor.

Other mascots
Blackpool – Bloomfield Bear ● Bournemouth – Cherry Bear ● Bradford City – Billy Bantam and City Gent ● Brentford – Buzzbee ● Bristol City – City Cat ● Bristol Rovers – Captain Gas ● Burnley – Bertie Bee ● Bury – Robbie the Bobby ● Cambridge United – Marvin the Moose ● Carlisle United – Foxy ● Chesterfield – Chester the Fieldmouse ● Colchester United – Eddie the Eagle ● Coventry City – Sky Blue Sam ● Crystal Palace – Pete the Eagle ● Crewe Alexandra – Gresty the Lion ● Darlington – Mr Q the Quaker ● Doncaster Rovers – Donny the Dog ● Gillingham – Tommy Trewblu ● Grimsby Town – Mighty Mariner ● Huddersfield Town – Terry and Trisha (Yorkshire Terriers) ● Ipswich Town – Bluey and Crazy Horse ● Leyton Orient – Theo the Wyvern ● Lincoln City – Poacher the Imp ● Luton Town – Happy Harry ● Macclesfield Town – Roary the Lion ● Mansfield Town – Sammy the Stag ● Northampton Town – Clarence the Dragon ● Norwich City – Captain Canary ● Notts County – Mr and Mrs Magpie ● Oldham Athletic – Chaddy the Owl ● Peterborough United – Ollie the Ox ● Port Vale – Boomer the Dog ● Preston North End – Deepdale Duck ● QPR – Jude the Cat ● Rochdale – Desmond the Dragon ● Scunthorpe – Sammy Saint (a St Bernard dog) ● Southend United – Elvis J Eel and Sammy the Shrimp ● Stockport County – Vernon Bear ● Swindon Town – Rockin Robin ● Torquay United – Gilbert the Gull ● Tranmere Rovers – Rover the Dog ● Walsall – Swifty (a bird) ● West Bromwich Albion – Baggie the bird ● Wycombe Wanderers – Bodger (a cartoon figure) ● Yeovil – Jolly Green Giant.

Some ancient jokes from a Chelsea FC programme of 1907

The 'Trotters' appear to have taken a great liking to trotting backwards and forwards between the First and Second Division.
(On Bolton Wanderers)

• •

We hear Big Bill Foulke has become a public house man and is no longer under the bar but behind the bar.
(On their famous ex-goalkeeper)

• •

Question: What is wrong with the goalkeeper's anatomy?
Answer: Why, his back's in front of him.

• •

Question: Why is a keen footballer like a fretful child?
Answer: Because he is always ready for the bawl.

• •

Boy: Mum, can I go out and play football?
Mum: Not with those holes in your socks.
Boy: No, with Harry next door, he's got a proper football.

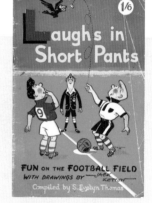

JOKES FROM THE 1940s TAKEN FROM *LAUGHS IN SHORT PANTS*

Hearing Things

Disgruntled schoolboy: We'd have won the game, ma, if our captain hadn't lost his head.
Mother: Mercy! Was it as bad as that? I heard it was only an ear.

Good Kick-off

Schoolmaster: Why were you late for school today, Sidney?
Small Boy: Please sir, I dreamed I was at a football match and the referee ordered extra time, so I stayed to see the finish.

Board and Lodger

An old lady was watching a match for the first time in her life.
'Could you tell me,' she asked the man next to her, 'whether those men between the posts get paid for what they do?'
'Well, of course,' he answered. 'They draw about eight pounds a week.'
'Do they really?' she exclaimed, and pondered a little. 'Don't you think it would be more economical to board up the space between the posts?'

Old jokes from *Topical Times* magazine of the 1970s. (Well, they were considered funny at the time …)

Liverpool's Kevin Keegan was shopping in a greengrocer's when his manager, Bill Shankly, came in.

'What are you doing here?' rasped Bill. 'You should be training.'

'I'm just buying a bag of potatoes, boss.'

'You get off to training. I'll get your potatoes.'

Off went Keegan, but within a couple of minutes in walked Billy Bingham, manager of rivals Everton.

'What are you doing here, Bill?' asked Bingham.

'I'm getting a bag of potatoes for Kevin Keegan,' replied the Shank.

'Oh, that's not a bad swop,' cracked Bingham.

* * * * * * * * * * * * * * * * * * *

It was said last season – 'Things are getting so bad at Old Trafford the players are giving away plastic replicas of petrol pump attendants.

* * * * * * * * * * * * * * * * *

When he was Manchester City's manager, Malcolm Allison phoned across town to the Manchester United manager, Tommy Docherty.

'Tom, we have developed a new system of training that might help you. I have my team playing a practice game against 11 dustbins.'

The following day Tommy rang back …

'Hey, Mal, it's not working … the dustbins won 2–0.'

* * * * * * * * * * * * * * * * * *

During last season's power crisis Sheffield United arranged a league game against Ipswich Town on a Tuesday afternoon.

The crowd was small – just over 10,000.

Up in the press box towards the end of the game one reporter shouted, 'Does anyone know the crowd?'

'Aye,' replied his colleague. 'Well, most of them, anyway.'

* * * * * * * * * * * * * * * * * *

Mr Alan Hardaker, secretary of the Football League, was phoned one morning by an irate club manager.

'The referee at our match last night was the worst ever,' ranted the caller. 'He cost us two goals. You're asking us to mark referees from 1 to 10 in our reports on them. Why don't you start at 0? That's more than this bloke is worth.'

Mr Hardaker considered the matter and replied quietly 'You wouldn't like to give him one for nerve just for daring to go out there, would you?'

More old jokes:

The players of Dundee are still telling this story …

After centre-half George Stewart had been spoken to in a European tie the referee came at him a second time, waving the yellow card that signifies a booking.

'Twist,' reacted Stewart, in the voice of one who has played a bit of pontoon in his day.

The manager of a relegation-haunted First Division club collapsed and went into a coma. He awoke in the city's Northern Hospital.

'Where am I?' he asked.

'You're in the Northern,' replied the nurse.

'And what happened to the Second, Third and Fourth Divisions?' came back the bedazed boss.

When Alan Ball was transferred to Arsenal a Highbury fan had this jingle published –
And now the Arsenal should not fail
To win the honours one and all,
Because they will be playing with
Britain's most expensive 'Ball'.

A father took his daughter to watch her first football match. The game was a little dull, to say the least, and the little girl piped up, 'Do Rovers ever score, Dad?'

'How should I know,' replied her Dad, 'I've only been supporting them for 10 years.'

Three fans were standing on the terraces moaning that their team was losing game after game.

'I blame the manager,' said the first. 'If he'd only sign eleven new players we could be a great side.'

'I blame the players,' responded the second. 'If they put in a bit more effort, they might at least score a few goals.'

'I blame my parents,' said the third. 'If I'd been born in another town, I'd be supporting a decent team!'

Trainer: Why are you late for training?

Player: I sprained my ankle.

Trainer: That's a lame excuse.

Insurance agent: This is a very good policy. We pay £10,000 for every broken arm or broken leg.

Dumb Footballer: Yes, but what do you do with them all?

Player: I've just been to the doctor and he says I can't play football.

Manager: Oh, when did he see you play?

The manager of a struggling Third Division (North) club was trying his hardest to gee up his team. 'Go out there, lads, and do your best,' he said. 'Then I can get enough money to replace you …'

• •

In church one Sunday the vicar opened his Bible to read the lesson. In a loud voice he proclaimed, 'Corinthians 7!'

A keen football fan who was dozing in the front pew woke up with a start and shouted. 'Who were they playing?'

• •

Reporter: Tell me, Mr Harris, will your £100,000 win on the football pools make any difference to your way of life?

Pools Winner: None at all. I shall carry on exactly as before.

Reporter: But what about all the begging letters?

Pools Winner: Oh, I'll keep sending them out as usual.

• •

'At our ground, they always play the National Anthem before every game.'

'Oh, why's that, are they very patriotic?'

'No, it's to make sure our team can stand up.'

• •

After the game, Freddy was moaning in the dressing room that nobody had passed to him.

'I might as well be invisible,' he said.

'Who said that?' asked the captain.

Jokes about famous managers and players, all said to be true …

In the days when players received a maximum wage and also different rates for the winter and summer periods, the legendary Tom Finney left the manager's office, having negotiated the coming season.

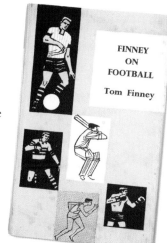

'What did you get, Tom?' asked his team-mate, waiting his turn.

'£12 a week, winter and summer,' replied Finney.

The team-mate took his place in the manager's office.

'Now, then, lad,' said the manager. 'You've not done bad, so I'm giving you a new contract. You'll get £12 a week in the winter and £8 in the summer.'

'But, gaffer,' protested the player. 'Finney's getting £12 a week all year!'

'Yes, son,' frowned the manager, 'but he's a better player than you.'

'Not in the summer, he's not!' was the explosive retort.

• •

Bill Shankly, the Liverpool manager, was once asked by an impertinent journalist if it was true that he had taken his wife to see a reserve team match as a wedding anniversary treat. 'It's not true at all,' said Shankly vehemently. 'That's a lie.' Then he paused and added. 'It was her birthday.'

Brian Clough, the famous Nottingham Forest manager, was in bed with his wife.

'God, your feet are cold,' she said to him.

'You can call me Brian in bed, dear,' replied Clough.

• •

Victoria Beckham comes back from the shops and finds her husband David jumping up and down in excitement.

'Forty-three days, forty-three days!' he shouts. 'I've finished this jigsaw in only forty-three days.'

'What's so good about that?' asks Victoria.

'Well,' says David. 'It says three to six years on the box!'

• •

Stanley Matthews was so fast that when he went to bed at night, he could turn out the light at the bedroom door and be under the blankets before the room got dark.

Above Stanley Matthews shows his pace at the 1953 Cup Final, which became known as the 'Matthews Final'.

Modern jokes

Steve Gerrard and Jamie Carragher were in a car park after the match, trying to unlock the door of Gerrard's sports car with a coat hanger. They tried and tried to get the door open, but the lock just wouldn't give. Carragher stopped to catch his breath. 'It's no use,' he said. 'We're never going to get in.'

'We have to,' urged Gerrard. 'It's starting to rain and the top's down.'

• •

A German family head out one Saturday to do some shopping. While in the sports shop the son picks up an England football shirt and says to his sister, 'I've decided to be an England supporter and I would like this for my birthday.'

His big sister is outraged by this and promptly whacks him round the head and says, 'Go talk to your mother.'

'Mum?'

'Yes, son?'

'I've decided I'm going to be an England supporter and I would like this shirt for my birthday.'

The mother is outraged at this, promptly whacks him around the head twice and says, 'Go talk to your father.'

'Dad?'

'Yes, son?'

'I've decided I'm going to be an England supporter and I would like this shirt for my birthday.'

The father is outraged and promptly whacks his

son around the head four times and says, 'No son of mine is ever going to be seen in THAT!'

About half an hour later they're all back in the car and heading towards home. The father turns to his son and says, 'Son, I hope you've learned something today.'

The son says, 'Yes, dad, I have.'

'Good, son, and what is it?'

The son replies, 'I've only been an England supporter for an hour and already I hate you Germans.'

• •

It is just before Scotland v Brazil at the next World Cup 2010.

Ronaldinho goes into the Brazilian changing room to find all his team mates looking at bit glum.

'What's up?' he asks.

'Well, we're having trouble getting motivated for this game. We know it's important but it's only Scotland. They're rubbish and we can't be bothered.'

Ronaldinho looks at them and says, 'Well, I reckon I can beat them by myself. You lads go down the pub.'

So Ronaldinho goes out to play Scotland by himself and the rest of the Brazilian team go off for a few jars.

After a few pints, they wonder how the game is going, so they get the landlord to put the teletext on. A big cheer goes up as the screen reads 'Brazil 1 – Scotland 0 (Ronaldinho 10 minutes)'. He is

beating Scotland all by himself.

Anyway, a few more pints later and the game is forgotten until someone remembers. 'It must be full time by now, let's see how he got on.'

They put the teletext on …

'Result from the Stadium: 'Brazil 1 (Ronaldinho 10 minutes) – Scotland 1 (Angus 89 minutes)'.

They can't believe it, he has single-handedly got a draw against Scotland!

They rush back to the Stadium to congratulate Ronaldinho. They find him in the dressing room, still in his gear, sat with his head in his hands.

He refuses to look at them. 'I've let you down, I've let you down.'

'Don't be daft, you got a draw against Scotland, all by yourself. And they only scored at the very, very end.'

'No. No, I have, I've let you down … I got sent off after 12 minutes.'

• •

Fan 1: Have you heard? We've just signed a new goalkeeper from Spain. He has a fish for a head and clothes pegs where his legs should be.

Fan 2: Where did we get him from?

Fan 1: Surreal Madrid.

A Watford player was talking to his friends.

'Our manager won't stand for any nonsense,' he said. 'Last Saturday he caught a couple of fans climbing over the wall and went bananas. He grabbed them by their collars and said, "Now you just get back in there and watch the game until it finishes."'

England v Andorra: against all expectations, Andorra dominate the first half and are thrashing England 10–0.

At half-time, England manager Steve McClaren makes the strange decision to take off Frank Lampard and replace him with a centipede. The crowd can't understand what is going through McClaren's mind, but they soon realize that the centipede is an amazing footballer – he scores 52 goals from penalties, free kicks and shots from every part of the pitch. England win by a record score!

After the match, the Andorra manager congratulates McClaren. 'Wow,' he says, 'that centipede of yours is a genius. But can I ask, why didn't you play him from the start?'

'Oh, I'd have liked to,' replies McClaren, 'but it takes him 40 minutes to get his boots on!'

Man offers marriage proposal to any woman with ticket for Leeds United v Sheffield United.

Must send photograph (of ticket).

Advert in *Yorkshire Post*, 1990

Jack and Joe sat down to watch a video of the 2007 Cup final. Jack bet Joe £5 that Chelsea would beat Manchester United. Chelsea did win, of course, but Jack said he wouldn't take his money as he already knew the score. 'So did I,' said Joe. 'But I didn't think Man Utd would lose a second time.'

First seagull: That's the new Wembley Stadium down there – the Cup final's just started. Look – there's Wayne Rooney.

Second seagull: Where? I can't see him.

First seagull: Yes, there he is – I'll spot him for you!

(Portuguese variant of the Brian Clough joke): **José Mourinho is in bed with his wife.**

'Meu Deus, vossos pes estão frios,' she says to him.

'Tu podes chamar-me José, minha querida,' replies Mourinho.

A supporter wearing red and white approaches a ticket tout before a Spurs v Arsenal game.

'How much for a ticket?'

'To you, £100.'

'Here's £50, then. I'm only going to watch one team.'

Two flies were playing football in a saucer. 'We're going to have to do better than this,' said one fly to the other. 'We're playing in the cup next week.'

Really awful 'knock-knock' jokes

Knock knock.
Who's there?
Kanu.
Kanu who?
Kanu open the door …

Knock knock.
Who's there?
Juno.
Juno who?
Juno what time's kick-off?

Knock knock.
Who's there?
Francis.
Francis who?
Francis where Arsène Wenger comes from.

Knock knock.
Who's there?
Beckham.
Beckham who?
Beckham and eggs, please.

Knock knock.
Who's there?
Micah.
Micah who?
Micah cuppa tea, please.

Knock knock.
Who's there?
Aladdin.
Aladdin who?
Aladdin the street wants you to come out and play football.

Knock knock.
Who's there?
Buster.
Buster who?
Buster White Hart Lane, please.

Knock knock.
Who's there?
Distin.
Distin who?
Distin relative.

"IS THIS WEMBLEY?"
"NO IT'S THURSDAY!"
"SO AM I—LET'S HAVE A DRINK!"

A 'BAMFORTH' COMIC

Knock knock.
Who's there?
Police.
Police who?
Police come out and play
football.

●●●●●●●●●●●●●●●●

Knock knock.
Who's there?
Alison.
Alison who?
Alison to *Sports Report* on the
radio every week.

●●●●●●●●●●●●●●●●

Knock knock.
Who's there?
Godfrey.
Godfrey who?
Godfrey tickets for the game on
Saturday?

●●●●●●●●●●●●●●●●

Knock knock.
Who's there?
General Lee.
General Lee who?
Generally I support Chelsea
but today I'm going to Fulham.

●●●●●●●●●●●●●●●●

Knock knock.
Who's there?
Thermos.
Thermos who?
Thermos be a better team than
this rubbish lot.

●●●●●●●●●●●●●●●●

Knock knock.
Who's there?
Gladys.
Gladys who?
Gladys Saturday and we can go
to the game.

●●●●●●●●●●●●●●●●

Knock knock.
Who's there?
Waddle.
Waddle who?
Waddle you do if I don't open
the door?

●●●●●●●●●●●●●●●●

Knock knock.
Who's there?
Wayne.
Wayne who?
Wayne are you opening the
door?

●●●●●●●●●●●●●●●●

Knock knock.
Who's there?
Ashley.
Ashley who?
Ashley, I didn't mean to knock
at the door.

●●●●●●●●●●●●●●●●

From page 146

For Football Rules Quiz from pages 150–151
Answers: Thanks to Arthur Smith of the Referees'
Association for checking that the answers are still correct
today. **1.** A goal would be awarded. **2.** The trainer must not
go onto the field of play until the referee has stopped the
game and signalled to him. **3.** No. A goal cannot be scored
direct from a throw-in. The referee should award a goal-
kick. **4.** Yes. The game would continue in the same way as if
the ball had come off a cross-bar or goalpost. **5.** No. A
player cannot be off-side direct from a corner-kick. **6.** The
ref would award a goal, because a player cannot foul one of
his own side, but the ref may deem it unsporting behaviour.
7. Yes. **8.** No. The ref would order the corner-flag post to be
replaced before the ball is played. **9.** No goal would be
given. The ref would award a free kick against the penalty
kicker for playing the ball twice before it had been touched
by anyone else. **10.** No. The player must wait until the ball is
kicked off. **11.** Yes. According to the rules, the ref is only
required to 'signal' – and he can do so in any manner he
chooses. But it is the custom, of course, for a whistle always
to be used.

9. Collecting

R. MORRIS.

T. BADDELEY.

NEW BROMPTON.

Football memorabilia

Say you are a keen football fan aged 10. Say from now to the end of your life, you keep every programme and every ticket from every match you go to, plus every football mag or comic you ever buy, plus every sticker you have been silly enough to spend your pocket money on – well, you could end up with a collection worth, possibly, maybe, quite a great deal.

In 60 years, you might have 2,000 football items. The stickers, alas, are likely to be worth nothing, but every programme, ticket and mag will have some value, however small. The programmes you have kept from this season, the one we are now in, could be worth £10–£15. (As that's what 1950s programmes are worth today.)

All in all, counting on both hands, you could end up with a collection worth £20,000. And that's without taking inflation into consideration. And all for nothing, in the sense that you would have bought all these things anyway.

But where to keep them might present a problem. You'll need to live in a very large house or have a wife/husband/partner/children/ parents who don't mind you cluttering up the place with all your rubbish – sorry, 'treasures'. Just think of the fun. Don't think of the dust.

Football fans tend to be collectors. They collect facts in their heads, they remember goals and incidents, records and achievements, players and

Above Programme for a Blackpool v Chelsea match from the 1959–60 season, now worth around £10.

Opposite Only worth collecting in order to laugh at those absurd 80s bouffant hairdos on the sleeve: Hoddle and Waddle's venture into the world of pop.

Far right An issue of the magazine *The Captain*, 1903.

managers, even if they don't actually collect physical bits of paper and objects.

But many do and always have done. It's so much more satisfying to settle an argument by producing the newspaper report of a game, or a photograph or a programme. It's a way of refreshing your own mind about what happened, especially if you yourself were present at the match.

Most famous players, when they were young, tried to get the autographs of their own favourite players, or cut out photos of them from the newspapers.

Football memorabilia today has turned out to be a good investment – far more valuable than it has ever been before. Some

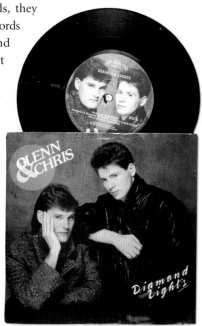

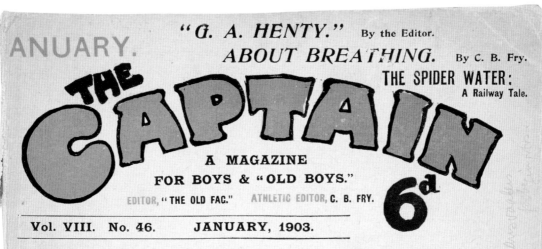

ANUARY.

"G. A. HENTY." By the Editor.

ABOUT BREATHING. By C. B. Fry.

THE SPIDER WATER:
A Railway Tale.

THE CAPTAIN

A MAGAZINE
FOR BOYS & "OLD BOYS."

EDITOR, "THE OLD FAG."   ATHLETIC EDITOR, C. B. FRY.

6^d

Vol. VIII. No. 46.   JANUARY, 1903.

TMRWHITWELL

GEORGE NEWNES, Limited, 7-12, Southampton Street, Strand, W.C.

famous shirts, as worn by famous players, have fetched incredible prices. Prices generally of any decent items have doubled in the last five years.

On the whole, football memorabilia is bought by football fans, as opposed to city slickers or investors looking for a fashionable investment. Prices therefore should not collapse in the years ahead when investment fashions change.

More and more fans these days have a lot more money than they did in the old days – for a start, you have to be well off to buy a Premiership season ticket. There's also a growing interest in the history of the game, and its legends.

So, collecting football memorabilia could turn out to be very worthwhile. But that should never be your aim. Love of the game, an interest in football for its own sake, its history and development – that should be your main motivation.

TIPS FOR COLLECTORS

Collectors usually begin as accumulators. Accumulators are people who don't throw anything out. They just accumulate.

The next stage is to actively go out, look for, buy, beg or swap for something you haven't got but would like to add to your existing collection.

You can pick up things for pennies at jumbles, car boots, charity shops. Or spend a few pounds at collectors' fairs, antique markets, specialist shops. Or lash out big money at the famous auction houses like Sotheby's and Christie's. At one time they were a bit snooty about football stuff, but now they are desperate for any half-decent football memorabilia, especially if it's pre-war.

Before you start on this madness – for it can grow into a disease if you are not careful – there are a few basic rules and guidelines to think about.

Below Merchandising specially produced to coincide with major football tournaments doesn't hold its value.

1. **Follow your own interest.** Collect objects you personally like and enjoy, or about clubs and players you like. Don't be influenced by what other people are collecting or what appears to be fashionable.

2. **Be selective.** You can't keep everything. So decide which clubs or players to concentrate on, what sort of objects to collect, what period to concentrate on. If you are trying to collect programmes, then try to stick to them, don't be side-tracked by medals or shirts.

3. **Objects produced to be collected are not really worth collecting.** This applies to first-day covers produced by the Post Office or 'special limited editions', plus most so-called 'collectors' items' advertised in newspapers and magazines. It also includes most stickers which appear at World Cup times. They are rarely of any lasting value. Stamp fairs are filled with bins of first-day covers which cost £5 to buy and are now sold off in job lots for 50p each.

4. Beware autographed objects. There are so many of them these days, on framed glossy photographs or football shirts, some of them with supposed certificates of authenticity. There are lots of cheats out there trying to rip off trusting fans. If you must collect autographs, try to get them yourself, directly from a player. Most will agree, if you ask nicely and pick a suitable moment. Explain it's for your own collection, not to sell to a dealer.

5. Go for content. An old photograph of a football team is more interesting if the team is named, and the players, or if it's a medal which actually says to whom and when it was given. The best content is in old programmes or in old football magazines, such as *Charlie Buchan's Football Monthly*, which ran from 1951 to 1971. They will give more fun, information and interest than an old autograph or shirt, however valuable those may supposedly be. You can't read a shirt.

6. Go for condition. The better nick it is in, the more valuable it will be. So keep your treasures in some sort of plastic folder or box, not just crammed in your sock drawer.

Above **A pewter medal from the 1950s with a football theme.**

7. Arrange things nicely. Keep them in some sort of order, such as chronological, with captions and details. For your own pleasure, and also to let your chums enjoy what you have done.

8. Don't expect your money back. Not with ordinary objects, and not for some time. This is because the dealer or stallholder will have at least doubled what he paid – so if you want to sell it back to him, or to any other dealers, the chances are you might only get half what you paid. Hence buy for pleasure. Then wait.

9. Buy the best you can afford. That's if you are hoping to have something pretty valuable in years to come. If, for example, you have £100 to spend. For that you might be able to buy 100 programmes from the 1980s at £1 each or one good one from the 1920s costing £100. Obviously, 100 programmes will give a chap lots of reading and amusement, and you might consider that enough, but in five years' time the chances are they will still be worth the same amount. A good 1920s programme worth £100 today, however, should be worth £200 in five years' time.

10. Keep a note of the price you paid – but do it in pencil, in code. This is so your mum/dad/wife/husband/partner/children will not be aware how potty you have been. In years to come, you'll have forgotten the code. Which will probably be just as well …

PROGRAMMES

These are the easiest, cheapest items of football memorabilia. And, according to many collectors, by far the most interesting because they are the historical records of football itself. They first appeared in the mid-1870s and were little more than a card, a team sheet, just one page, with the names of the players on one side and upcoming fixtures on the other.

If you look at the earliest ones, you'll notice that they don't have a price on them. That's because they were free, given out to directors or VIP guests, not to ordinary fans. There were very few of them, which explains the big prices today when they come up for sale.

The highest price paid so far for a programme was in May 2006, when a programme for the 1889 Cup final between Preston North End and Wolverhampton Wanderers was sold at Sotheby's in London for £19,000. It was just one sheet, listing the teams. Apart from its age and rarity, this programme is of special interest to football historians for many reasons. That Preston team, the side known as the 'Invincibles', had already won the first-ever League. The names of the umpires were: Lord Kinnaird, Mr Clegg and Major Marindin. All of them were important figures in the early history of football. Preston won 3–0.

The record was almost broken at Sotheby's in November 2006, when a 1901 Cup final programme made £18,000. The match was between Sheffield United, of the First Division, and Spurs, who were in the Southern League at the time. The game ended in a 2–2 draw. In the replay, Spurs won 3–2, becoming the only club to win the FA Cup as a non-league side.

Right and opposite This single sheet of card showing the teams for a Grimsby v Walsall fixture in 1897 doesn't bear much resemblance to today's glossy productions. Yet even at this early stage, advertising (on the reverse) from local firms was a key component. Cost in 1897: free, today: £500.

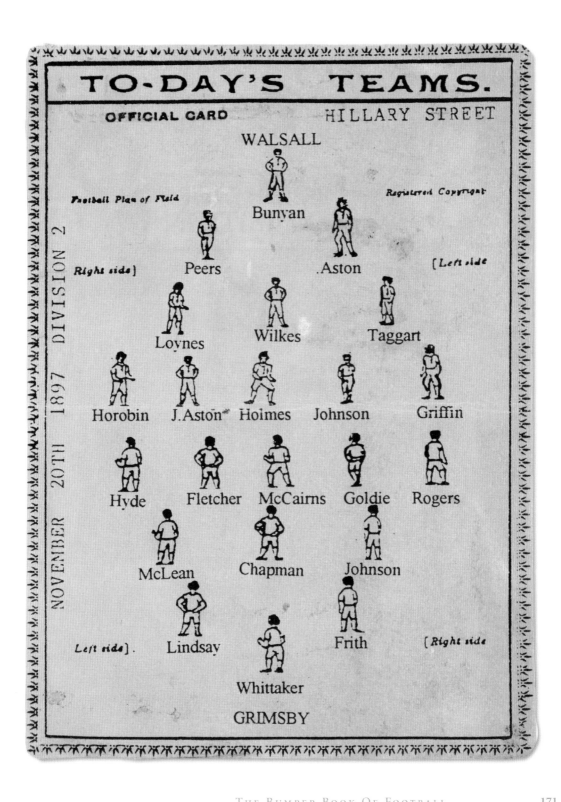

'I have never ever seen a programme for the 1901 Cup final replay,' says Graham Budd, who runs football auctions for Sotheby's. 'If one of them ever turned up, I'm sure that it would fetch the world record.'

That 1901 programme, the first one, was just one sheet, on a stiff piece of paper, but it folded at the sides to reveal some advertisements for football boots, pads and balls on sale at Gamages, one of Edwardian London's best-known department stores. Football clubs had realized that putting some adverts on the team sheet helped pay the cost of printing it. And they also had the idea of making the sheets a bit bigger, and selling them to the fans.

By 1900, most programmes cost a penny and most contained adverts and two or four pages of news about the club. By 1910, some of the programmes had grown to 12 or 16 pages, such as Aston Villa's and Sheffield Wednesday's. Chelsea's programmes for 1907, as we know, contained jokes, poems and competitions as well as football news and stats.

These early programmes are fascinating for the adverts, especially for the local music halls, where many fans proceeded after the game. And so did the players. If they'd had a good win, they would get in for nothing and be invited up on the stage and the whole audience would cheer.

FA Cup final programmes did not become official until 1921. Until then they were simply free sheets given to the nobs, though there were unofficial programmes produced by outside commercial bodies, such as a Sunday newspaper, and sold on the streets outside.

For the 1923 Cup final, the first at Wembley, the FA produced a very handsome, artistic programme of 28 pages.

One of the most interesting developments in football programmes took place in Liverpool. For 30 years from 1904, Liverpool and Everton shared the same programme. Depending on which first team was at home, that team would get the main coverage, but each programme would also cover the other team's reserves, who would also be playing that day. It's a shame that neighbouring football clubs don't share resources today.

After the last war, programmes were fairly thin and poorly produced, partly because there was still paper rationing for some time. Some clubs, such as Arsenal and Spurs, had thin programmes because they were refusing to take any commercial adverts, either inside the ground or in their programmes. They considered it lowered the tone. One didn't do that sort of thing. This attitude had changed by the 1980s, by which time all clubs had become obsessed by merchandising and sponsorship. By then, most clubs were opening club shops selling repro shirts and souvenirs. Programmes became big and glossy – and very expensive. For the Cup final of 1993, the FA managed to charge the huge sum of £5. By 2007, it was £10.

In August 2002, to celebrate their arrival in the Premiership, West Bromwich Albion produced the first known 100-page programme for an ordinary league game. It was pretty good, with lots to read, and reasonably priced at £2.50.

Opposite The splendid programme produced by the Football Association for the first Cup final at Wembley, in 1923. Yours for threepence then, but now expect to pay £1,000 …

And yet, despite growing bigger and more expensive, modern programmes are not rated very highly by collectors or dealers. Perhaps it's because there are just so many. Or perhaps most have become little more than extended merchandising catalogues filled with glossy photographs and adverts, but with not much editorial content. Collectors much prefer to look out for the older programmes.

Programme prices

Wartime programmes have suddenly shot up in price, some of them up to £50, even though they are very thin and on poor paper. This is because so few were printed or survived.

The 1950s programmes are now also slowly increasing in value, having been worth very little for many years. If you were looking for bargains, 1960s programmes would be the best to buy, as they will surely start increasing in value soon.

As a rule of thumb, 1950s programmes are worth £10, 1960s £5, while those of the 1970s are worth £3. Programmes from the 1980s, 1990s and the present day are usually little more than £1. But there are exceptions, for unusual or greatly sought-after programmes.

Above A programme for a Barcelona game in 1958; even in those days, Barça were a hugely successful club.

While an ordinary 1960s programme is still very cheap, there are two at least which command a lot of money. A programme for the 1967 European Cup final, which Celtic won when they beat Inter Milan in Lisbon, will cost at least £200. This is because most Celtic fans, if they ever did return home, have kept their programme. You won't find them at jumble sales.

Programmes for the 1966 World Cup are also very desirable – but take care to buy the right one. The programme for the final, between England and West Germany, is the valuable one, worth £150. There is also a souvenir programme for the whole competition which is worth only £30. This is because one million of the souvenir ones were printed.

Perhaps the most valued postwar programme is the one for the Man Utd v Red Star Belgrade game in February 1958. This was the game Man Utd was returning from when the Munich air disaster occurred and so many of the Busby Babes featured in the programme lost their lives. Today, that programme is worth £2,000–£3,000.

Now for some other football memorabilia to collect:

CIGARETTE CARDS

After football programmes, the most popular item over the last 100 years for football fans to collect has been cigarette cards. Unlike programmes, they were free, or at least they came free as long as you bought a packet of cigarettes, which most adults did during the 1920s and 1930s.

The idea arrived in Britain in the 1890s from America and became a vital sales tool in the battles between the rival cigarette manufacturers. Adults bought the packets of cigarettes and small boys pounced on the cards inside. The manufacturers, once they realized this, deliberately produced series of cards on topics which would appeal to small boys, such as soldiers, sailors and, most popular of all, sportsmen. Among the earliest to feature footballers were sets produced by Ogden's in 1896.

Manufacturers then created special albums in which to stick each set once you had collected them all. The albums usually looked pretty enough, but what a mistake they have turned out to be. Once the picture cards have been stuck in the albums, it becomes impossible to read the reverse side which contained fascinating facts and descriptions. Today the price of stuck-in cards is about half that of loose ones.

Cigarette cards were often little works of art, with good-quality photographs or illustrations. They were neat and portable, easy to carry around, easy to swap or store. And of course it became a challenge to try to collect all 50 of Player's, Churchman's or Wills' Famous Footballers.

It's estimated that between 1900 and 1939 there were 10,000 different cards produced on a football theme. As for total numbers, they must have run into several millions. During that period, almost every professional club appeared on at least one set of cards and so did every professional player in England and Scotland. As a record of facts and figures and faces, they are invaluable. They are also of interest because of the changing hairstyles, shirts and team colours.

Cigarette cards all but died out after the last war, being eventually replaced by stickers, such as those made by Panini. The principle is much the same. You are encouraged to complete sets or swap doubles – but unlike the old ciggie cards, you have to pay for modern stickers.

Below The first two of these 1906–08 cigarette cards, left to right, show famous players of the day, while the one on the far right, from a different series depicting team strips, shows that of New Brompton, forerunner of Gillingham FC.

T. BADDELEY.

R. MORRIS.

NEW BROMPTON.

Pre-war cigarette cards, from the 1930s, are still quite cheap – often only £1 or 50p each. And if they are stuck in albums you can get a whole set for as little as £10. Sets from 1900, not in albums, can sell for up to £3,000.

TICKETS

At one time, just 10 years ago, match day tickets were totally overlooked. Unlike programmes, which fans have been keeping and treasuring for well over 100 years, tickets were immediately thrown away after the match. No dealer was selling them. No one seemed to be collecting them. And you can understand the reason why: there's not much content in a ticket, apart from the name of the game and the number of the seat.

But in the last 10 years tickets for big games, or games which later became famous, have become very expensive and possibly even overpriced when you consider that they are nothing but small, used scraps of paper – usually, in fact, only the counterfoil, not even the whole ticket. Nonetheless, a used ticket for the 1966 World Cup final will now cost £150.

One way to start a ticket collection, without spending too much money, would be to collect Wembley tickets – tickets from Wembley matches, the old Wembley, before it closed to be rebuilt. From the 1990s and 1980s they are still only a few pounds each. But they are now part of football history. However, any pre-war Wembley tickets, especially for Cup finals, are very rare and tend to be hugely expensive. The highest price so far paid by a collector for a ticket was £3,200 for the FA Cup final of 1923.

EMPIRE STADIUM
WEMBLEY

WORLD CHAMPIONSHIP
1966
Jules Rimet Cup

FINAL TIE

SECRETARY.
THE FOOTBALL ASSOCIATION

SATURDAY JULY 30
KICK-OFF 3 p.m.

SOUTH STAND
£5

(SEE PLAN & CONDITIONS ON BACK)
TO BE RETAINED

ENTER AT
K
TURNSTILES

ENTRANCE
36

ROW
9

SEAT
37

SHIRTS

Meaning shirts actually worn by players in real games, subsequently signed by them, not replica shirts bought in the club shop or from a street stall. In the last few years, some of these have changed hands for huge sums – but the market for them appears to be lessening, thanks to all the fiddling that was going on. What proof is there that the star signed it? How do you know it was the exact shirt from that exact game? (Players often wear two shirts, changing into a clean one at half time.) And what do you do with a signed shirt anyway? It's very hard to display.

Most people paying inflated prices for signed football shirts were not ordinary fans but owners of sports bars and clubs who wanted to display them for publicity reasons. Many of the big prices were realized at charity auctions, so at least the money went to good causes, but they were not always as they seemed. (It has been known for a club to send a repro shirt, not one worn in a game, and for a club secretary to sign it.)

On the pitch today, you will see players swapping shirts after a game, competing with each other to grab the star. This is usually for their own use, in their own big

Above A great match to have seen, and if you kept the ticket, it's now worth £150.

Right top Vintage football shirts (front, an England 1966 World Cup final shirt) awaiting auction.

Right below World Cup stamps from France (top) and Sweden.

luxury homes, where they have lashings of space and ginormous trophy cabinets. Famous footballers are impressed by other famous footballers, just like the rest of us. Well, many of us.

STAMPS

Football stamps, meaning postage stamps with a football-related scene, are generally overlooked by both football memorabilia fans and stamp collectors. That means they are cheap to buy. You can get a bundle of them for a few pounds, though they will turn out to be all modern ones, issued by countries you've hardly heard of, with no football history. These are little more than labels, produced to be collected, so have little value or interest.

The interesting ones are the historic ones, produced by countries to celebrate their success at the Olympics or World Cups. If you get used ones, they cost no more than a few pounds each. The earliest stamp with a football theme was issued by Uruguay in 1924 in honour of their victory in the Olympic Games – but it didn't actually show a footballer. The first stamp with an actual player came from Holland in 1928 to mark the Olympics.

The first World Cup stamps were issued by the Italians, the hosts in 1934, which are very attractive, as are those issued by France in 1938 and Sweden in 1958.

Opposite Huge numbers of young football fans in Britain once owned Subbuteo sets. There are now many websites dedicated to this popular flick football game.

Below An older form of football game was Blow Football, in which the ball was propelled by blowing down a tube or straw. This set dates from the 1930s.

England's World Cup stamps of 1966 are still plentiful (as are a lot of first-day covers). However, unlike most first-day covers, they are well worth collecting.

GAMES AND TOYS

Toys with a football theme are as old as football itself, dating back as far as the 1860s. Victorian manufacturers who kept up to date with the latest printing methods could easily add a footballer or a football to simple card games or board games. Creating a toy football game, which you could actually play – that was a bit more complicated, but games of table football were appearing as early as 1884. Then came Blow Football, the easiest football game to make and play, which sold millions up to the last war.

After the Second World War, and until the advent of computer games, the best-known football game was Subbuteo, devised in 1947 by Peter Adolph in his home in Tunbridge Wells, Kent. He was a keen bird watcher and took the name from the Latin for 'hobby hawk' (*Falco subbuteo*). Old Subbuteo sets have now become collectors' items.

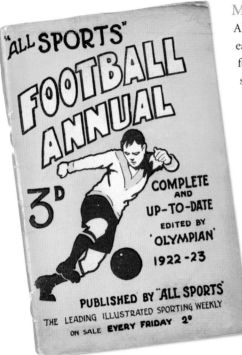

MISCELLANEOUS MEMORABILIA

Almost any object with a football theme, if it is old enough (i.e. earlier than the 1960s), is worth collecting, such as photographs, football magazines, comics with football stories, and newspaper supplements on big matches.

Pre-war football annuals are now fetching high prices – from £30 to £100 – the sort usually produced by a newspaper, national and regional, at the beginning of each season. They have a long history, back to 1868. Among the best known are *Athletic News* annuals, which began in 1887 and are still appearing today, though now produced by the *News of the World*. Some of them were several hundreds of pages long and full of riveting information.

Most football memorabilia fans like to have the early editions of *Rothman's Football Yearbook*, which began in 1970. It's now called the *Sky Football Yearbook*.

Pre-war postcards, showing photographs of famous teams, are now very expensive: £50 to £100, but if it's just an ordinary local Sunday team, not named, they can be had for £3.

Rare items, hardly seen, include Baines cards. They were a very early version of modern-day stickers, but ever so artistic and attractive. They came in different shapes, such as a circle, diamond or a heart, and usually featured a well-known team or player along with a slogan such as PLAY UP, WELL SHOT, WELL WON. They came in sets, which you had to buy, and were on sale between 1887 and the 1920s. Today one in reasonable condition, showing a well-known team, could cost you £30.

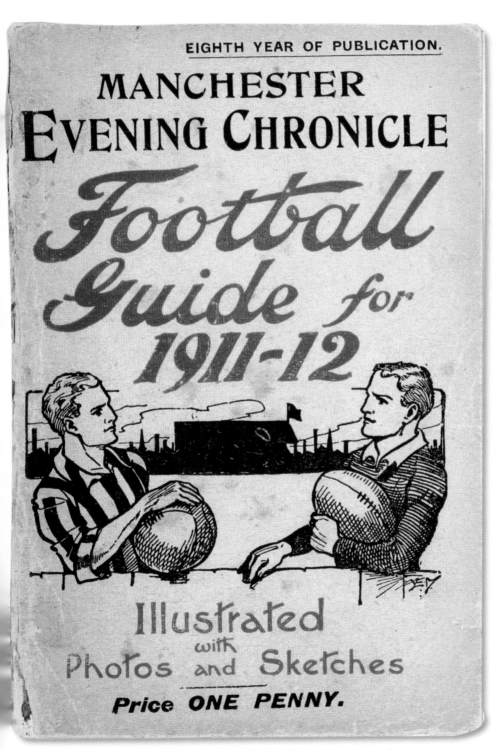

Left and far left Examples of informative and compendious football yearbooks from the early 20th century.

Left below Two cards made by John Baines of Bradford. In their heyday, many millions of these colourful cards were sold in the north of England and Scotland.

Famously expensive football items

Going to the Match **by L. S. Lowry** – £2 million
Lowry did this painting showing Burnden Park, Bolton, in 1953. In 1999 it was bought by the Professional Footballers' Association and is normally on show at the Lowry Gallery in Salford. The fact that it is by Lowry is, of course, the main reason for its high price, but it is the best-known football painting of the 20th century and the most expensive ever football-related item.

FA Cup – £488,000
The most expensive item of a purely football nature ever sold. This was the real FA Cup, in use from 1896 to 1910. It was presented to Lord Kinnaird in 1911 to mark his 21 years as President of the FA. In 2005 it came up for auction at Christie's in London and was bought by David Gold, chairman of Birmingham City. In 2007, it went on temporary show at the National Football Museum in Preston.

World Cup medal – £164,000
Awarded to Alan Ball after the 1966 World Cup win. Sold at Christie's in 2005. Record price so far for a medal. (Bobby Moore's medal, which in theory might have fetched more, was sold, along with other Moore items, to West Ham for an undisclosed sum.)

Pele's shirt – £157,750
The one he wore at the 1970 World Cup final. Sold at Christie's in 2002. Likely to remain the most expensive football shirt ever, now shirt prices are falling.

Geoff Hurst's 1966 World Cup final shirt – £91,750
Sold at Christie's in 2000.

Most expensive cap – £43,200
Alan Ball's 1966 World Cup final cap. Sold at Christie's in 2005.

Most expensive football – £37,500
It was used in the 1888 FA Cup final.

Most expensive football programme – £19,000
As mentioned already, this was paid in 2006 at Sotheby's for a single sheet of paper – which happened to be the programme for the 1889 FA Cup final between Preston North End and Wolves.

Most expensive football book – £800
This was paid at Sotheby's in 2006 for a copy of Marriot and Alcock's *The Rugby Union Game, the Association Game*, published in 1903.

Opposite First won by Sheffield Wednesday in 1896, the FA Cup that came up for auction in 2005 was a replacement for the original trophy, which was stolen from a Birmingham shop window in 1895.

Below Cover of the 1905–06 *Association Football and the Men Who Made It* by Arthur Gibson and William Pickford, a fine but expensive collectible.

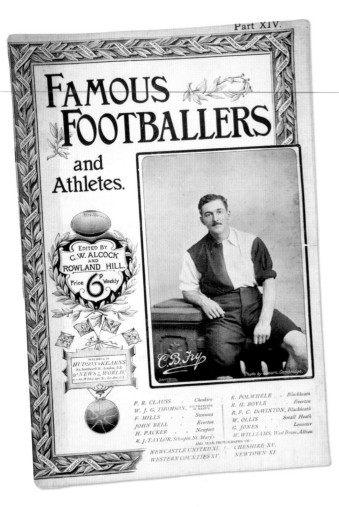

Above Title page and player profile from *Famous Footballers*. Featured is C.B. Fry, an outstanding all-round sportsman, who played rugby union and football at the highest level, held the world long-jump record and captained England at cricket.

There are two other classic and very beautiful books about the early days of football, copies of which usually sell for around £500 each: *Famous Footballers* by Alcock and Hill, 1895, and *Association Football and the Men Who Made It* (four volumes) by Gibson and Pickford, published in 1905–06.

MUSEUMS

It you can't afford to bid for items of historic interest, then you can still ogle them by visiting some of the football museums which have opened in the last 10 years.

National Football Museum

Opened in Preston, Lancashire, in 2001. It's under the stand of the recently developed Deepdale, home of Preston North End. A bit out of the way for soft southerners, but a fitting home for our national treasures as, of course, Preston North End won the first football league in 1888. The museum has over 1,000 items on show, including the world's oldest international shirt as worn by Arnold Kirke Smith while playing for England against Scotland in the first proper international in 1872.

The National Football Museum has the oldest known moving images of football. They are of a game played between Blackburn Rovers and West Bromwich Albion at Ewood Park in 1898. The reel is just four minutes long. The museum also has a slightly longer film of a 1910 game at Old Trafford.

The Scottish Football Museum

This is located in the newly built Hampden Park, Glasgow. Scotland, of course, has as good a claim as England to be the home of the game and its earliest footballers. Very strong on old shirts, boots, tickets and programmes. For example, this museum boasts the world's oldest match ticket, from that same 1872 Scotland v England game.

Club Museums

Most clubs, big and small, have a trophy room or a cabinet holding relics which used normally never to be open to the general public. You had to be a friend of a director, a visiting VIP or similar, though sometimes they could be viewed during organized tours of the stadium and ground.

But more and more of the Premiership clubs, especially the big names like Arsenal, Liverpool and Manchester United, are opening proper museums – with a designated curator, exhibits arranged in a proper order, and regular opening hours.

Below **Charlie George of Arsenal (centre) celebrating his team's 1971 FA Cup win over Liverpool, a match in which he scored the winning goal in extra time. The shirt he wore on this memorable occasion is now displayed in the museum at the Emirates Stadium.**

Very often they are combined with a tour of the ground. For all of which you pay, of course. They're not daft.

Naturally, each club concentrates on its own history, but they are nonetheless of interest to all real football fans. And of course awfully educational.

There are, at present, seven Premiership clubs with proper museums, plus one in Scotland, each well worth visiting.

Arsenal's museum first opened in 1993 and boasts the largest collection of a single club's memorabilia in Britain. It's now housed at the new Emirates Stadium in what's called the Northern Triangle Building. Here you can see the shirt Alex James wore in the 1936 Cup final and Charlie George's from the 1971 final.

Manchester United's is big, modern and very flashy, as one might expect. It was opened in 1998 by none other than the legendary Pele. The museum takes you through the history of the club from its founding in 1878, including the Munich air crash. It attracts around 200,000 fans a year which, at £9.50 (adult admission price in 2007 for the museum and tour), means they must be taking in well over £1 million annually, enough to pay Rooney's wages for quite a few weeks.

Below Promotional literature for the museum of Liverpool FC, England's most successful club bar none.

Liverpool's museum is also very impressive and high-tech and boasts that it has more trophies to show than anyone else, 'As we are England's most successful club.' With a grand total of 18 League championships, 14 League and FA Cup wins, three UEFA Cups, and – the crowning glory – five European Cups, nobody could argue with that. Two films are constantly on show at the museum, one revisiting the heady days when the Kop was an all-standing hotbed of support, and another recalling the astonishing night in Istanbul in 2005 when Liverpool came back from 3–0 down against AC Milan to lift their fifth European Cup. When they move to their new super-stadium, the museum will be extended to include a repro of their famous Boot Room. Let's hope they can recreate the smell.

West Ham's museum opened in 2002 at a cost of £4 million. Its highlights include the 1966 World Cup shirts, caps and medals of Bobby Moore, Geoff Hurst and Martin Peters, West Ham players one and all.

Manchester City calls its museum and tour 'The Manchester City Experience'. They don't quite have as many trophies to boast about as Liverpool or Man Utd, but their new museum has won a local tourism award.

Newcastle United have recently opened their own museum, which you enter through the café at the redeveloped Gallowgate end. You can visit the museum on its own, or as part of the stadium tour. (Most clubs

CELTIC VISITOR CENTRE - IT'S A LEARNING EXPERIENCE

Admission: Adults £8.50, Children £5.50, Family Ticket £20
(2 adults and 2 children or 1 adult and 3 children)

To book your tour call 0141 551 4308 or email visitorexperience@celticfc.co.uk

lump them together.) Exhibits include Jackie Milburn's medals and Michael Owen's hat-trick ball from England's famous 5–1 win over Germany in 2001. Not exactly a Newcastle trophy, as he was playing for Liverpool at the time, but near enough.

Chelsea now have a museum, though a modest one, which can be seen as part of the stadium tour. 'Our trophy cabinet is ever growing,' they boast, hopefully.

Celtic's museum, at Celtic Park, or Visitor Centre as they like to call it, has among its many other attractions a 1903 jersey – historic stuff as this was the first time they wore green hoops.

Rangers have not got a separate museum, as such, but you do get a chance to see their trophy room during stadium tours.

Elsewhere, there are a few town and local museums, scattered around the country, which often feature items related to the local professional club. They include:

Watford Museum, in Watford High Street, containing some interesting material on Watford FC;

The Bridewell, in Bridewell Alley, Norwich, which has a Norwich City display;

In Wales, Wrexham's County Borough Museum, in the County Buildings, has a Welsh football collection.

And, if you are visiting Carlisle, do pop into Tullie House Museum, near the cathedral, where you can see some excellent memorabilia relating to the famous Carlisle United …

Above Celtic Visitor Centre offers a fascinating insight into one half of Glasgow's 'Old Firm'. The Celtic trophy cabinet isn't short of domestic silverware, though they haven't claimed a European title since 1967.

A MORAL DILEMMA FOR WAYNE
Part Three

United's academy director had told Wayne not to tell anyone about their interest in him – either people at school, because it would just make them jealous, or outsiders. 'Best to keep these things private,' so he had added.

However, Wayne did tell Darren, his best friend. Darren was made up for him, so he said, well impressed, but promised to keep it dead secret.

Fortunately, the big talking point at school all week was the forthcoming final of the Camden Cup when little Brookpark Primary were going to meet the might of the King's Cross Boys Club. They had their own proper coaches, trained three nights a week on the Astroturf, and over the years had provided many young players for both Arsenal and Spurs.

By chance, Brookpark Girls' team was also doing well that season. They too had reached the final of their competition, which was to be played on Saturday morning on Hampstead Heath.

Wayne and Darren arranged that they'd go together to watch the game, cheer on the girls. It was only fair, as the girls had cheered them on.

'You can't go,' said Wayne's father on Saturday morning. 'I want you here all morning. There are three fellers coming to see me, and they want a word with you as well.'

Wayne's mother was doing the hoovering and cleaning, which she did every Saturday. During the week, she worked as a cleaner in one of the big houses near Hampstead Heath.

'Look, there's no need to do all that now,' said Wayne's father. 'I don't want you here, making all that noise, when they come. Is that clear?'

'It's got to be done,' she replied. 'If I don't do it, who will? You certainly won't. This flat is a right dump.'

'We'll be leaving here soon,' said Wayne's dad, with a wink to Wayne. 'And we'll be hiring a proper cleaner …'

'What are you on about?' said Wayne's

mother. 'Get out of my way. I thought you were taking the twins out to play?'

'Come on then, let's go,' said Wayne's dad. 'But I don't want you here when I get back in half an hour.'

Wayne and his sisters set off with their dad to the shops as they did most Saturday mornings while their mum cleaned the flat. He usually bought them an ice cream while he popped into the bookies to put on a bet.

The twins were on their bikes, riding ahead. When they were out of earshot, Wayne's dad explained that both Arsenal and Spurs had been on the phone during the week wanting Wayne to have another trial. The scout for a northern club had also turned up at the door, wanting Wayne to sign for them without even being given a trial.

'We could do well out of this,' said his dad, 'if we play it properly. They've all been dropping hints about a few perks …'

'You mean free tickets?' asked Wayne.

'And the rest,' said Wayne's dad. 'They all noticed how beat up my car is. Said they could get it sorted. One of them even said it must be awkward, living on the ninth floor …'

'So they'll move us to the ground floor?' said Wayne. 'I didn't know clubs could do

that. That would be good. I could then get to the Den quicker than Darren …'

The official letter, on headed notepaper, came from United a week later, in the week of the final of the Camden Cup, just as Wayne was leaving to go to school. His father was still in bed. Wayne could see United's crest on the back of the envelope, so he tore it open.

'Dear Wayne,

On behalf of London United Football Club, I am very pleased to offer you a place at our Football Academy for the

season 2007–2008.

Our coaching staff were very happy with your trial and, as a consequence, we hope you will form an important part of our special group of Academy players. To this end, you will need to set excellent examples to your fellow Academy players and also to your fellow pupils at your school, for whom of course you will not be allowed to play in future.

You will be required to attend training sessions on Tuesday and Thursday evenings from 5.00pm to 6.30pm, plus playing for our Academy team on Saturday mornings against another Academy team from the London and South East region.

If you or your parents would at any time like to discuss your progress, please contact me.

I would ask you and your parents to complete the two copies of the attached form then forward one copy to me by return post in the enclosed SAE.'

Wayne read the letter so quickly he didn't at first take in all the words, some of which he didn't understand anyway.

'What's an SAE, mum?' he said. 'Is it something to do with Save All the Environment? We've been doing that at school all week.'

His mother explained it meant they had sent an envelope already stamped and addressed for him to return the form.

It was easy enough to fill in, just asking basic information – place and date of birth, home address, any medical conditions or operations. When they had done so, Wayne and his mother each signed it.

'When your lazy dad gets up,' she said, 'I'll get him to sign it as well, then I'll get it posted. Now, you better hurry, Wayne, or you'll be late, and so will I …'

At school, in morning assembly, the Head Teacher Miss Henn announced that the Parent–Teachers Association had hired two coaches so that any parents who wanted could come along and support the school at the Camden Cup final.

'And, on behalf of the whole school,' said the Head, 'I'd like to wish Wayne Wright and all the team the very best of luck.'

The whole school cheered and clapped. Wayne felt himself going a bit red. On the pitch, he was always confident, not to say cocky, but off the pitch he was basically very shy and easily embarrassed.

Wayne came home with Darren, as he usually did, to find the flat empty. He'd already told Darren, in confidence, about the letter, and naturally Darren wanted to see it. There was no sign of the top copy and the SAE envelope, but Wayne found the other copy lying on the kitchen table.

Darren was much better at reading than Wayne, even though he did read quite slowly, his lips moving with every word. He went through the letter several times. He even knew what SAE meant without Wayne having to tell him.

'So what will you do about the school team?' asked Darren.

'Score three goals for them, that's what,' replied Wayne.

'No, I mean, you can't play for them any more.'

'What are you on about, you wally?'

'Look, it says here,' said Darren, 'at the end of this paragraph. Once you've joined them, you can't play for the school any more.'

'You what!' Where? Show me.'

Wayne studied the letter carefully. Practically the whole of Brookpark Primary was turning out tomorrow to watch him play. Loads of parents were coming in special coaches. It was going to be the biggest day in Brookpark's history.

He couldn't let them down at this stage. He was the captain, the star player, the one they all depended on.

'Have you signed the form yet?' asked Darren.

'Yeh, and my mum's posted it.'

'Oh, God!' said Darren. 'But you've GOT to play for the school. We'll have no bleedin' chance without you …'

'But if I do play,' said Wayne, 'United will chuck me out – even before I've joined them. And I've dreamt about playing for United all my life. They're MY team. Always have been. Oh no, what am I going to do? I've waited 10 years for this moment …'

'Actually, nine and three quarters,' corrected Darren, who was good at maths as well as English. 'You're not 10 for three months …'

What is Wayne going to do? How will he solve his dilemma? Rush at once to page 224.

10. Fascinating facts

(WORLD CUP WINNERS 1966)
ENGLAND

Records and stats about England managers, transfers, club names, goal scorers, foreign players, oh, and lots of other things . . .

ENGLAND MANAGERS

The first one in modern times was Walter Winterbottom, appointed in 1946. Before him, the England team was usually chosen by a committee.

Although Sven-Göran Eriksson was derided after England's failure in the 2006 World Cup, his percentage of wins during his time in charge is still the best of all the England managers … so far.

The top 10 England managers' all-time win record

			Played	Won	
1	Sven-Göran Eriksson	2001–06	67	41	61.2%
2	Sir Alf Ramsey	1963–74	113	69	61.1%
3	Glenn Hoddle	1996–99	28	17	60.7%
4	Ron Greenwood	1977–82	55	33	60%
5	Walter Winterbottom	1946–62	139	78	56.1%
6	Sir Bobby Robson	1982–90	95	47	49.5%
7	Don Revie	1974–77	29	14	48.3%
8	Terry Venables	1994–96	23	11	47.8%
9	Graham Taylor	1990–93	38	18	47.3%
10	Kevin Keegan	1999–2000	18	7	38.8%

Below Terry Venables (seen here in his playing days at QPR) managed England from 1994 to 1996. Ten years later, he was brought back to act as assistant manager to Steve McClaren.

First games

How they fared on their first game as manager did not have much relation to their later success. Sir Alf Ramsey is the only England manager since the war to lose his first game – beaten 5–2 by France.

Sven-Göran Eriksson: England 3 Spain 0, friendly at Villa Park, 23 February 2001

Kevin Keegan: England 3 Portugal 1, Euro qualifier at Wembley, 27 March 1999

Glenn Hoddle: Moldova 0 England 3, World Cup qualifier, Republican Stadium, Kishinev, 1 September 1996

Terry Venables: England 1 Denmark 0, friendly at Wembley, 3 April 1994

Graham Taylor: England 1 Hungary 0, friendly at Wembley, 12 September 1990

Sir Bobby Robson: Denmark 2 England 2, Euro qualifier at Idraetsparken, Copenhagen, 22 September 1982

Ron Greenwood: England 0 Switzerland 0, friendly at Wembley, 7 September 1977

Don Revie: England 3 Czechoslovakia 0, Euro qualifier at Wembley, 30 October 1974

Sir Alf Ramsey: France 5 England 2, Euro qualifier at Parc des Princes, Paris, 27 February 1963

Sir Walter Winterbottom: Northern Ireland 2 England 7, British Championship, Windsor Park, Belfast, 28 September 1946

Steve McClaren: England 4 Greece 0, friendly at Old Trafford, 16 August 2006

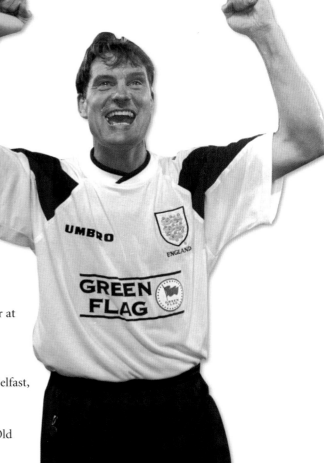

Below **Divine inspiration? Glenn Hoddle's record as England manager wasn't that bad, but he was sacked in a controversy over his religious beliefs in February 1999.**

First seven games

Alas, after that excellent win over Greece in his first match in charge, Steve McClaren did not do so well in his next six games. In fact, his record in his first seven games became the joint worst of any England manager.

Below England coach Steve McClaren paces the touchline. Well might he have looked worried after his first seven games in charge.

Sven-Göran Eriksson (2001–06)

P7	W6	D0	L1	F19	A5	Wins % 86%

Glenn Hoddle (1996–99)

P7	W6	D0	L1	F13	A3	Wins % 86%

Graham Taylor (1990–93)

P7	W5	D2	L0	F11	A3	Wins % 71%

Walter Winterbottom (1946–62)

P7	W5	D1	L1	F23	A6	Wins % 71%

Don Revie (1974–77)

P7	W4	D3	L0	F13	A2	Wins % 57%

Terry Venables (1994–96)

P7	W4	D3	L0	F10	A1	Wins % 57%

Sir Bobby Robson (1982–90)

P7	W4	D2	L1	F19	A5	Wins % 57%

Ron Greenwood (1977–82)

P7	W4	D2	L1	F10	A4	Wins % 57%

Sir Alf Ramsey (1963–74)

P7	W4	D1	L2	F22	A12	Wins % 57%

Kevin Keegan (1999–2000)

P7	W3	D4	L0	F13	A4	Wins % 43%

Steve McClaren (2006–07)

P7	W3	D2	L2	F11	A4	Wins % 43%

GOALSCORING RECORDS

On Tuesday 9 August 2006, the 500,000th goal was scored in English League football since the League first began in 1888. The player who happened to knock in the milestone-setting goal that evening was not one of the Premiership stars but Gary Taylor-Fletcher of Huddersfield Town. He got it in the 78th minute – after 62 other goals had been scored earlier in other League matches that evening, bringing the grand, all-round total up to exactly 500,000. It was in a League One game at home to Rotherham – Huddersfield won 3–0.

Gary, a 25-year-old utility player, did not realize until after the game that he had gone into the record books.

'It was only when friends started sending me messages on my mobile that I knew I'd done something unusual. Luckily it was a good goal, one of the best in my career. Certainly not a tap in …' Well done.

Above **Unsung hero: Gary Taylor-Fletcher (left) of Huddersfield Town, scorer of the 500,000th League goal, in 2006.**

First League goal was scored by Aston Villa's Gersham Cox (own goal, for Wolves, in the 30th minute) on 8 September 1888. This was not the quickest goal in a match that day, but Fred Dewhurst's second-minute goal for Preston against Burnley came in a game that kicked off later in the day.

100,000th goal: the 65th goal scored on 5 October 1929.

200,000th goal: the 49th goal scored on 8 February 1952.

300,000th goal: the 99th scored on 24 August 1968.

400,000th goal: the 30th scored on 29 August 1987. (An absence of exact goal timings makes it impossible to identify the individual scorers of the landmark goals so far.)

Most League goals in a career: Arthur Rowley (433 goals), Dixie Dean (379), Jimmy Greaves (357).

Most goals by one player in a single League season: 60, by Dixie Dean for Everton in 1927–28.

Most goals by one player in a League game: 10, by Joe Payne for Luton Town v Bristol Rovers on 13 April 1936.

Most goals scored by a club in a League season: 134, by Peterborough, Fourth Division, 1960–61.

Most goals conceded by a club in a League season: 141, by Darwen, Second Division, 1899.

Most goals in an English game: 17, when Tranmere beat Oldham 13–4 on 26 December 1935, in the Third Division (North). The next-best tally in England was 14, three times – most recently when Tottenham beat Everton 10–4 in October 1958.

Fastest League goal: four seconds, by Jim Fryatt for Bradford Park Avenue v Tranmere on 25 April 1964.

Fastest League hat-trick: two minutes, 20 seconds, by James Hayter, for Bournemouth v Wrexham on 24 February 2004.

Most goals in any British senior game: 36: scored by Arbroath against Bon Accord, Scottish Cup, 1885.

Premiership's 15,000th goal: on 30 December 2006, during Fulham's 2–2 draw with Chelsea at Stamford Bridge, Moritz Volz of Fulham scored the 15,000th Premiership goal since the Premier League began in 1992–93. He earned his club a prize of £15,000 from the sponsors Barclays – not much these days to a Premiership footballer, but it was donated to charity.

Volz, a German, is unusual among modern Premiership players in not being known for his conspicuous expenditure. He has been seen arriving at Craven Cottage on a fold-up bicycle, as opposed to a Ferrari. Sometimes he even walks.

Right Goal-poacher extraordinaire Dixie Dean (right) notches up another one for Everton, this time against Arsenal at Hughbury in 1936.

ENGLISH TRANSFER RECORDS

● The first four-figure transfer fee in English football saw centre-forward Alf Common move from Middlesbrough to Sunderland for £1,000 in February 1905.

● The first £2,000 transfer took place in December 1912 when Danny O'Shea left Southern League side West Ham United and moved to First Division Blackburn Rovers. The following year Chelsea paid a then-record £2,500 for Tommy Logan from the Scottish club Third Lanark.

● The first £5,000 transfer took place in February 1922 when Syd Puddefoot left West Ham United for Falkirk. Shortly afterwards Sunderland also signed two players for £5,000 – Mick Gilhooley from Hull City and Warney Cresswell from South Shields.

● David Jack moved from Bolton Wanderers to Arsenal in October 1928 for a reported £10,000 – the country's first five-figure fee.

● The first time a goalkeeper was sold for a five-figure fee was in June 1950 when Reg Allen joined Manchester United from Queens Park Rangers for £11,000.

● The first £20,000 transfer in Britain took place in November 1947 when England centre-forward Tommy Lawton moved from Chelsea (who had bought him two years previously for £11,500) to Third Division Notts County.

● The first £25,000 transfer was in March 1949 when Johnny Morris switched from Manchester United to Derby County.

● Jackie Sewell was the first player involved in a £30,000 deal – moving from Notts County to Sheffield Wednesday for £34,000 in March 1951.

● Inside-forward Eddie Quigley became the first player to be involved in transfers totalling more than £50,000 when he moved from Sheffield Wednesday to Preston North End to Blackburn Rovers over a period of two years: 1949–51.

● The first English club to pay more than £50,000 for a player was Manchester City who signed Denis Law from Huddersfield Town in March 1960 for a fee totalling £55,000.

OGDEN'S CIGARETTES.

A. COMMON.

Above **Big money –
then.** In 1905, the
princely sum of
£1,000 was paid to
secure Alf Common's
services at Roker
Park.

Right **Back in England after his brief stint in Italy, Denis Law rounds Leicester City keeper Gordon Banks to score in the 1963 Cup final, which Man Utd won 3–1.**

● Denis Law was also involved in the first six-figure transfer involving a British club when he moved from Manchester City to the Italian club Torino for £100,000 in July 1961. Manchester United brought him back to the UK for £115,000 a year later.

● The first £100,000 footballer transferred between two English clubs was England's World Cup winner Alan Ball who moved from Blackpool to Everton in August 1966.

● The first £200,000 player in British football was Martin Peters who switched from West Ham United to Tottenham Hotspur in 1970.

● Kevin Keegan became the first £500,000 footballer to leave an English club, transferring to Hamburger SV from Liverpool in June 1977.

● David Mills was the first half-a-million pound player to move from one English club to another – joining West Bromwich Albion from Middlesbrough for £514,000 in January 1979 (signed by Ron Atkinson).

● Trevor Francis moved from Birmingham City to Nottingham Forest in February 1979 to become the first £1 million footballer (£975,000 plus VAT = £1.15 million).

● Clive Allen was the first player to be transferred twice for £1 million – signed by Arsenal from QPR in June 1980 and by Crystal Palace from Arsenal two months later.

● Bryan Robson became the first £1.5 million footballer when he left West Bromwich Albion for Manchester United in October 1981. In the same deal, the Albion midfielder Remi Moses, valued at £500,000, moved to Old Trafford – thus making this also the first £2 million transaction in British football.

● In 1996 Alan Shearer was sold for a then world-record £15 million when he moved from Blackburn Rovers to Newcastle United.

● The first £30 million transfer involving two English clubs saw defender Rio Ferdinand switch from Leeds United to Manchester United in 2002.

● Wayne Rooney was the first teenager to be transferred for more than £25 million when he joined Manchester United from Everton for £27 million in 2004.

● In January 2006, Theo Walcott became Britain's first £10 million 16-year-old when he joined Arsenal from Southampton. An initial payment of £3.5 million was agreed with a further £6.5 million to come after a set number of appearances and goals scored.

WORLD RECORD TRANSFER FEES

£46 million	Zinedine Zidane	Juventus to Real Madrid	2001
£37 million	Luis Figo	Barcelona to Real Madrid	2000
£31 million	Christian Vieri	Lazio to Internazionale	1999
£23 million	Denilson	São Paolo to Real Betis	1998
£19.5 million	Ronaldo	Barcelona to Internazionale	1997
£12 million	Gianluca Vialli	Sampdoria to Juventus	1992
£6 million	Ruud Gullit	PSV Eindhoven to Milan	1987
£922,000	Johan Cruyff	Ajax to Barcelona	1973
£142,000	Luis Suarez	Barcelona to Inter	1961

Left Playing for France, Zinedine Zidane loses – and uses – his head in the World Cup final of 2006.

WHAT'S IN A NAME?

Team names

And the winner is ... United!

In the season 2007–08, out of the 92 clubs in the Premiership and Football League, there were:

13 Uniteds: Manchester, West Ham, Newcastle, Sheffield, Leeds, Colchester, Southend, Scunthorpe, Rotherham, Carlisle, Peterborough, Hartlepool and Hereford.

12 Cities: Manchester, Cardiff, Coventry, Norwich, Leicester, Bristol, Birmingham, Stoke, Hull, Lincoln, Bradford, and Chester.

12 Towns: Ipswich, Shrewsbury, Luton, Yeovil, Swansea, Huddersfield, Northampton, Cheltenham, Swindon, Mansfield, Grimsby and Macclesfield.

3 Wanderers: Bolton, Wolves and Wycombe.

3 Athletics: Wigan, Charlton and Oldham.

and only two ...

Counties: Derby and Notts.

Players' names

Christian names in football, as in ordinary life, go in fashions. You can almost tell the age of someone by their first name. Charlie, for example, has almost disappeared among footballers whilst Wilfred is extinct. The last Wilfred to play for England was back in the 1930s.

Above Ralph is hardly a common name for modern footballers, but it was in Ralph Squire's day (seen here in 1895). You don't see many moustaches like that nowadays, either ...

Among Premiership players in the 2006–07 season, the most common first name was James, which is not surprising as James is still one of the most popular names for a boy. Eleven Prem players were called James: McFadden, Beattie, Vaughan (all Everton), Chambers (Watford), Collins (West Ham), Bullard (Fulham), Morrison (Boro), Thomas (Charlton), Milner (Newcastle), Keene (Plymouth) and Harper (Reading).

Kevins are getting a bit thinner on the ground, and on the pitch, since the heyday of Kevin Keegan, but even so there were still five Kevins – Nolan (Villa), Davis (Bolton), Lisbie (Charlton), Kilbane (Everton) and Doyle (Reading).

Five players were called Lee, or seven if you count variations on the name – Hendrie (Villa), McCulloch (Wigan), Cattermole (Boro), Bowyer (West Ham), Carsley (Everton) plus Leigh Bromby (Sheffield United) and Leon Osman (Everton).

There were four Jasons – Roberts (Blackburn), Brown (Blackburn), Euell (Charlton) and Kennedy (Boro).

Three Ashleys – Cole (Chelsea), Young (Villa), Williams (Man City).

Three Waynes – Rooney (Man Utd), Bridge (Chelsea) and Routledge (Spurs).

Three Scotts – Parker (Newcastle), Loach (Watford) and Carson (Liverpool).

American players

In the 2006–07 season, there were 12 Americans playing in the Premiership: Brad Friedel, Blackburn Rovers' goalie, had notched up most games, over 250 since he first joined Liverpool in 1997.

The other Americans were: Johann Smith (Bolton), Cory Gibbs (Charlton), Carlos Bocanegra and Brian McBride (Fulham), Tim Howard (Everton, on loan from Man Utd), Claudio Reyna and DaMarcus Beasley (Man City), Marcus Hahnemann and Bobby Convey (Reading), Jonathan Spector (West Ham) and Jay DeMerit (Watford).

Above **Brad Friedel, in goal for the USA, pulls off a save against Polish striker Cesar Kucharski in the 2002 World Cup.**

Foreign players in the Premiership

We all know that every club has loads of them, but of course it varies from week to week, and game to game, just how many are actually on the pitch.

During the weekend games of 10 to 11 February 2007, the London *Evening Standard* worked out, in percentages, exactly how many foreign players had been in each team, including subs on the bench.

Out of the 272 players on duty that day, only 107 were English – or just 39%.

Arsenal had the smallest percentage of English players that day – just 14% – which was actually a relatively high percentage for them, as they sometimes play with no English players at all. Sheffield United fielded the most English players, with 69%.

France was the most heavily represented foreign country, with 19 players, followed by the Republic of Ireland with 12. The complete breakdown was as follows:

Manchester United: Kuszczak (Poland), Neville, Ferdinand, Vidić (Serbia), Evra (France), Fletcher (Scotland), Scholes, Giggs (Wales), Park (South Korea), Rooney, Saha (Fr). Subs: Larsson (Sweden). 38% English players

Chelsea: Cech (Czech Republic), Diarra (Fr), Ferreira (Portugal), Bridge, Essien (Ghana), Makelele (Fr), Lampard, Kalou (Ivory Coast), Drogba (Iv Coast), Shevchenko (Ukraine). Subs: Robben (Holland), Wright-Philips, Geremi (Cameroon). 29%

Liverpool: Reina (Spain), Finnan (Ireland), Carragher, Agger (Denmark), Riise (Norway), Pennant, Sissoko (Mali), Gerrard, Zenden (Hol), Bellamy (Wales), Kuyt (Hol). Subs: Crouch, Arbeloa (Spain), Guthrie. 36%

Arsenal: Lehmann (Germany), Hoyte, Touré (Iv Coast), Djourou (Switzerland), Clichy (Fr), Walcott, Fàbregas (Spain), Gilberto (Brazil), Rosický (Czech), Baptista (Brazil), Henry (Fr). Subs: Aliadière (Fr), Adebayor (Togo), Flamini (Fr). 14%

Bolton: Jääskeläinen (Finland), Hunt, Meite (Iv Coast), Ben Haim (Israel), Gardner (Jamaica), Nolan, Speed (Wales), Teymourian (Iran), Giannakopoulos (Greece), Anelka (Fr), Diouf (Senegal). Subs: Thompson, Tal (Israel), Pedersen (Den). 21%

Reading: Hahnemann (USA), Murty (Scot), Bikey (Cam), Ingimarsson (Iceland), Shorey, Little, Harper, Sidwell, Hunt (Ireland), Lita, Long (Ireland). Subs: Oster (Wales), Kitson. 46%

Portsmouth: James, Johnson, Pamarot (Fr), Campbell, Traoré (Fr), O'Neill, Davis, Pedro Mendes (Portugal), Taylor, Cole, LuaLua (Congo). Subs: Kranjcar (Croatia), Lauren (Cam), Kanu (Nigeria). 50%

Everton: Howard (USA), Neville, Yobo (Nig), Stubbs, Lescott, Van der Meyde (Hol), Carsley, Fernandes (Portugal), Arteta (Spain), Cahill (Australia), Johnson. Subs: Beattie. 50%

Newcastle: Harper, Taylor, Onyewu (USA), Bramble, Babayaro (Nig), Solano (Peru), Parker, Bolt, Milner, Dyer, Martins (Nig). Subs: Duff (Ireland), Sibierski (Fr). 54%

Blackburn: Friedel (USA), Khizanishvili (Georgia), Samba (Congo), Nelsen (NZ), Berner (Switz), Emerton (Australia), Dunn, Tugay (Turkey), Bentley, Gallagher (Scot), McCarthy (South Africa). Subs: Todd, Roberts (Grenada), Jeffers. 29%

Tottenham: Robinson, Chimbonda (Fr), Dawson, Rocha (Portugal), Assou-Ekotto (Cam), Jenas, Zokora (Iv Coast), Tainio (Finland), Malbranque (Fr), Keane (Ireland), Berbatov (Bulgaria). Subs: Defoe, Mido (Egypt). 31%

Middlesbrough: Schwarzer (Australia), Davies, Xavier (Portugal), Pogatetz (Austria), Taylor, Morrison, Boateng (Hol), Arca (Argentina), Downing, Viduka (Australia), Yakubu (Nig). Subs: Euell (Jam), Rochemback (Brazil), Christie. 36%

Aston Villa: Sørensen (Den), Bardsley, Mellberg (Sweden), Cahill, Barry, Agbonlahor, McCann, Petrov (Bulgaria), Maloney (Scot), Carew (Norway), Young. Subs: Berger (Czech), Davis (Northern Ireland). 46%

Fulham: Laštůvka (Czech), Volz (Germany), Queudrue (Fr), Knight, Christanval (Fr), Rosenior, Brown, Diop (Senegal), Davies (Wales), McBride (USA), Helguson (Iceland). Subs: Radzinski (Canada), Smertin (Russia), Montella (Italy). 21%

Sheffield United: Kenny (Ireland), Geary (Ireland), Jagielka, Lucketti, Armstrong, Kazim-Richards, Tonge, Montgomery, Quinn (Ireland), Hulse, Stead. Subs: Fathi (Egypt), Bromby. 69%

Man City: Isaksson (Sweden), Richards, Dunne (Ireland), Distin (Fr), Jihai (China), Barton, Ireland (Ireland), Dabo (Fr), Ball, Corradi (Italy), Vassell. Subs: Samaras (Greece), Beasley (USA). 36%

Wigan: Kirkland, Hall, Boyce, Jackson, Baines, Taylor, Landzaat (Hol), Skoko (Australia), McCulloch (Scot), Wesley, Aghahowa (Nig). Subs: Haestad (Norway), Valencia (Ecuador), Kilbane (Ireland). 50%

West Ham: Green, Neill (Australia), Ferdinand, Davenport, McCartney (N Ireland), Benayoun (Israel), Reo-Coker, Quashie (Scot), Etherington, Harewood, Zamora. Subs: Spector (USA), Boa Morte (Portugal), Tevez (Argentina). 50%

Charlton: Carson, Sankofa, Bougherra (Algeria), Diawara (Sen), Thatcher (Wales), Rommedahl (Den), Song Billong (Cam), Holland (Ireland), Faye (Sen), Ambrose, M. Bent. Subs: Hughes, Zheng (China), Lisbie (Jam). 36%

Watford: Foster, Mariappa, DeMerit (USA), Mackay (Scot), Stewart, Smith, Mahon, Francis (Jam), Cavalli (Fr), Henderson, Kabba. Subs: Bangura (Fr), Shittu (Nig), Ashikodi (Nig). 50%

Below Enjoy it while it lasts, lads … Sheffield United, a side that fielded the highest percentage of English players, celebrate promotion in 2006. But after just one season, the Blades found themselves back in the Championship.

FOOTBALL FIRSTS

The first televised game was on 29 August 1936 between Arsenal and Everton.

The first League game to be broadcast live on radio was on 22 January 1927 between Arsenal and Sheffield United. It ended 1–1.

The 1966 World Cup final between England and West Germany was the first international to be shown live in colour on TV.

In 1975, Kettering Town were the first English club to have a sponsor's name on their shirt. The FA told them to stop it, at once!

The first legal use of a sponsor's name was by Liverpool in 1979, promoting Hitachi.

The first black professional in England was Arthur Wharton, who joined Preston North End in 1886.

The first black player to win a full England cap was Viv Anderson in 1978.

The first black footballer to captain England was Paul Ince in June 1993 against the USA.

The first black player to captain a Cup final side was Viv Anderson of Sheffield Wednesday in 1993.

The first player to score a hat trick in an FA Cup final was William Townley playing for Preston North End in 1890.

The first FA Cup final goal scored at the old Wembley was by David Jack of Bolton Wanderers in 1923.

The first Footballer of the Year was Stanley Matthews in 1948.

The first manager of the year was Jock Stein in 1966.

The first player sent off while playing for England was Alan Mullery in June 1969 against Yugoslavia.

'Abide with me' was first sung at a Wembley Cup final in 1927.

The first British club to play in Europe was Hibernian in 1955–56.

The first British player to earn £100 a week was Johnny Haynes of Fulham in 1961.

Nottingham Forest were the first club to be relegated from the Premiership when they finished bottom in 1992–93.

Left Arthur Wharton, England's first black professional footballer.

● The first artificial ('Astroturf') pitch to be used in England was at QPR in 1982.

● The first player to score a hat trick in the Premiership was Eric Cantona – for Leeds United in their 5–0 win over Spurs, 25 August 1992.

● Dave Beasant was the first goalkeeper to captain a winning FA Cup side when Wimbledon beat Liverpool 1–0 in the 1988 final.

● The first German to play in a League game was Max Seeburg, who appeared for Spurs against Hull City in September 1908.

● The first Egyptian to play in the Premiership was Mido of Spurs on 5 February 2005 against Portsmouth.

● The first substitute to be used in a League match was Keith Peacock in 1956, playing for Charlton.

● The first 5–5 draw in the Football League was between Blackburn Rovers and Accrington on 15 September 1888.

● The first 6–6 draw did not take place until 21 April 1930, in a game between Leicester City and Arsenal at Filbert Street.

● The first player to appear in 1,000 Football League games was goalkeeper Peter Shilton in December 1996, playing for Leyton Orient against Brighton.

● England's first captain was Cuthbert John Ottway of Oxford University, England v Scotland, November 1872.

● The first football club in the world was Sheffield FC, founded in 1857, according to the FA, though Cambridge University Football Club claims it is older, having formed its first rules in 1856.

Above Mido scores in his first game for Spurs in 2005.

Top at Christmas – but what does it mean?

In the first 15 seasons of the Premiership, from 1992–93 to 2006–07, only six clubs who led the League at Christmas went on to win the Championship.

		Finished	Champs
92–93	Norwich	3rd	Man Utd
93–94	Man Utd	1st	Man Utd
94–95	Blackburn	1st	Blackburn
95–96	Newcastle	2nd	Man Utd
96–97	Liverpool	4th	Man Utd
97–98	Man Utd	2nd	Arsenal
98–99	Aston Villa	6th	Man Utd
99–00	Leeds Utd	3rd	Man Utd
00–01	Man Utd	1st	Man Utd
01–02	Newcastle Utd	4th	Arsenal
02–03	Arsenal	2nd	Man Utd
03–04	Man Utd	3rd	Arsenal
04–05	Chelsea	1st	Chelsea
05–06	Chelsea	1st	Chelsea
06–07	Man Utd	1st	Man Utd

Gretna

When Gretna won the Scottish First Division title in 2007, they entered the Scottish Premier League for the first time and completed what must be the most extraordinary rise in any of the world's professional football leagues. Gretna was hardly more than a Sunday pub team ten years before, playing in the English minor leagues. In 2002, they joined Division Three of the Scottish League, finishing fifth. Their meteoric rise then began. Gretna (population 2,705) is the smallest town with a top League club anywhere in Europe. In comparison, Thun in Switzerland (pop. 40,000), Molde in Norway (24,000) and even Paralimni on Cyprus (11,000) are all metropolitan giants.

… and one more Scottish fact

Prime Minister Gordon Brown is a keen football fan. He is still an avid supporter of his local team, Raith Rovers. As a schoolboy in Kirkcaldy, wee Gordon used to sell match-day programmes so that he could get in free at half-time.

How do the pros promote themselves?
Find out in the next chapter …

11. Player profiles

The pros' public image

Since football began, all football fans have been interested in the personalities of our players as well as in their football prowess. We like to feel the flavour of them, not just the facts. On the pitch, we can make up our mind about how they play, but we can only guess at their real characters.

Football newspapers and comics, magazines and programmes have catered to our curiosity by trying to find out personal details about our heroes, their backgrounds, how they became footballers, their home lives, their likes and dislikes, their favourite colours, their favourite players. Within reason, of course. The tradition, until very recently, has been to be reverential, keeping up appearances, revealing nothing nasty about them or asking really horrid questions.

And yet, if you study player profiles and interviews, ghosted first-person columns, or questions and answers from the last 100 years, you'll find that, back in ye olden days, writers could sometimes be a bit critical.

In 1895, in a publication called *Famous Footballers*, Millwall's full-back J. Graham was said to 'play more for the spectators than was necessary'. In other words, he did a bit of showboating, showing off, just as some players often do today.

Reading these player profiles, you can see the game changing, with different heroes, styles, language and attitudes. Imagine a footballer from the past being asked the cheeky, not to say rude, questions in today's *FourFourTwo* magazine …

Right The splendidly moustachioed full-back J. Graham, pictured in 1895. Clearly a man who was very conscious of his public image.

- -

1905

Steve Bloomer

It would be interesting to know where Steve Bloomer purchases his shooting boots, for he is certainly the most prolific goal scorer playing. Born at Cradley Heath, in 1874, Bloomer is now in the veteran stage, as players go, but the game cannot stale the versatility of his play. To a young player, it is a liberal education to see the Derby County man upon the field. No matter what team he may be playing against, it is the same old tale. Give him the semblance of a chance, no matter what the angle may be, and the ball is flashed into the net. Working like a Trojan, Bloomer has over and over again pulled a match out of the fire, and to this deadliness of aim the County has had to ascribe many of its victories in the past, and, judging by his displays already this season, he will have to be put in the eleven again when the International caps come to be distributed. He has a unique record, in this respect, for on over twenty occasions, writing from memory, he has represented England. He ascribes his success upon the football field to temperate living. "A man must look after himself to be any good," he says. "You cannot live well, and then turn out twice, and sometimes more, during the week, and feel fit for your work." These

From a Photo. by]

J. GRAHAM.

[Symmons & Thiele, 66, Chancery Lane.

GRAHAM, the Millwall Athletic back, and captain of the team, has had a somewhat brief, but a brilliant, career. He was born at Derby in 1873. At an early age he came to the Metropolis, and acquired his first knowledge of football with a school eleven. His first real entry upon the game, however, was when he joined the Magpie F.C., at that time one of the leading junior teams. Then, after a time, he became associated with the Cray Wanderers, one of the strongest of the Kentish elevens. In the season 1892-93 he was selected and played for the county in the majority of their engagements. In one of these fixtures, against Middlesex, contested on the Millwall ground, he attracted the attention of the local executive. An offer was made him to become one of the Athletic team, an offer which he accepted. Since then he has played regularly for the team, while he has, also, been included in the Middlesex eleven. He is a consistent performer. Although somewhat prone in his earlier engagements to play more for the spectators than was necessary, Graham has now quietened down, and, in a hot attack, is one of the mainstays of the eleven. His height gives him an advantage in "heading" the ball out of danger, while he is also possessed of considerable speed. He is a great favourite with the local spectators, while it is considered he is about the best back in the South of England.

From *Famous Footballers*, 1895.

Photograph by BROWN, BARNES & BELL   31, Bold Street, Liverpool.

ENGLISH TEAM.

N. L. JACKSON.   L. V. LODGE.   J. REID (Referee.)   J. W. SUTCLIFFE.   R. E. LYTHGOE.
           J. REYNOLDS.   J. HOLT.   E. NEEDHAM.   J. CRABTREE.   C. J. HUGHES.
      W. J. BASSETT.   S. BLOOMER.   J. GOODALL.   R. C. GOSLING.   S. SMITH.

Above The England squad of 1895 pose for a team photo before their match against Scotland. Steve Bloomer is second from left on the front row.

words of advice might be remembered by some of the budding footballers, and also by more than a few spectators, who, the first to induce a man to forget his training duties, are also the first to rail should he show a falling away in form. There is no fear of this happening with Bloomer, however; if he had been going to be spoilt, that would have happened years ago.

From *The Pictorial Magazine*, 14 October 1905

1908

Percy Humphreys

Humphreys was clearly a favourite of the Stamford Bridge faithful when this profile appeared. The next season, however, he transferred to Spurs and had the temerity to knock his old team out of the FA Cup at home in the second round.

CHRONICLES OF THE CHELSEA FOOTBALL CLUB

CHELSEA F.C. PROFILES

No. 31.

If ever there was a genuine ninety-minute "trier" it is PERCY HUMPHREYS. From "whistle to whistle" he throws off more radio-activity than a whole ounce of radium would in a fortnight. He is a veritable glutton for work. No matter how the game may be going, Percy is as ready and eager for the fray as a schoolboy is for a holiday. There is little respite for the defenders whilst he is on the field. As the surf on the beach is beaten back only to hurl itself with renewed force at the pebbles, so does Percy throw himself time after time with undiminished vigour into the thickest of the fight. Hard knocks? He loves 'em!

If he ever has to leave the field, you know he really is hurt. Nature has endowed Percy with a sturdy frame and stout heart, and, – well, she has not misplaced these gifts, for he makes the best possible use of them. As a splendid example of one of the never-say-die type of footballers, Humphreys is a player after the "man in the crowd" who appreciates to the full the sterling British qualities of pluck and determination. Like so many other Chelsea players, Humphreys has represented his country on the football field, having played for England against Scotland both in the International and Inter-League games.

" Irrepressible."

From the Chelsea programme, 1908.

How I Started Football

GEORGE WILSON
(Wednesday's English International Centre half)

FRED KEENOR
(The Welsh International who plays for Cardiff City)

I STARTED my football career on the Blackpool sands. I have vivid recollections of dribbling a ball round the pillars which support the piers there, and though at that time it was not a full-sized football, I fancy that this exercise of my boyhood days did something to teach me what is essentially the first lesson of all real football – the art of ball control.

If a lad can control a ball of the size of those with which lawn tennis is played, then he will not have a great deal of difficulty in learning to control the full-sized ball which is used in big matches.

TAKING CHANCES

Blackpool was my native place – the town in which I was born, and in which I really came to somewhere near the front in football. Of course, I played at school. My enthusiasm for the game knew no bounds; I was ready to run all sorts of risks of chastisement if I could get any sort of game.

In those days I rather fancied myself as a forward, and it was in this position that I got my first real leg upwards. From football in the Sunday School League – not Sunday football, mind – I was invited to go to play at Morecambe, and as a professional received fifteen shillings a week for appearing in West Lancashire League games there.

The news of the things I did at Morecambe drifted back to Blackpool, and in due course I made a first appearance in the second Division team of my native town. That was in the season 1911-12, and my position was centre forward. In 1912-13 I occupied all three inside positions at different times, but I suppose I did not impress to any considerable extent.

I GET MY CHANCE

Some months later there came a lucky day for me. The centre-half-back of the Blackpool team was unable to turn out. I was put into that place, and since then I have never played anywhere else. After the war I went to The Wednesday of Sheffield, and had the pleasure of acting as captain to England teams more than once. That luck played a part in my progress I am not prepared to deny. But the thing for every lad to do when he gets his chance is to struggle might and main to make the most of it. We can't all be top class footballers, but we can all do our level best to go on the field fit enough to stay the whole ninety minutes. That tells!

EVER since I can remember I have just loved soccer football. During my schoolboy days I am afraid it took up nearly all my spare time, and at a very early age I appreciated the fact that football demands physical fitness.

WATCHING GOOD MEN

I used to avail myself of every chance I could get to see a senior match. It is surprising what you learn by watching the experts. I owe much of my success to my efforts to improve my play by watching others far better than myself. Amongst my ideal masters were Steve Bloomer and Alf Common, when they played together for Middlesbrough. Middlesbrough came to Cardiff to play a friendly match against a side picked from the best clubs in Cardiff.

What an exhibition these two players gave. They made football look easy, and I picked up quite a useful number of hints on this particular afternoon. Indeed, I think it was this match that decided me to take up the game seriously.

Nearly every known honour had come my way during my schooldays – captain of the school team that had won the schools league without losing a match, and represented the town team and also my country.

MY TRY OUT

It was while I was playing for a junior side called Roath Wednesday that I was first approached by a director of the newly-formed Cardiff City football club, and asked to play in a trial match. That director happened to be my old school teacher, Mr. Walter Rider. Having played in this particular trial match and given satisfaction, Mr. Rider asked me to sign amateur forms for Cardiff. At this time I was only fifteen years of age, and my dad's permission had to be obtained before I dare consent.

After two seasons with the reserve side I got my chance with the first team – at seventeen years of age. Playing for my own town team was a thing I had never thought of, but I decided that whatever happened, I would not let my side down. I felt a bit nervous during the first few minutes, but after this everything went all right, and we won by three to one.

From that day to this I have always been considered a first team player, have played nearly five hundred games for my club.

1924

George Wilson and Fred Keenor

These two players met in a home international on 3 March 1924, at Ewood Park.
Wales ran out 2–1 winners. (From *The Boys' Book of Football*, 1924)

1935

Eddie Hapgood, George Barber, et al.

Footballers have always been keen on clothes. A profile of some of the Dapper Dans
of pre-war football. (From *Topical Times*, 1935)

THE SWELL GUYS IN SOCCER

Footballers are seldom associated with anything but football. Most spectators can only imagine them in their shorts and their jerseys. It is difficult to imagine them having private lives of their own.

But many well-known footballers are just as interesting "characters" in private life as they are on the soccer field.

Eddie Hapgood, for instance, Arsenal and England captain, always used to pride himself on being the best-dressed footballer in the game. His plus-fours are always immaculately cut, and his shirts and ties are chosen with great care.

BARBER GAVE THE BOYS A SHOCK

George Barber, of Chelsea, is another who takes a pride in his appearance. George left Luton on a free transfer for Chelsea. The week he got his first full pay he went out and bought a neat suiting. With bowler hat and a watch-chain across his middle, he turned up for training.

When he opened the door to the dressing-room, the boys got a shock. Jack Whitley, popular Chelsea trainer, rubbed his eyes. Then he found his voice.

"Wrong door, milord," he said. "Corinthians at the other end!"

George Barber is not only particular about his dress. He is also anxious to raise the tone of professional football.

Another gentleman of the game is Jack Crayston, of Arsenal. Jack never says a word out of place. Never gets ruffled. Always dresses quietly. Modest and obliging in everything he does.

CHARMING HERBIE ROBERTS

Then there's Herbie Roberts. Those who have seen this super-stopper and have gained the impression he is a "tough guy," have got him wrong.

Roberts is one of the most popular players on the Arsenal staff. He is another of the "obliging" type. Ask anyone who knows Herbie off the field. They will describe him as "one of the best". He is mild-mannered and always anxious to do his pals a good turn. He has a charm of manner all his own.

1938

Today, a player would save his best stories and memories for his ghosted autobiography, but before the last war, such books hardly existed. In 1938, the famous Arsenal player Cliff Bastin gave a very graphic account of his first Cup final eight years earlier, when he was only 18. This was the 1930 Cup final when Arsenal beat Huddersfield Town 2–0.

Of the game itself I will mention only one amusing incident. I was playing on the left wing, with Alex James at inside-left. As we were going to the ground, Alex had turned to me and said : "If we get a free kick, Cliff, I'll send it to you; you slip it back to me quickly and I'll put it into the net." "This was something of a joke among us, because Alex had hardly scored at all that season, though he had engineered plenty of goals for others.

But strangely enough, what he had suggested in joke actually happened. He was awarded a free kick and, taking it quickly, he sent the ball to me. Dodging the full-back, I centred to Alex, who took the ball in his stride and sent it in a right-footed shot that entered the net like a rocket. I

have seldom seen such a perfectly timed shot. The Huddersfield goalkeeper was left standing. Although we scored again later, that goal was the real match-winner, and we were all delighted that when at last Alex's luck did change it should have done so in the most important match of all.

The final whistle naturally brings very mixed feelings to the players. Before the match you are keyed up. Afterwards, if you have won, comes a tremendous excitement; if you have lost, a "pricked-bubble" sensation. But for both sides is a relief that it is all over. I have been on both the winning and losing sides at Wembley. I know now how the losers feel; but even on this occasion I remember thinking of our unfortunate opponents as we walked up to the Royal box to receive our medals. After a hard season they had come within sight of victory, only to have it snatched from them at the last moment, and the chance of obtaining the Finalist's medal might never come again.

Two years later, after we had lost to Newcastle, I experienced the feelings that the Huddersfield men had now. On that occasion, however, I at least had the knowledge that I had already been in one winning team at Wembley. But if they were disappointed, the Huddersfield men were also great sportsmen, and at the joint dinner afterwards they joined in our celebration in a way that fully upheld the high tradition of Britain's greatest sport.

From *Boy's Own* magazine, April 1938

1946

Frank Swift

Most players during the last war were called up into the services, and this was reflected in their profiles. Frank Swift, Man City's star goalkeeper, survived the war but was killed in the Munich air disaster of 1958. (From *Football Stars*, 1946)

FRANK SWIFT
Manchester City and England

See Frank Swift on the field. He's tall (6 ft. 3½ in.), quick to move into position, double-quick to intercept a centre or beat out a surprise shot. He has the greatest hand expansion recorded in the game— 11½ in. Meet him off the field. maybe at Withington, the Manchester suburb, where he is the teetotal host of the " local." He is dark, good looking, well dressed, well spoken, and a witty conversationalist. Everyone in football likes Frank. Frank likes everyone in football—except one or two notoriously rugged centre-forwards !

1965

George Best

In 1965, George Best was 19 and had just got into Man Utd's first team. He talked to Hunter Davies of *The Sunday Times* about his hopes for the future – when none of us knew what his future might hold.

GEORGE BEST is a very shy, quiet boy, of nineteen. He has a soft Belfast accent and a Beatle haircut. His wage for the week before last was £175.

Mr Best plays for Manchester United and is the boy wonder of football.

"When I first went to the ground and I'd seen all those big lads, I thought, there's no chance here. I'll never make the grade. I was 15 and sharing digs with another Belfast boy. After two weeks, I packed up and went home. I was just so homesick.

"But my father talked me into coming back, and I stayed. I've changed a lot since those days. If somebody in a shop gave me change out of ten bob and I'd given them a pound, I'd be too shy to complain.

"You've got to have confidence to be a foot-baller. I think in the last two months I've got it. I used to lie in my bed on Friday nights, imagining how I was going to beat everybody. Funny, I never did badly, always well, when I was doing this thinking. Now I never think about the match at all.

"I used to wear very quiet clothes. Now, if I see something smart, no matter what anybody else says, I buy it. I've got a black and white striped jacket. The lads in the team are always saying, 'Here comes the butcher.'

"I used to write home three or four times a week. Now, well, I haven't written at all for a few weeks, it's terrible. That's one thing I've gone down on.

"But I can talk to my parents, the way I never used to, as if I'm grown up. I can talk about girls. I never had the nerve before.

"I thought I wouldn't be able to talk to Denis

Law and Bobby Charlton, the ones I'd always hero-worshipped as a kid. But your opinion changes. They're just like ordinary blokes in the street.

"They're all married in the first team, so after training I get a bit bored. I thought at first they didn't want me to mix. They do, but they've got families. The afternoons, I either play snooker or go bowling. Pictures perhaps twice a week. I'm getting very lazy. I read a bit. Horror stories, comics, that sort of thing.

"I don't drink or smoke. Perhaps on a rare occasion, I might have a lager. Then it gets back to the boss, Mr Busby, that you're drunk. I share digs with another footballer. I would like to have a flat on my own. But the boss thinks there might be temptation. Perhaps, when I'm twenty-one. I've no complaints. I like my landlady.

"One thing you never realise until you actually play, is that other footballers are always talking to you on the pitch, though no one else can hear. One bloke every time he got near me said, get your hair cut, scruff. They try to nark you, break you down.

"I've found that footballers never read reports of their own matches. They're just not interested. They know what happened. I read them. I'm young.

"I save most of my money. Last week's £175 was very unusual – I had three matches, one an international. Often it's down to £50 a week.

"What I'd like to be is a millionaire, that's what I'd like. If it meant not playing football again from this minute on? Well, perhaps I don't want to be a millionaire after all."

Right A fresh-faced George Best pictured in 1964.

1970s

Sam Allardyce

One of the many joys of reading old *Shoot* magazine profiles from the 1970s is their focus on players who are star managers or pundits today. Big Sam likes roast beef and Yorkshire pud, which he surely does not allow his players today. (From *Shoot*, 1976)

1980s

Kenny Dalglish

Kenny Dalglish interviewed in the Scotland v England programme for 24 May 1980.

KENNY DALGLISH

(LIVERPOOL AND SCOTLAND)

With more than seventy international appearances, you are Scotland's most capped player. Does one game stand out more than any other?

My first cap. The night at Pittodrie 1971 when I came on as substitute for Alex Cropley against Belgium. Alongside that, I place my first full-cap against Holland in Amsterdam. Sandy Jardine, Davie Hay, Billy Bremner and Archie Gemmill were all in the team. A marvellous memory!

You are in line to join the elite of British soccer stars who have played a hundred times for their country. Does that excite you?

Of course it does. I just hope the legs last that long!

How much does playing for Scotland mean to you

For me it means everything. It's all about passion and pride. It's an experience which never fails to make you feel proud to be a Scot. Some cynics say money plays a paramount part in it. Don't believe that – there's a marvellous feeling when you pull a Scotland jersey over your head.

Looking back on your Celtic days, which of the many honours gave you the biggest thrill?

It's a double answer. The day I signed for them, and the day I was made captain. For me these were magic moments.

You have played seven times against England – which of these games do you remember most?

The three we won! Playing against England is something special – to win is a great compensation.

Has your immense success with Liverpool come as a surprise to you?

Whatever success I have gained playing in England is equally shared by my colleagues at Anfield. Not just the lads on the field but the entire staff who have given me so much help. While individualism is always a necessary asset, we must never lose sight of the fact that it's a team game.

If you could change one rule in football what would it be?

To make the goals bigger when we're attacking and smaller when we're defending!

As a young man with Cumbernauld did you have a football hero?

The great Denis Law. To me he stood for everything that was just right in football. He showed great pride and passion for the game.

Have you any superstitions?

Not really. I don't like a No.13 shirt, and I don't intentionally walk under ladders. But that apart, I am not superstitious.

Have you a particular dislike in football?

Referees who are inconsistent. One game you get the official who works in harmony wih his linesman and all goes well. The next, you get the ref who ignores his linesmen's every signal, and it's chaos.

Have you any football ambitions as yet unfulfilled?

Not really. Except that I want to go on playing well for Liverpool and for Scotland. Success is a great spur – I never lose sight of it.

● *Sponsored by Mackinlay's Old Scotch Whisky.*

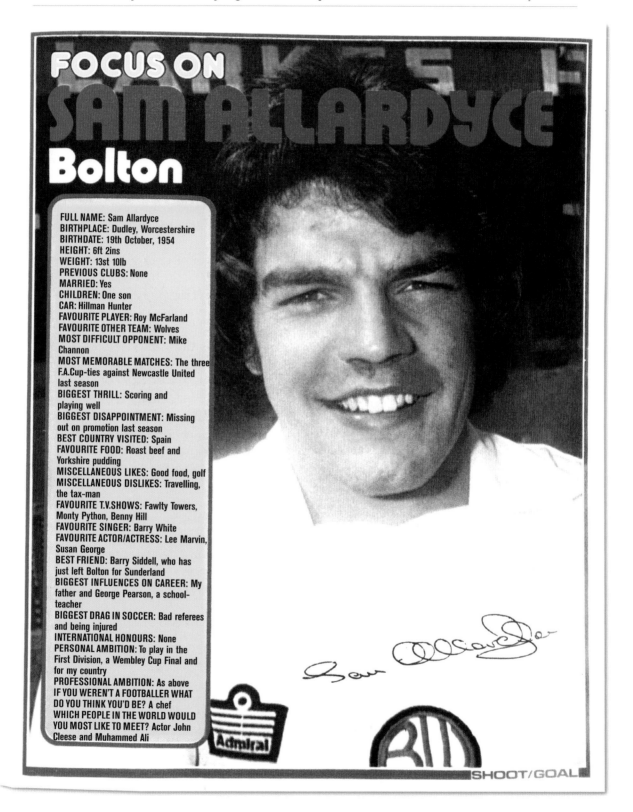

FOCUS ON
SAM ALLARDYCE
Bolton

FULL NAME: Sam Allardyce
BIRTHPLACE: Dudley, Worcestershire
BIRTHDATE: 19th October, 1954
HEIGHT: 6ft 2ins
WEIGHT: 13st 10lb
PREVIOUS CLUBS: None
MARRIED: Yes
CHILDREN: One son
CAR: Hillman Hunter
FAVOURITE PLAYER: Roy McFarland
FAVOURITE OTHER TEAM: Wolves
MOST DIFFICULT OPPONENT: Mike Channon
MOST MEMORABLE MATCHES: The three F.A.Cup-ties against Newcastle United last season
BIGGEST THRILL: Scoring and playing well
BIGGEST DISAPPOINTMENT: Missing out on promotion last season
BEST COUNTRY VISITED: Spain
FAVOURITE FOOD: Roast beef and Yorkshire pudding
MISCELLANEOUS LIKES: Good food, golf
MISCELLANEOUS DISLIKES: Travelling, the tax-man
FAVOURITE T.V.SHOWS: Fawlty Towers, Monty Python, Benny Hill
FAVOURITE SINGER: Barry White
FAVOURITE ACTOR/ACTRESS: Lee Marvin, Susan George
BEST FRIEND: Barry Siddell, who has just left Bolton for Sunderland
BIGGEST INFLUENCES ON CAREER: My father and George Pearson, a school-teacher
BIGGEST DRAG IN SOCCER: Bad referees and being injured
INTERNATIONAL HONOURS: None
PERSONAL AMBITION: To play in the First Division, a Wembley Cup Final and for my country
PROFESSIONAL AMBITION: As above
IF YOU WEREN'T A FOOTBALLER WHAT DO YOU THINK YOU'D BE? A chef
WHICH PEOPLE IN THE WORLD WOULD YOU MOST LIKE TO MEET? Actor John Cleese and Muhammed Ali

SHOOT/GOAL

1990s

Paul Gascoigne

The arrival of the internet has meant that stories and details can be broadcast about famous players – even when the stories are untrue, unfair and often obscene. In his autobiography, Paul Gascoigne listed some of the stories spread about him – and said which were true or not.

1. One hour after playing for England, met 'showbiz pals' Danny Baker and Chris Evans in a Hampstead pub while still wearing his full kit … boots included.

2. When asked for his nationality before an operation, told the nurse 'Church of England'.

3. On a trip to London, jumped out of his car to demand 'a go' on a workman's pneumatic drill. After getting the go-ahead, happily pounded the pavement to the amusement of shoppers.

4. On first meeting with Lazio's president to discuss his big-money move to the Italian club, was quick to tell the esteemed gentleman that he reminded him of Russ Abbot.

5. Organizers of Italia 90 TV coverage had the splendid idea of augmenting team line-ups with footage of each player mouthing his own name. Gascoigne's genius led him to subvert the process by, instead, mouthing 'f***ing w****r'. Broadcasters across the world had to use it all the way through the tournament.

6. Booked a series of sunbed sessions for then Newcastle team-mate Tony Cunningham. Who, of course, is black.

7. Asked by a Norwegian camera crew if he had a message for England's upcoming opponents, he immediately responded with, 'Yes. F*** off, Norway.' Then ran off laughing.

8. Turned up for England training the morning after then manager Bobby Robson had called him 'daft as a brush' with a brush sticking out of his sock.

9. When asked for a footballing comment while at Lazio, burped enthusiastically into a TV microphone.

10. Decided it would be a great idea to have massive hair extensions. Looked a fool and had them taken out a day later.

11. After paying for ex-wife Sheryl's breast implants, sent flowers to the hospital after the operation addressed to 'Dolly Parton'.

12. Astounded commuters in London by jumping on a double-decker in London's Piccadilly Circus and asking if he could have a drive. The bus driver said yes, and the passengers thoroughly enjoyed Gazza's impromptu appearance.

13. Sent a rose round to the Wimbledon dressing room for Vinnie Jones after the infamous ball-squeezing incident. Got a toilet brush in return.

All were true, he said, except for 4 and 11.

Top **Always one to court controversy, Gazza wound up Celtic fans when he was playing for Rangers in an Old Firm derby in 1994 by mimicking flute-playing, an activity associated with the Protestant Orange Order.**

2006

Peter Reid

Some of the silliest and rudest interviews today appear in *FourFourTwo* magazine:

ASK A SILLY QUESTION

PETER REID

Afternoon, Peter, if you were a wrestler, what stage name would you use – bearing in mind Ray Stubbs recently opted for 'The Stubb Dogg'?
'The Stubb Dogg.' Good name. I think it'd have to be something to do with me head, 'cos they call me Gorilla Head.

Do they really?
Yeah, they do. Why don't we go for Grilla? …

Right, onto business: have you ever left home without any pants on?
Yes.

Yes! When? And indeed why?
All the time. And why not?

What's wrong with pants?
What's f…ing right with them, more like. If you wash yourself and keep your-self clean, I don't see why you should wear underpants.

Are you wearing any as we speak?
No, just me jeans. …

How much can you glug before you forget your name?
I'm not bad, to be fair?

What does that mean?
It means that I'm not bad, I can kick on.

Have you ever drunk booze from a shoe?
From a shoe? Not that I can remember. When I was a young lad I was in Ibiza and I drank vodka and Listermint [laughs]. We'd run out of mixers so mouth wash seemed like a good idea. My breath smelt great afterwards, but I was bollocksed [laughs again].

When did you last flounce about in women's clothes?
[Ponders for some time] Er, I haven't worn women's clothes, it's not my bag.

I'd love to say it was, but it's not. I'm sure there's a feminine side of me to find but I've not gone looking for it [laughs].

What was the first thing you ever shoplifted?
The first thing? I can't remember, I think it was probably a Lucky Bag from a newsagent called Forbuoys. You know, those bags with sweets and toys in 'em.

Did you get away with it?
Well, up to now I have, yeah [laughs]. But if I get a visit from the police, I'll know who to blame [laughs].

When was the last time you slept in your shed?
[Laughs heartily, for some reason] I've got a couple of sheds but I've never slept in either of them. I slept on a bench once, but never in the shed.

Was it a park bench? Were you drinking with the tramps again?
No, I just got home late one night and had lost me keys and couldn't wake anyone up, so I slept on the bench round the back … a bad night's kip [laughs].

Had you been out with Robbo?
No, no, not on this occasion, although I'd had a drink [laughs].

Alright, Grilla, last question, and given that this is a World Cup Special, a token nod to football with this one: why oh why oh why didn't you just kick Maradona square in the swingers when you had the chance?
If I'd been on what he was on I'd have caught him, let's put it that way [chuckles].

It's been a pleasure, Grilla. Bye.
No problem, ta-ra.

A MORAL DILEMMA FOR WAYNE
Part Four

Wayne and Darren were in the Den, taking turns at shots on goal, trying to curl it in, but neither was trying very hard. It was the evening before their Cup final, so they were meant to be taking it easy, but neither seemed to have much energy.

'You could wear a beard,' said Darren.

'Oh, shurrup!' said Wayne.

'Or a mask, one of them horror masks from Halloween. Oooh, sorry, didn't realise you was wearing one anyways …'

'Ha ha,' said Wayne.

'The thing is,' said Darren, being serious, 'you gotta play. We won't win without you.'

'Yeh, I know,' said Wayne.

'Big head,' said Darren.

They did some more shots on goal, then sat down, heads in their hands.

'What a mess,' moaned Wayne. 'I don't want to muck up my place at the Academy – but I also want to play for the school.'

'What does your dad think?' asked Darren.

'He says all big clubs have these rules. Once you join them, that's it, you can't play for your school any more. They are training you a certain way, they don't want you injured.'

'My dad,' said Darren, 'says he's seen your dad driving around the estate in a big flash car with that bloke with the leather jacket. It looked like a demonstration drive, so my dad thought.'

'So?' said Wayne. 'What's your point, Darren? What you incinerating?'

'Insinuating,' said Darren. 'Incinerating is when you set fire to something.'

'And that's what I'll do to you, if you don't pack it in.'

'I think you should play,' said Darren. 'But when you score the winning goal and all the press and scouts rush up, you give your name as Kevin Wright, Wayne's twin brother…'

'I ain't got no twin brother …'

'Of course you ain't, you noodle.'

'I'm fed up with this,' said Wayne. 'I'm going home.'

'See you tomorrow,' said Darren. 'Sleep well …'

'No chance,' said Wayne.

Brookpark's team was already on the team coach, plus Mr Wilkins, the sports teacher, Miss Henn, the Head Teacher, and a couple of parents who were going to act as trainers, carrying sponges and freeze packs.

'Where the hell is Wayne,' said Mr Wilkins. 'He's five minutes late. Darren, have you seen him?'

'I called for him, sir, but he wasn't in.'

'I've rung his dad on my mobile,' said Mr Wilkins, 'but he's not answering.'

At that moment, Wayne could be seen running up the hill to the gates of Brookpark school, along with his mother who seemed to be out of breath. She pushed Wayne onto the coach, then the door closed and the coach departed.

Mrs Wright could then be seen running down the hill again – and for some reason she then disappeared into the bookie's. Which was strange. Unlike her husband, she never put a bet on any horse.

Darren had kept a place empty beside him at the back of the coach where Wayne threw himself down.

'So what happened?' said Darren.

'Oh, they've just had a huge row,' said Wayne, 'me mum and dad, about who did what, who didn't do what, usual stuff. I don't want to talk about it …'

'Well, I'm glad you're here anyway. What decided you to play?'

'I felt I just had to. I couldn't let the school down. I promised …'

Brookpark were three up by half time, all scored by Wayne. He couldn't put a foot wrong.

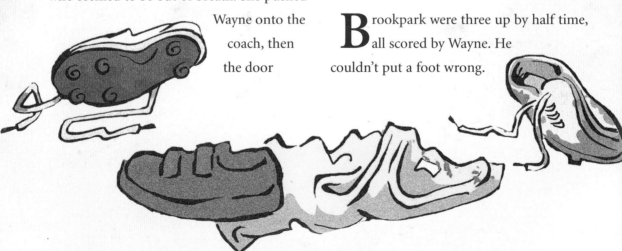

Every pass was accurate, on every run he beat at least two of their players, every shot was on target.

One goal had been a pure fluke. King's Cross's giant central defender had taken a massive swipe at an easy clearance, but missed his footing. He sliced the ball and it span over the goalie's head. The goalie, desperately diving backwards to try and save it, crashed into Wayne and brought him down. The ball struck the crossbar and rebounded into play – hitting Wayne on his bum as he lay on the ground. Dead jammy. But his other two goals were blinders.

At half time, the Brookpark fans were jubilant, dancing up and down and singing 'We're going to win the Cup … Are you Holloway Road in Disguise … Wayne, Wayne, give us a wave … Wayne Wright, Wright, Wright, Wright …'

A few of the top class were singing some rather ruder words, but not in Miss Henn's hearing. Anyway, she was jumping up and down herself and shouting 'Come on, Brookpark!'

At the start of the second half, King's Cross regrouped, bringing on two subs, one of whom was detailed to mark Wayne, kicking him at every opportunity.

They got a breakaway goal after 10 minutes and suddenly started playing much better. Brookpark were taken by surprise, thinking it was going to be as easy as the first half.

King's Cross got a penalty, a dubious one, for which Darren was yellow-carded for protesting. He got one hand to it, but it crept in off the post. They then got a third when Wayne, of all people, lost the ball on the halfway line. He seemed to be tiring, as if he'd had a bad night's sleep. That made it 3–3.

In extra time, Wayne sprang back into life, determined to make amends for his mistake, and scored his fourth goal, a header from a corner. But in the dying minutes, King's Cross equalised, once again, making it 4–4. And so it went to penalties.

After four penalties each, everyone had scored, including Wayne and Darren. King's Cross got their fifth which meant that Brookpark's final penalty taker, Rupert, who had come on as sub, had to score.

Rupert took a huge run at the ball – and sent it miles over the bar. That was it. Brookpark had lost their first and probably only ever chance of winning the Cup.

Wayne immediately went across to console Rupert, saying it wasn't his fault. Any one of them could well have missed.

Wayne was made Man of the Match, which was well deserved after four goals, and was immediately surrounded by a group of people congratulating him, including reporters from the Camden Journal and the Ham and High – and also five scouts. Wayne recognised one of them as the scout from United.

Darren rushed in before they could all get to Wayne and led him away to the dressing room.

'Well played, mate,' he said, putting his arm around Wayne.

'Gerroff!' said Wayne. 'Leave me alone.'

'I never thought it would end like this,' said Darren. 'We lost the final and I suppose you'll now lose your place at the Academy as well …'

But will he? Read the final episode on page 280.

12. Cartoons

Referee : " Be reasonable. I can't be all over the field at once."

Player : " Can't you ? You wait until this game's over ! "

Drawing funny conclusions

Right Early Chelsea programmes, such as this one from 1907, usually had a cartoon on the cover featuring a figure known as The Pensioner.

Below 1920s footer funnies: two comic picture postcards and the cover of Tom Webster's 1924 annual.

Football cartoons or caricatures have been around for well over a hundred years in football magazines, comics and books. Many club programmes had a resident artist who did a cartoon for the cover, or an amusing drawing of a star player for the inside pages.

Before the First World War, almost all of Chelsea's and also Spurs' programmes had a cartoon on the cover. With Chelsea, there was a figure known as The Pensioner, who represented Chelsea. With Spurs, their cartoons featured Cocky – a reference to the Spurs emblem. A lot of the references, to topical events or to games then being argued about, don't make a lot of sense today, but often they do, as the same subjects keep coming up over and over again.

By the 1920s, football cartoonists in the national papers had become very well known and books of their collected cartoons were often published at the end of each year, such as those of Tom Webster of the *London Evening News* and *Daily Mail*. Since then, books of football jokes and cartoons have been a regular feature of Christmas.

"WELL SAVED."

Off side !!! the poor referee.

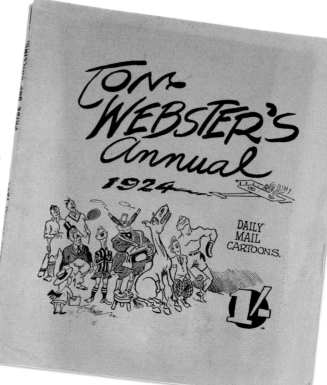

The CHELSEA F.C. Chronicle

OFFICIAL PROGRAMME

of

The Chelsea Football & Athletic Company, Limited.

[ENTERED AT STATIONERS' HALL.]   MEMBERS OF

The Football League (Division 1), South Eastern League (Division 1).

VOL. III. No. 2.]   September 7th, 1907.   [ONE PENNY.

THE GUNNER'S "MATE."

The Pensioner was trying his shooting boots : " My word," said the Gunner
(as he struggled into his jersey) " aint 'e 'OT " !

AND SO SAY ALL OF US!

CRICKETER : "Well Cocky, au revoir, and I sincerely hope the weather will be kinder to you than it has been with me."

COCKY : "Carried unanimously."

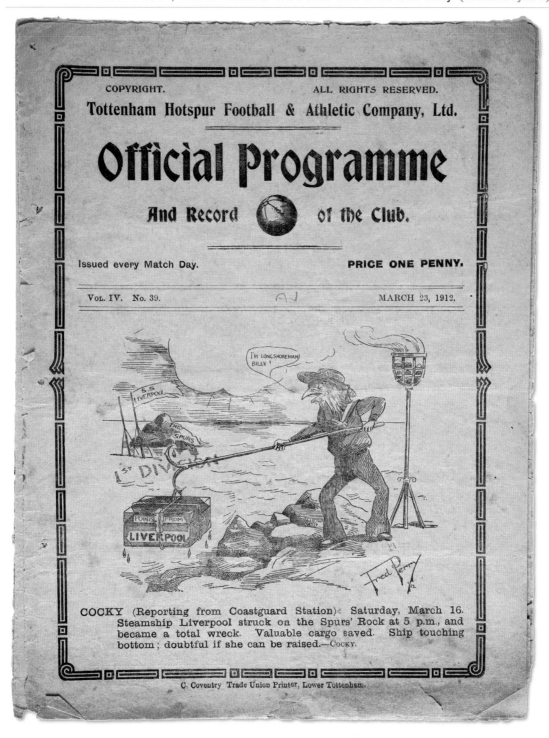

Left 1910s: Early Spurs programmes featured a cartoon character called Cocky, still with us at White Hart Lane. 'Bye 'bye cricket, hello footer for a new season – a message which is still understandable today.

Above Complicated joke after Spurs had stuffed Liverpool in 1912. The 'valuable cargo' was of course the points ...

THE CUP FINAL OF 1923

THIS AFTERNOON BOLTON WANDERERS' MEET WEST HAM IN THE CUP FINAL.

BOLTON WANDERERS SAY THAT THEY WILL WIN.

NOW ALTOGETHER— WE SHALL WIN!

ABSOLUTELY

POSITIVELY

INDUBITABLY

NEVERTHELESS

THAT IS NOT TRUE WHAT THEY ARE SAYING.

WEST HAM REFUSE TO BELIEVE THIS SO THERE APPEARS TO BE THE MAKINGS OF A GOOD ARGUMENT. AT ANYRATE IT WILL BE NO BATTLE OF FLOWERS

WE ARE TOLD THAT THE BOLTON TEAM DEPARTED FOR LONDON ON THURSDAY AFTERNOON TO THE CRIES OF "FIVE GOALS" FROM THE ONE SUPPORTER WHO HAS BEEN LEFT BEHIND TO LOOK AFTER THE TOWN.

WE ARE ALSO TOLD THAT 5000 BOLTON SUPPORTERS WILL BE PRESENT. (OF WHICH THIS IS ONE) IF THEREFORE WEST HAM SCORE THERE WILL BE 5,000 PEOPLE SAYING NOTHING - EXCEPT PERHAPS SOMETHING IN AN UNDERTONE.

REGARDING THE STATISTICS OF THE GAME. AT THE BUFFET BARS THERE WILL BE 200,000 SANDWICHES — HALF OF WHICH WERE LEFT OVER FROM LAST YEAR'S CUP FINAL.

THERE WILL BE 104 TURNSTILES AND 72 CORRIDOR ENTRANCES TO THE GROUND. IT IS TO BE HOPED THAT THE TWO TEAMS DON'T GO UP THE WRONG CORRIDOR

HI! WE WANT TO PLAY YOU!

WELL COME OVER HERE - WE CAN'T GET OUT.

AND GET WEDGED IN WITH THE CROWD.

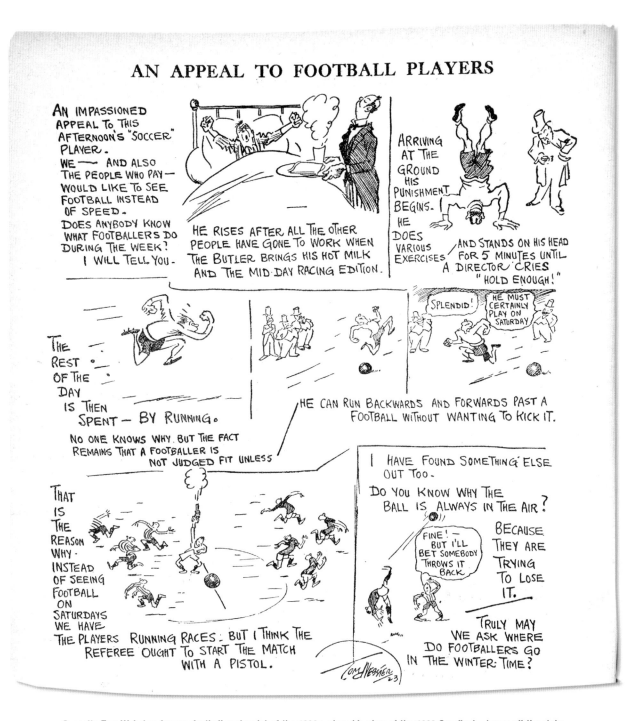

Opposite Tom Webster, famous football cartoonist of the 1920s, gives his view of the 1923 Cup final – hence all the stats.

Above ... and mocks footballers for their training methods.

CARTOONS

A CUP-TIE AT CHARLTON

LAST YEAR CHARLTON ATHLETIC PLAYED IN THE NEIGHBOURHOOD OF PLUMSTEAD. NOW THEY HAVE MOVED TO CATFORD. HAVING SEEN CHARLTON ATHLETIC PLAY I KNOW NOW WHY THEY HAVE TO GET A NEW GROUND EVERY SEASON. — THEY ARE TRYING TO DODGE THEIR SUPPORTERS.

PLEASE DON'T FOLLOW US ABOUT-OUR GOAL-KEEPER SAYS YOU'VE BEEN STARING AT HIM FOR 3 MONTHS AND HE CAN'T STAND IT ANY LONGER.

Above Tom Webster's 1923 joke about Charlton and their problems with grounds was still apt many years later.

Right 1936: Players trying to intimidate refs isn't a new phenomenon – from *The Football Weekly.*

Right 1946: Three cartoons from the book *Laughs in Short Pants.*

Referee : " Be reasonable. I can't be all over the field at once."
Player : " Can't you ? You wait until this game's over ! "

" This running commentary comes to you from the City Football Ground."

" . . . yes, I must admit I've been out of the game for a season or two !"

" We lost 10-0 last week and every time I picked the ball out of the net I saw that ruddy poster !"

THE PENALTY KICK

How the Goal appears to—

(A) : The Penalty-Taker.

(B) : The Goalkeeper.

"One says he's a Blackburn Rover and the other a Wolverhampton Wanderer!"

Opposite and right
1946: Some cartoons
hardly date ... More
fun from *Laughs in
Short Pants*.

"I reckon there's a limit to this introduction of young blood!"

JENKINS

Consulting the Linesman

1950s cartoons from
*Charles Buchan's
Football Monthly.*

"We'll play with the telly cameras behind us!"

"It's not teenagers I'm against—it's
their ridiculous clothes!"

"Perhaps you'd feel better if you went
to the ground and booed someone!"

... and a selection of 1970s cartoons from *Topical Times.*

CARTOONS

Above 1970s: From *All Star Parade*.

Right and below More from *Topical Times* of the same era.

"Got him! I've been trying to get that loud mouth all day."

"—and where d'you think you're going?"

"Never mind a better view, get back between those sticks."

"And watch out for their dirty centre-forward. He'll try and trip you the first chance he gets."

13. Believe it or not

Strange but true...

It's a funny old game, football, so football people often say – usually when something not very funny has happened, such as getting stuffed when they expected to win.

But over the decades there have been many funny, peculiar, interesting, unusual incidents, stories and records worth recalling. Not major events, just a bit odd ...

● The royal family has been more interested in horse racing than football over the centuries, though since the First World War the monarch has usually turned up at the FA Cup final and presented the medals. Today, however, Prince William, who has recently been made President of the FA, is a genuine football fan. He played the game at school, has been seen at Arsenal and is said to support Aston Villa.

The first royal connection with football came in 1892 when the Prince of Wales, later Edward VII, became a patron of the FA despite having little interest or much knowledge of the game, being far keener on cards and actresses. But he did attend the

Left Some weird and wonderful footballing trivia from a 1950s *FA Book For Boys*.

FA Cup final of 1889 between Wolverhampton Wanderers and Preston North End, held at the Kennington Oval, where he was seated next to the Preston chairman, William Sudell.

The prince was clearly alarmed by all the crunching tackles and flying limbs, but what amazed him most was when in a crowded penalty area a player rose and headed the ball.

'I say, Sudell,' he exclaimed. 'That man kicked the ball with his head …'

● In November 1888, during the very first season of the Football League, the *Sporting Chronicle* described some unseemly behaviour at the game between Notts County and Everton. One player 'struck another in the back in a piece of ruffianism which produced a lively verbal encounter.' Supporters were heard to shout 'Dog' and 'Pig'. Just as well such things do not happen today.

● In September 1894 the referee, Mr Ted Kirkham, arrived late for the Div One game between Sunderland and Derby County. His deputy started the game, but at half time, when Derby were 3–0 down, Mr Kirkham arrived. He asked the players what they wanted to do and they agreed to re-start the game from scratch. Sunderland still went on to win 8–0. This was the first known game of three halves …

Above **Well played, Your Highness! Prince William displays some nifty ball control during an inter-house tournament at Eton in 2000.**

● In January 1895 Woolwich Arsenal, later Arsenal, had their ground, Manor Park, closed because of crowd trouble in a game against Bolton Wanderers. This is thought to be the first time football hooliganism caused a ground to be closed.

● For two seasons, 1930–32, a team called Thames played in the Football League, Division Three (Southern). Their ground was West Ham Stadium in Custom House, London, E16 which had a capacity of 120,000. In 1932 they withdrew from the Football League.

● In 1891 Blackburn Rovers were playing their deadly rivals Burnley at Ewood Park. Two massive brawls between the players resulted in all the Blackburn team marching off the pitch – except for their goalie, Herby Arthur. According to local legend, he appealed successfully for the offside, then refused to take the kick because he had no one to pass to. The referee was then forced to abandon the game.

● Patsy Gallacher, the legendary Celtic player, scored one of the strangest ever goals. In the 1925 Scottish Cup final against Dundee, he ran into the box and appeared to

Above **Everton** (in white shirts) get the ball in the net in the 1933 FA Cup final, as Manchester City's No. 22 makes a despairing lunge.

lose control of the ball. Somehow, despite all the Dundee defenders around him, he managed to wedge the ball between his heels – then he somersaulted over the goal line, with the ball, into the net.

● The Baseball Ground, Derby County's home until 1997, was once occupied by a group of gypsies who, when they were chucked out in 1895, put a curse on the club. In 1946, when Derby, after a defeat in three FA Cup finals, made the final once again, their captain sought out some gypsies before the game. He persuaded them to lift the curse. Derby beat Charlton 4–1 after extra time.

● Everton were the first football team to wear the numbers 1–11 when they appeared in the Cup final of 1933 against Manchester City, who were numbered 12–22. Everton won 3–0.

● The first Northern, working-class team to win the FA Cup was Blackburn Olympic in 1883 when they beat Old Etonians. Until then, the Cup had been won by Southern clubs made up mainly of ex-public schoolboys or Oxbridge graduates, all amateurs who did not need to play – or indeed often work – for a living. Blackburn that day consisted mainly of working men – three weavers, one spinner, one cotton worker, one iron worker, a dentist's assistant, a picture framer, a plumber, plus two who probably were playing professionally, although professionalism was not legally recognized until two years later. The game was a watershed in that the North from

Above The flamboyant Roger Milla, star of the 1990 World Cup, performs his famous samba around the corner flag after scoring against Colombia.

then on took over English football and it soon became the sport of the working classes.

● In January 1966, in a Fourth Division game against Bradford City, Port Vale lined up with five teenagers in their attack – Alex Donald (17), Paul Bannister (18), Roddy Georgeson (17), Mick Cullerton (17) and Paul Ogden (19). They got beaten 2–0.

● The smallest known crowd at a Football League match was on 7 May 1921 at Old Trafford – but it did not involve Man United. Stockport County, whose own ground was closed, were playing Leicester Fosse on the last day of the season. Both of them had already been relegated. Only 13 spectators paid to see them.

● The first person to take part in a League game and First Class County Cricket game on the same day was Chris Balderstone, on 15 September 1975, when he turned out for Leicestershire and then for Doncaster Rovers.

● Goal celebrations today can be very complicated, often rehearsed beforehand, with the whole team joining in, but in the 1960s Denis Law of Man Utd kept things very simple. All he did after scoring a goal was point one finger in the air. In the 1970s Mick Channon of Southampton used to rotate an arm like a windmill. Roger Milla of Cameroon in the 1990s did a dance around a corner flag.

● Many football chants cannot be repeated in a respectable book, being read by respectable chaps. Mostly they are meant to be abusive, but witty or topical at the same time. One of the best known is an anti-Liverpool chant originating in the 1980s when they were winning everything. It was usually sung by supposedly more affluent fans of Southern teams, mocking Scousers and their allegedly deprived backgrounds.

> *In your Liverpool slums*
> *You look in the gutter for something to eat*
> *You find a dead cat and you think it's a treat*
> *In your Liverpool home.*

In 1997, in a UEFA Cup match in Monaco, between Monaco and Newcastle United, football writer Alex Leith heard the Newcastle fans singing a new version of the Liverpool chant:

In your Monaco slums
You look in the gutter for something to eat
You find a dead lobster and think it's a treat
In your Monaco slums.

● Liverpool's first League game was on 2 September 1893, in Division Two against Middlesbrough Ironopolis. All 10 of their outfield players were Scottish – McLean, Hannah, Henderson, McQue, McBride, Gordon, McVean, Stott, M. McQueen, H. McQueen. The goalie, McOwen, had a Scottish name but was in fact English. They won 2–0.

● Gary Sprake, goalkeeper for Leeds in a game against Liverpool in 1967, changed his mind at the last second as he was about to throw the ball out to a colleague – and threw it into his own net instead.

● In the olden days, balls often burst during a game. It was relatively easy for the leather outer case to be pierced by a stud or a splinter and the rubber bladder inside

Right Gary Sprake training for Leeds in 1970. After his infamous blunder against Liverpool, wits in the Kop (of whom there are many) launched into a Des O'Connor number, 'Careless Hands' ...

to get a slow or a quick puncture. The first time it happened at a Cup final was in 1946 between Charlton Athletic and Derby County.

Amazingly, four days later the same two teams met in a League game – and the ball burst again. A year later, Charlton were again in the Cup final, this time against Burnley, and once more the ball burst. So a hat-trick of burst balls to Charlton.

● While playing for Arsenal against Blackpool in 1956, Dennis Evans heard what he thought was the final whistle. To celebrate his side's 4–0 win, he gleefully whacked the ball into his own net. The whistle had in fact come from someone in the crowd: 4–1 to Arsenal, then.

● Denis Law, in front of 59,000 Man Utd fans, scored with a back heel for Man City at the end of the 1973–74 season to give City a 1–0 win and send Man Utd down into the Second Division. Law, who had once been an Old Trafford hero, left the field in tears.

● In the game between Newcastle Utd and Portsmouth in December 1931, there were no corners – the only recorded League game which was cornerless. The final score, not surprisingly, was 0–0.

● In a Premiership game in November 1992 between Nottingham Forest and Southampton, Forest had 22 corners to Saints' two – but they still lost the game 2–1.

● Ricardinho Neves of Brazil juggled a football for 19 hours 5 minutes and 31 seconds to set a world record on 15–16 July 1994.

● A player for the Argentinian club San Lorenzo picked up the ball in a game against Estudiantes, thinking it had gone out of play. It hadn't and the ref awarded a penalty. Estudiantes scored and two players were sent off for manhandling the ref. At the end of the game, the ref was escorted off the pitch by the riot police.

● After a game against Rangers in 1988, a Hearts director was so incensed by the referee that he locked him in his room for 18 minutes, then left the ground with the key. He was later fined £1,000 by the Scottish League.

● That famous all-time scoring stat, known about by all boys for over 120 years, which records that Arbroath beat Bon Accord 36–0 in a Scottish Cup tie on 5 September 1885, hides the fact that, on the very same day, in the same competition, Dundee Harp beat Aberdeen Rovers 35–0.

● The smallest player ever to appear in a League game was Freddy Le May of Thames playing against Watford in Division Three (South) on 1 October 1930. He was only 5ft tall and weighed 7st 10 lbs – though he later shot up to 5ft 2ins and 8 stone.

Opposite **Chelsea's foreign legion at The Dell on Boxing Day 1999. From left to right: Leboeuf, Flo, Poyet and Deschamps.**

● In 1951 Bill Nicholson won the League playing for Tottenham Hotspur. In 1961 Spurs won the League again with him as manager, the first person to do both with the same club.

● On 29 August 1955 Accrington Stanley fielded an all-Scottish-born team against Rochdale: McQueen (goal), Ashe and Harrower (fullbacks), Hunter, Ryden, Sneddon (halfbacks), Scott, Wright, Stewart, Dick and McCredie (forwards).

● On Boxing Day 1999 Chelsea fielded an all-foreign side for the Premiership game at Southampton: De Goey (from Holland), Ferrer (Spain), Babayaro (Nigeria), Deschamps and Leboeuf (France), Thome (Brazil), Petrescu (Romania), Di Matteo (Italy), Flo (Norway), Poyet (Uruguay) and Ambrosetti (Italy). Jody Morris (born in London) came on as substitute.

● In November 2002 Fulham fielded a team of 11 internationals from 11 different countries for their League Cup tie against Bury. The countries represented were Cameroon, Denmark, France, Republic of Ireland, Jamaica, Japan, Latvia, Morocco, Northern Ireland, Scotland and Wales.

Above If you want
to get ahead, get a
cap. Bobby Charlton
pictured in 1970,
when he had won
100 caps for England.

Opposite Melchester
Rovers' star striker
Roy Race spanks it
into the onion bag
once again … Cover
of the 1960 *Roy of
the Rovers* Yearbook.

● A cap has traditionally been awarded to a player who has made an appearance for his national team. Early footballers did actually play in caps, a hangover from their public school days when the colour and design of their cap represented which house they were in, or which school they played for. In 1886 the FA decided that 'all players taking part in future internationals be presented with a white silk cap, with a red rose on the front, these to be termed "international caps"'. These days an England player does not always get an England cap for every England game he plays. When he plays in a tournament, he usually gets one cap to cover all the matches in that tournament.

● 'Addicks' is the nickname for Charlton Athletic. The obvious explanation is that it is a variation on Athletic, but some believe it goes back to the club's foundation in 1905 by some local youths. A local fishmonger agreed to reward them with a free fish supper after every game. If Charlton lost, they got cod. If they won, they got the more expensive haddock, pronounced 'addock' which turned into 'addick'.

● 'Bhoys' is the nickname for Glasgow Celtic. When they were founded in 1888, they were known as the Bold Boys. Because of their Irish Catholic origins, it was decided to try and Irish-ify the spelling and pronunciation, so Boys got turned into Bhoys.

● Yellow and red cards were first used in the World Cup finals of 1970. They were the brainwave of a former English referee, Ken Aston, who had been appointed chairman of FIFA's referees' committee. A controversial incident had recently occurred in an England–Argentina game in which Jack Charlton was cautioned, but only became aware that he had actually been booked when he read the next day's paper. The match referee was German, spoke little English, and had not made it clear that he was booking the player. As Mr Aston was driving his car and waiting for a set of traffic lights to change from red to green, it suddenly occurred to him that holding up a yellow or red card to signify an offence would overcome any language problems.

● The word 'soccer' dates back to the 1880s and the early years of Association Football when it was used to differentiate Association Football from Rugby Football. 'Soccer' is a slightly tortuous shorthand, taken out of the word 'association'. The person credited with coining it was Charles Wreford-Brown who was then a student at Oxford University. When asked one afternoon if he was going to play rugger, he replied 'No, I'm going to play soccer.' There was a fashion at the time for shortening words, and then adding an 'er' to the end, which of course still goes on to this day.

Wreford-Brown later played for England and became an FA vice president. In the United States, association football has always been known as soccer because football, to Americans, refers to American gridiron football.

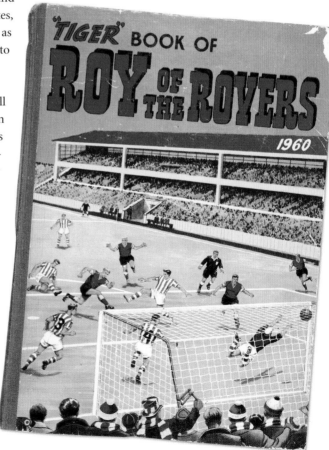

● Roy of the Rovers, a mythical figure still conjured up lovingly by commentators when something unexpected and romantic has happened, such as an unknown player becoming an overnight hero. Roy Race of Melchester Rovers was a fictional character who first appeared in 1954 in a comic called *Tiger* and then later in a comic named after him, *Roy of the Rovers*. He was a handsome, blond, swashbuckling striker who won everything in the game, beating everyone. He was never sent off in over four decades, by which time he had scored 5,000 first-class goals. (Thus beating Dixie Dean by well over 4,000.) His career finished dramatically in 1993 after a helicopter crash. In reality, falling sales killed him off. However, he lives on in the minds of all those who used to enjoy reading about his exploits. In 2007 he was being revived in the pages of a Northern football magazine.

● Billy Meredith played for Man City in an FA Cup semi final in 1924 at the age of 49. City lost. After over 1,000 games for City, Meredith never played for them again.

● In 1974 against Portsmouth, three different Notts County players took the same penalty – and all failed to score. The first was retaken as the ref said the goalie had moved; the second went in but the ref hadn't signalled; the third was saved.

● Stoke City and Burnley in 1898 played possibly the most boring match ever recorded outside Italy. They each needed one point to stay in Div One and managed to finish the game without either team having one shot on goal.

● Len Shackleton was one of the star players of the 1940s and 1950s, known as the 'Clown Prince of Soccer' for his ability to entertain the crowds on and off the pitch. In 1947 he joined Newcastle United from Bradford Park Avenue and on his debut scored six goals. In 1948 he was transferred to Sunderland, for the then record fee of £20,050, and stayed with them for the next 10 seasons. He was adored by the Roker Park crowd and most football fans, but was always suspected by the England selectors of being too much of an individual and not enough of a team player. In consequence, his opinion of the men who ran soccer was always pretty poor. In 1955 Shack published his autobiography *Clown Prince of Soccer*. Chapter Nine was entitled 'The Average Director's Knowledge of Football'. The chapter consisted of only one page – which was left completely blank. The football world was most amused, but not the football directors. The book had been a serious account of his life, apart from that dig at directors, but the following year he did a wholly humorous football book, amongst the first ever written, called *Shack's Guide to Soccer*. In it he took the mickey out of players, directors, football reporters and referees. One of his mischievous suggestions was that in future the numbers on the backs of players' shirts should be in Braille – so that referees could read them better …

Chapter 9

The average director's knowledge of football. *

Left and opposite **Len Shackleton**'s 1955 autobiography was a frank account of this much-loved player's life in soccer. Chapter Nine spoke volumes about what he thought of club directors.

* *Publisher's note:* This chapter has deliberately been left blank in accordance with the author's wishes.

78

Incredible injuries

● In February 2007, Cristiano Ronaldo of Man Utd was substituted in their European Championship game against Lille. He was so furious at being taken off that he kicked a tray of water bottles and injured his foot.

● Dave Beasant, the Wimbledon goalie, missed the start of the 1993–94 season with a foot injury caused when he dropped a bottle of salad cream on the floor.

● Darren Barnard of Barnsley slipped in a pool of urine left by a puppy and was put out of the game for several months with torn knee ligaments.

● Everton's James McFadden once broke a foot playing head tennis.

● Rio Ferdinand, whilst at Leeds, hurt his knee while reaching for the remote control on his TV with his foot up on a coffee table.

● Svein Grondalen of Norway was forced to pull out of an international match after colliding with a moose while jogging.

● Paul Gascoigne, while at Spurs, strained a thigh getting out of bed.

● Thierry Henry in his Arsenal days once hurt himself in the eye with a corner flag while celebrating a goal. (Better take some dance lessons from Roger Milla, Thierry.)

● Paulo Diogo of the Swiss club Servette did even worse self-damage during his goal celebrations. He jumped into the crowd, caught his wedding ring on a fence and tore off the top of his finger. The ref booked him for excessive celebration.

● In the 1970s, Man Utd goalkeeper Alex Stepney dislocated his jaw yelling at his defence.

● In the 1930 World Cup, the USA trainer ran on to treat an injured player. He tripped and broke a bottle of chloroform and was carried off unconscious.

And now for quotable quotes from some of football's great characters…

14. Quotations

Talking a good game

Footballers are not normally known for having a way with words, preferring to stick to clichés and stock replies – and indeed why should they? Their feet should always do the talking, not their mouths. But many soccer sayings and wisdoms have passed into the language, and many famous people have offered their views on football. Footballers themselves can be quick and streetsmart, especially if they are sticking the boot in – metaphorically, of course.

Put-downs

● Beckham can't kick with his left foot. He can't head the ball, can't tackle and doesn't score many goals. Apart from that, he's all right. (George Best, 2000.)

● I was on holiday in Portugal when we signed Bradbury, but I can tell you this – we would definitely, definitely, definitely, definitely not have signed him if I'd seen him play. (Francis Lee, former chairman of Man City, three years after manager Alan Ball had spent £3 million on Lee Bradbury, Man City's record buy.)

● Paolo [di Canio] often storms off the training pitch in the middle of a game if something's not going right. Maybe it's the Italian way, or he's a nutter. (Neil Ruddock.)

● If Stan could pass a betting shop the way he can pass a ball, he'd have no worries whatsoever. (Ernie Tagg, Crewe manager, on Stan Bowles.)

● The oldest 24-year-old I've ever met. He wears pyjamas, slippers, everything your granddad would wear. (Rio Ferdinand on Danny Mills, his then Leeds Utd and England colleague.)

● That David Seaman is a handsome young man but he spends too much time looking in his mirror rather than at the ball. You can't keep goal with hair like that. (Brian Clough on England goalkeeper David Seaman's ponytail.)

● If brains were chocolates, he wouldn't have enough to fill a Smartie. (Alan Birchenall on Robbie Savage.)

Opposite **David Seaman of Arsenal and England sporting the trademark ponytail that incurred Cloughie's displeasure.**

Left **Poetry in motion: Wizard Welsh winger Ryan Giggs floating over the ground for Man Utd.**

● Apart from Oliver Kahn [the German national goalkeeper], if you put all the players in a sack and punched it, whoever you hit would deserve it. (Franz Beckenbauer, former German captain, on Germany's chances in the 2002 World Cup. They got to the final.)

● Emile could probably pick up Gareth Southgate and throw him the length of the pitch, yet he has developed the art of dropping like a sack of spuds whenever he is touched. (John Gregory, Aston Villa manager, on Emile Heskey.)

Build-ups

● I remember when I first saw him, he was 13 and he just floated over the ground like a cocker spaniel chasing a piece of silver paper in the wind. (Sir Alex Ferguson on Ryan Giggs.)

● The worst part is that Gareth is such a nice guy. You never normally hear him utter a single swearword. (David James on Gareth Southgate.)

● The moment I turned up for training and saw Zola, I knew it was time to go. (Scotland striker John Spencer on the Italian's impact on Chelsea, 1997.)

● I went to have a look at him playing for Wealdstone on a stinking night at Yeovil. After eight minutes he put in a thundering tackle and the Yeovil winger landed in my wife's lap. I said to her 'That's it. I've seen enough. We're going home.' (Bobby Gould, remembering how he signed Stuart Pearce for Coventry in 1991.)

Self-aware remarks

● It's not nice going into a supermarket and the woman at the till is thinking, 'Dodgy keeper'. (David James.)

● My addictions are always there, waiting for me. They're doing press-ups outside my door. (Paul Merson on his fight against alcoholism, gambling and drugs.)

● I'm a bit anxious. I think every manager out there hates me. (Robbie Savage.)

Famous quotes

Quotes which keep on being quoted, and often misquoted, so you might as well get them right:

● Martin Peters is a player 10 years ahead of his time. (Alf Ramsey, England manager, 1968.)

Below Descartes, Sartre, Cantona ... One in a line of great French philosophers, Eric the King signs autographs at Old Trafford.

● The great fallacy is that the game is first and foremost about winning. It's nothing of the kind. The game is about glory. It's about doing things in style, with a flourish, about going out and beating the other lot, not waiting for them to die of boredom. (Danny Blanchflower, Spurs captain, 1960s.)

● Football is not art, but there is an art to playing good football. (Rudi Krol, star of Ajax and Holland, 1970s.)

● It's like going to a different country. (Ian Rush, after his transfer from Liverpool to Juventus, 1988.)

● For all his horses, knighthoods, and championships, he hasn't got two of what I've got. And I don't mean balls. (Brian Clough, 1990s, on Sir Alex Ferguson's failure to win successive European Cups.)

● When the seagulls follow the trawler it is because they think sardines will be thrown into the sea. (Eric Cantona, Man Utd, on the media reaction to his kung-fu kick at an abusive fan at Crystal Palace in 1995.)

● Beware of the clever sharp men who are creeping into the game. (William McGregor, 1909, founder of the Football League.)

… plus some of the inanities we all cherish

● Ronaldo bears comparison with the incomparable George Best. (David Pleat, 2007.)

● History doesn't have a history of repeating itself. (John Helm, commenting on a Newcastle United game, Channel 5, 2007.)

● The new West Stand casts a giant shadow over the pitch, even on a sunny day. (London *Evening Standard* report on Arsenal's new Emirates Stadium.)

● Scotland are staring down the barrel of a wooden spoon. (Commentary on Radio 5 Live.)

● Now is the time to draw a line under the sand. (Radio 5.)

● Middlesbrough have turned the tide of the game on its head. (Jonathan Pierce.)

● Most managers would give their right arm for a European Cup and Bob Paisley had three. (Local Liverpool radio station.)

● Scholes walked away a bit gingerly. (Radio 5 on the 2007 Cup final.)

● People need to understand what kind of goldfish Wayne Rooney lives in. (Graham Taylor.)

Literary and other allusions

The good and the great aren't beyond commenting on the people's game:

● Am I so round with you as you with me
   That like a football you do spurn me thus?
   (William Shakespeare, *The Comedy of Errors*, 1590.)

● And life itself is but a game of football. (Sir Walter Scott, 1815.)

● To say that these men paid their shillings to watch 22 hirelings kick a ball is merely to say that a violin is wood made of catgut, that *Hamlet* is so much paper and ink. For a shilling, the Bruddersford United AFC offered you conflict and art. (J. B. Priestley in his novel *The Good Companions*, 1929.)

● All that I know most surely about morality and the obligations of man, I owe to football. (French writer and philosopher, Albert Camus. While studying at the University of Algiers in the 1930s, he played in goal for the university team.)

● Anything you say must be used in Everton against you. (John Lennon *In His Own Write*, 1964.)

● I know more about football than I know about politics. (Harold Wilson, Prime Minister, 1974.)

● I should rather like the 'Match of the Day' theme played at my funeral. (Cardinal Basil Hume, 1986.)

● Five days shalt thou labour, as the Bible says. The Seventh day is the Lord thy God's. The sixth day is for football. (Anthony Burgess).

Period quotes

About players and references long gone, but the point often lingers on …

● Playing Stan is like playing a ghost. (Johnny Carey of Man Utd on Stanley Matthews, 1930s.)

● We play at Wembley Stadium, not the London Palladium. (England selector's reason for not picking the 'Clown Prince' Len Shackleton, 1950s.)

● Joe Jordan strikes quicker than British Leyland. (Scottish banner at Wembley, 1970s.)

● It's just like playing alongside Barbra Streisand. (Mike Summerbee on his Man City colleague, Rodney Marsh, 1973.)

● For those of you watching in black and white, Spurs are in the yellow strip. (John Motson, 1970s.)

● Lord Nelson! Lord Beaverbrook! Sir Winston Churchill! Sir Anthony Eden! Clement Attlee! Henry Cooper! Lady Diana! Maggie Thatcher! Your boys took a hell of a beating! (Norwegian commentator after his country beat England in a 1981 World Cup qualifier.)

● We've lost that Terry Phelan, ohhh-wooh, Terry Phelan. We've lost that Terry Phelan. Now it's Vonk Vonk Vonk … (Man City fans, to the tune of the Walker Brothers, take it out on Michael Vonk after he replaced Terry Phelan in a game.)

● He's fat, he's round, his car is in the pound, Jan Molby! (Rival fans after Liverpool's Jan Molby got into a spot of bother for reckless driving, 1980s.)

● One team in Tallinn, there's only one team in Tallinn. (Scottish fans at a 1996 World Cup qualifier in Estonia. Their team kicked off against no opposition, because Estonia had protested over the kick-off time.)

● You should see his boots. They're like something you hang from your car mirror. (Middlesbrough chairman Steve Gibson on signing the diminutive Brazilian Juninho in 1995.)

● You can spend £2 million and find the player can't trap the ball. (Graham Taylor bemoans the inflated transfer market, 2001.)

● He's fat, he's round, he's never in the ground, Captain Bob! (Oxford United fans on the attendance record of their chairman, Robert Maxwell, 1980s.)

Modern quotes

● I just don't like talking about myself or being talked about. I would rather people talked about something else. It's nice, I suppose, but if I'm honest, I'd rather not be spoken about. (Paul Scholes, Man Utd, 2006. An unusual and refreshingly self-effacing comment from a modern footballer.)

● I will be cremated in the jersey I wore the night I was first made captain of Rangers. I have already decided that I will be clothed in that light blue shirt when they send me to that big dressing room in the sky. Morbid? Maybe, but the truth is that the arrangements for what I wear in my coffin are already made. That's the last will and testament of Barry Ferguson and it has been settled for a while now. (Barry Ferguson, January 2007, just after being relieved of the captaincy after a difference of opinion with the Rangers' manager, Paul Le Guen. Not long afterwards, the manager got the sack and Ferguson returned as captain.)

● There's only one Gordon Ramsay, one Gordon Ramsay! (Chelsea fans when playing Norwich City in the FA Cup, February 2007. Norwich's main shareholder was Delia Smith, a well-known cook.)

Below Happy days at the Manor Ground. Cap'n Bob pours the bubbly in the heady days when Oxford United were in the top flight.

Right **Ending on a high note: in his final season as Liverpool manager in 1974, Bill Shankly saw his side lift the Charity Shield and the FA Cup.**

Opposite **A bronze statue of Shanks reminds the Anfield faithful of their greatest-ever manager.**

The best of Bill Shankly

Bill Shankly, Liverpool manager from 1959 to 1974, was famous not only for his many achievements but also for his sayings and comments. Born in Ayrshire in 1913, he went over the border for his playing career, first at Carlisle United and then Preston North End. Even as a young player in the 1930s, his strong, determined character was noted by the media, as in this paragraph from *Topical Times* on 3 September 1938:

> *Bill Shankly, Preston's international right-half, is one of the fittest and strongest men in the game. He never eases up for a second. In a charity game an opponent said to him – 'Say, Bill, take it easy. This is only a friendly, not a cup-tie.' Bill's reply was – 'Friendly or not, they're all the same to me, sir. When I'm playing football, I'm playing!' That's Bill all over. He can only play one way. Hard all the time!*

In 1949 he went into management back at Carlisle United. After that it was a long, slow struggle in the lower divisions, including spells at Grimsby and Workington. His appointment as Liverpool's manager in 1959 was seen as a slight surprise, though at the time Liverpool were languishing in the Second Division. It wasn't until 1964 that he won his first trophy with Liverpool, the Division One championship. He repeated that triumph in 1966 and 1973 and also won the FA Cup twice.

Shankly laid down the tactics, style of play and conviction which kept Liverpool at the top for over 20 years, making them one of Europe's dominant teams of the 1980s. He also created the 'boot room dynasty', with successive managers being promoted from inside the coaching staff.

Shanks died in 1981. Throughout his lifetime, he was known for his passion and devotion to Liverpool, while his observations on the game of football will live on in Britain as long as the game is being played.

His best-known quotation is often shortened to make it more dramatic, but his original words, in an interview given in 1973, were as follows: 'Some people think football is a matter of life and death. I don't like that attitude. I can assure them it is much more serious than that'.

And here are some more words of wisdom from the great man:

● He belongs in the company of the supremely great, like Shakespeare, Rembrandt and Beethoven. (Shankly honouring the memory of Dixie Dean.)

● Football is a simple game made complicated by people who should know better.

● The trouble with you is that your brains are all in your head. (Shankly to an unnamed Liverpool player.)

● When you play for Scotland you look at the dark blue shirt and the wee lion looks up at you and says: 'Get out there after those English bastards!'.

● He's got a heart the size of a caraway seed. (On a player he sold.)

● The trouble with referees is that they know the rules but they don't know the game.

● I don't drop players. I make changes.

● If a player isn't interfering with play or seeking to gain an advantage, then he should be.

● There are two great teams in this city. Liverpool … and Liverpool reserves.

● Professional footballers should have more sense than to consider marrying during the season. Anybody who does isn't behaving professionally as far as I'm concerned.

● Look, laddie, if you're in the penalty area and aren't quite sure what to do with the ball, just stick it in the net and we'll discuss your options afterwards.

● He's worse than the rain in Manchester. At least the rain in Manchester stops occasionally. (On the loquacious Brian Clough.)

Old Big 'Ead – the genius of Brian Clough

Finally, no section on football quotations would be complete without the wit and wisdom of one of the most gifted and garrulous men ever to have graced the game. Clough was an inspiring manager, taking Nottingham Forest to European Cup glory in successive seasons (1979 and 1980), and had a ready quote for every occasion. Fittingly, he was even responsible for coining his own nickname, quipping that the OBE he had been awarded stood for 'Old Big 'Ead'. He also said 'I call myself Big 'Ead just to remind myself not to be'.

Here, then, are some gems from a man who never knew how it felt to sit on the fence:

- I wouldn't say I was the best manager, but I was in the top one.

- Football hooligans? Well, there are 92 club chairmen for a start.

- I just don't like him. (On the Leeds manager Don Revie, 1970s.)

- A fat dumpy lad who lives out of a frying-pan, but give him a ball and some grass and he becomes Picasso. (On John Robertson, the Nottingham Forest player who scored the goal that defeated Hamburger SV in the 1980 European Cup final.)

- He was a very unattractive young man. If I ever felt off-colour I'd sit next to him because compared with [him] I was Errol Flynn. (Also on John Robertson.)

- The only person certain of making the bus to Wembley is Albert Kershore, because he's driving it. (To his Nottingham Forest players before the 1989 League Cup final.)

- No problem. If he can find a ground where he scored a league goal, I'll meet him there. (Responding to a request from Jimmy Hill for an open debate.)

- He wasn't that big, but he had a huge arse. It came down below his knees, and that's where he got his strength from. (On Kenny Dalglish.)

- Anyone who can do anything more than make a jumper in Leicester has got to be a genius. (On Martin O'Neill, when the latter was manager of Leicester City.)

Next: as Eric Cantona would say, plus ça change . . .

15. Some things never change ...

History repeating itself

Studying old footer programmes, comics, magazines and books, which is a healthy activity for any chap, of any age, and keeps him well out of mischief, you will find the same old moans and complaints being trotted out, the same subjects coming up and the same observations being made.

Referees are idiots and/or blind. Football hooligans should be banned. Too many football clubs are corrupt. Paying footballers all this money will ruin football, it will never be the same again, etc. and, oh, oh, why don't we have the Wizards of Dribble, the Prince of Players, the way we used to have them, men of principle and loyalty, who played fair, didn't cheat, and loved the beautiful game ...

In fact, football today is technically better than it ever was. The players are fitter, more skilful and better trained.

The biggest-ever crowds at English football games came after the last war, when servicemen returned and there were few other attractions. In the 1948–49 season, there was a record total attendance at English League matches of 41 million – a figure that is unlikely to be beaten. It then dropped dramatically and, by the 1980s, it had gone down to 16 million. It was a time when the moaners had a point: that football, as we knew it, would never be the same again. Today, football is on a high once more and the annual attendance in the four English Leagues is around 30 million.

Right One of the football annuals, guides and handbooks that proliferated after the Second World War. Attendances in this period were huge.

Below Arsenal's new home, the Emirates Stadium, has an all-seater capacity of almost 60,500.

Today the Premiership grounds are all-seater and hold fewer than they did in the 1940s, although even that is beginning to change. Old Trafford has got bigger and bigger, now holding 76,000. Arsenal has moved into a larger ground and Liverpool and others aim to follow.

So, while the total gates might not be as high as in ye olden days, there are waiting lists at most Premiership clubs, all seats taken at most games. Millions watch every week on TV. Billions of pounds pour into football every year from commercial sources. An established player in a Premiership club expects to earn one million pounds per year from all sources. By most criteria, football is arguably more popular and more successful than it has ever been.

So, bear all this in mind whenever you hear people harking back to the 'Good Old Days'.

All the same, it is interesting, illuminating and amusing to look back, see where we've come from, and what fans in the past thought and worried about ...

1887 – On refs, rough play and jokers

In a match the other day a forward was watching the ball, which had been kicked off from his own goal, without in any way intending to impede an opponent, when he was violently charged from behind and felled to the ground. No notice was taken of this occurrence by either spectators or players, which shows that a widespread ignorance of the law on this point exists. We hold that such cases are instances of rough play, and referees would be justified in cautioning players indulging in them. Persistent offenders should be ordered out of play.

Another common error is that a player may push with his hands an opponent facing his own goal. As a matter of fact, no player may, under any circumstances, use his hands or arms to push an opponent.

The Hon. Sec. of the Corinthians was lately much surprised on receiving from a correspondent, whose name was unknown to him, a grateful acceptance of an invitation to represent that club in one of its matches. The writer, it was afterwards discovered, had been the victim of some practical joking on the part of some undergrads, who, it is hoped, will not repeat what at the best is but weakly wit.

In a recent Cup tie a referee allowed a goal which was palpably off-side, whereupon several of the claimants said, 'Thank you, sir,' in their sweetest tones, and the referee felt like a philanthropist.

(An excerpt from *Pastime*, 23 November 1887.)

1909 – On women

From the Tottenham Hotspur programme, 23 October 1909:

> We hope we shall not be considered ungallant in making public a complaint sent to us regarding some of our lady patrons. Probably it is one they have heard before if they are in the habit of going to theatres, although it is somewhat rare for it to come from the football field. It appears that owing to the prevailing fashion for wide brims and mountainous trimmings in the matter of head gear, there have been persons in the grand stand who have seen too much of hats and too little of the play, even though the seats are in tiers. We have no doubt that the wearers look very charming in them, but might we tell them in a whisper that there would be less grumbling if they wore their smallest chapeaux on these occasions. We believe the men would even see beauty in a bonnet.

1913 – On deadly rivals

In the Spurs programme of 13 March 1913, the club was clearly very incensed at the prospect of Woolwich Arsenal moving to North London from South London. They and the 'Orientals' – a reference to Leyton Orient – considered Arsenal should stay where they belonged. Arsenal didn't stay, of course, and the rivalry with Spurs has continued to this day:

Woolwich Wanderers

After what occurred at the meeting of the League Management Committee on Saturday, there appears to be little doubt that Woolwich Arsenal will be playing on a ground near Gillespie Road, Highbury, next season. Our Chairman was present at Glasgow, and made out a strong case in conjunction with our Oriental neighbours, against the Arsenal's suggested removal, but the Management Committee declined to interfere. It is idle to contend, as the Committee stated in giving their opinion, that there is ample scope for the Arsenal in a district that is already well catered for by ourselves and the Orient. The presence of another League club within three miles of our enclosure and that of the Orient must have the effect of attracting support that would otherwise be accorded to the clubs who have developed League football in North London, and we consider it very unfair that this competition should be set up. What is difficult to understand is why the Arsenal should come to North London instead of settling in a South London area where there is plenty of room for a first-class club.

Left **March 1914: Arsenal and Fulham battle it out at Highbury, Arsenal's new ground, which had opened only six months previously. The Gunners' move to North London from the Manor Ground in Plumstead was the subject of controversy.**

1907 – Harassed football officials

In a Chelsea programme in 1907, the club is moaning about supporters daring to ring up the club with stupid questions. Or were they just boasting that the club had a 'phone?

What a number of telephone-enquiring 'Supporters' the leading football clubs have, to be sure!

On the morning of every League match the wires must get nearly red-hot – the poor secretaries and their staffs certainly do – with the constant ringing up. 'What time is the kick-off, please?'

After half-an-hour's play the 'ting-a-ling' tattoo re-commences, – 'What is the half-time score, please?'

You are called upon to answer this question twice every minute until nearly full-time, and THEN!!!

Oh, dear! – that blessed bell! For three solid hours this is what goes on:

'Hull-O! Yes, we're the Chelsea Football Club.' 'Can you tell me the result, please?'

'Who are you?' – 'Eh?' – 'What's your name, please?'

'Oh! you wouldn't know my name, I'm a Supporter.'

'Thank you! Who scored? What was the gate? Was it a good game? Anybody hurt?' – Well, there would be if we could only heave a brick along the wire sometimes.

Worst of all are those who, instead of enquiring, 'Are you the Chelsea Football Club?' – requiring a simple 'Yes' in reply, lead off with 'Who are you?' Just as though (having asked for Chelsea Football Club) they expected to be switched on to Harrods Stores or Woking Crematorium.

We begin to understand why the F. A. are not on the telephone. Wise birds!

The funny thing about these enquiries is – they are all 'supporters'. Just that.

Why don't they attend a match occasionally, just for a change, and see for themselves?

Opposite The FA Cup final of 1921, played at Stamford Bridge.

Below Spurs' original 'gallant rooster'. The famous emblem is thought to have its origin in cock-fighting, in which the birds wore spurs.

1921 – Historical notes

In the Spurs handbook of 1921 there was an interesting item on the giant copper cockerel standing on a ball which had perched on the roof of the West Stand since 1909. The article pointed out how much bigger it was than most spectators might realize.

It also said that inside the cockerel were souvenirs of the club's entry into Division One in 1909 and some current coins.

In 1958 the cockerel was moved to the top of the East Stand. In 1989, while the East Stand was being refurbished, the cockerel was cleaned up and opened, just to see what was there. The only item was a very soggy handbook from the 1909 season. No sign of any coins.

Today, the original copper cockerel stands in state within the East Stand executive area. Its two offspring are on the top of the West Stand and the East Stand – but they are only fibreglass replicas.

The gallant rooster that is perched with lofty grace on the highest pinnacle of the grand stand, is considerably more well-proportioned than many of our readers would imagine. The following are the measurements and particulars of the emblem which is made entirely of copper: Height from base to top of bird 9ft 6in., Ball 31in diameter; size of Bird: 5ft. high; 3ft. 6in. from beak to tail; 15in. thick. Contract carried out by F. Braby & Co., Coppersmiths, Euston Road. Actual cost £35. Inside the ball are the souvenirs of the Club's entry into the 1st Division of the Football League in 1909 when the stand was erected; also some current coins. The bird was made and fixed by an old Amateur Spurs player, W. J. Scott, of Edmonton.

1948 – On corruption in football

Almost from the beginning, there were allegations of underhand payments being made in football – so-called amateurs finding a few pound notes stuffed in their boots after a game. Then, when the transfer system started, there were always rumours of various fiddles, illegal payments behind the scenes, middlemen taking a cut, or 'bungs' as we now call them.

In *Picture Post* in November 1948 (opposite) the Labour MP J. P. W. Mallalieu sounded off about the transfer system itself, saying that it was unfair because it allowed the then big boys, who included Arsenal, Chelsea and Manchester United, to buy their way to success at the expense of the less wealthy clubs. So what else is new?

1924 – When countries were female

In the programme for the England–Scotland game at Wembley in 1924, there was a note about the Home Nations. Wales was top, which was interesting in itself, but all four national teams were referred to as 'she' or 'her', something which doesn't happen today:

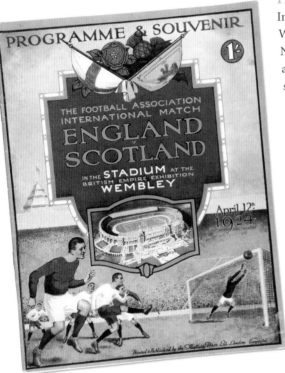

'According to the matches that have been played up to date, and this is the last game of the series, the four nations stand in the following order :

>*Wales*
>*Scotland*
>*Ireland*
>*England.*

Wales, as already stated, has won all her matches.

This afternoon, England is given the opportunity of winning her first game this season, for up to the present, she has not gained a single victory.

On the other hand, Scotland has one win to her credit and, whatever the outcome of this game, cannot be ousted by her rival from the position which she holds in the table.'

1937 – When boots were big ...

'When the Hungarians opposed England at Highbury on 2 December 1936, they wore football boots weighing 1.5 lbs each. The weight of a football boot worn by a British player is 3.5 lbs.'

(From 'Soccer Items in Brief' in the programme for the Scotland v England game at Hampden Park, 1937.)

TRANSFERS: IS THERE CORRUPTION?
by J. P. W. MALLALIEU, M.P.

Professional football has been both a business and a pleasure.
Now dirty business under the transfer system is spoiling some
of the pleasure. This evil, if unchecked, may wreck the game.

1905, THE FIRST £1,000 STAR
Alf Common, bought from Newcastle by
Sunderland for the first four-figure fee.

Millions of people find their greatest happiness each week in watching professional soccer. But not everything is happiness about the game. There were streaks of rottenness about it when it was first organised in 1885. They have widened and deepened with the years. Since the war they have become a serious menace. They are all summed up in the transfer system.

A good sixty years ago, directors of English professional clubs agreed that it was no use trying to treat each other as gentlemen. If one lot, by their own efforts, built a good team, another lot stole it. So clubs which were members of the newly-formed Football League fell back on legislation to protect themselves from each other. Thenceforward a player was to be his Club's property. he could not move to any other League club without his own club's permission: and the 'owning' club had the right to demand cash in exchange. If Preston wanted a Blackburn player, the Preston and Blackburn directors sat down to bargain. Only if Preston agreed to pay what Blackburn asked, and the palyer agreed to move, did he become the property of Preston instead of Blackburn.

That, in essence, is the transfer system. It has good points. A club which finds and develops a star does not now have the fruits of its labour snatched from it without compensation by an unscrupulous rival. Further, it helps struggling clubs to pay their way. Even in the First Division of the Football League there is a wide difference in the incomes of clubs. Arsenal, Chelsea, Aston Villa, Newcastle, the two Manchester clubs, all in densely-populated areas, can normally expect higher 'gates' and therefore higher incomes, than clubs such as Huddersfield or Portsmouth. The difference in income between First Division clubs and the small clubs of the Third Division is even more marked. Sometimes these poorer clubs can only provide stands for their supporters, or wages for their players, by selling a star.

But even when the transfer system is practised strictly according to the rules of the Football League it has serious defects. It still encourages directors and managers to use their cheque books instead of their heads. Between October, 1945, and March, 1948, Newcastle United spent £89,000 on other people's players. In fact, they bought their way back into the First Division and are still spending, or trying to spend, money to stay there.

1954 – Scottish boasts

On the glories of Hampden Park, taken from the Scotland v England programme of 3 April 1954:

Some Facts About Hampden

Newcomers to Hampden – and every year hundreds of football lovers visit the stadium for the first time – would like to have some facts and figures about the great ground of which Glasgow and the whole of Scotland is so proud.

First of all, it is the property of the Queen's Park F.C., Scotland's premier club and the only amateur club now competing in a major British league.

It is the third home of the club, which was founded in 1863, and it was opened in 1904 with a Scottish League match – Queen's Park v. Celtic.

16½ Acres

The stadium occupies 16½ acres and the entire Queen's Park property comprises 33½ acres.

When the ground was extended in 1935 it was measured to accommodate (including passages) 183,000, and was limited to 150,000.

The record crowd was in 1937, at the Scotland–England game, when 149,547 saw the spectacle. In the same year there were 146,433 at the Celtic and Aberdeen Scottish Cup Final.

Nowadays the crowd is limited to 134,000.

900 feet apart

The man standing at the top of the east terracing – that's the higher one – is 60 feet above the pitch, and he is 325 feet from the nearer goal and 685 feet from the west goal. He is also 900 feet from the man at the top of the west terracing.

There are 355 steel barriers keeping the crowd in position.

The south stand accommodates 10,008, and the north stand 4,485.

Crowd control is from the tower at the east end of the Press gallery. You may be able to see the police officers up there. They not only position the crowd inside the ground by means of loud speakers and wireless to officers on the terraces, but they receive a constant stream of messages from the traffic control.

Press facilities

Other towers of the Press gallery are for home and overseas broadcasting, and the towers at the rear of the stand are used by the newspapers for sending pictures by telephoto and by wireless. There are also a number of dark rooms for the photographers.

No other sports ground in the United Kingdom has such complete reporting facilities as Hampden. There are seats for 208 journalists with batteries of telephones and teleprinter equipment.

Opposite In the 1946 Scotland v England fixture at Hampden, watched by 139,468 spectators, the home side ran out 1–0 winners when, as a contemporary Pathé newsreel put it, 'Lady Luck took a last-minute hand.'

SOME THINGS NEVER CHANGE...

1959 and 1967 – When they were young

In April 1959, a young chap named John Motson, then at his public school, wrote a jolly interesting letter to *Charles Buchan's Football Monthly* – and it was published!

> ## Good idea
>
> Why not some new attractions among seasonal representative matches? For instance, why not Division I v. Division II or Division III v. Division IV? On paper, Division I should beat Division II.
>
> But the latter possess more stars than folk realise. There's Johnny Haynes and Graham Leggat, of Fulham, Alan A'Court, of Liverpoool, Brian Clough, of Middlesbrough - all internationals, to name but a few - **JOHN MOTSON - Culford School, Bury St. Edmunds, Suffolk.**
> *Why not, indeed!*

Opposite **Poster boy of the 1950s – Johnny Haynes of Fulham and England endorses a widely used men's grooming product. Decades later, David Beckham also took part in an advertising campaign for Brylcreem.**

In the same magazine, another public schoolboy, the future novelist Sebastian Faulks, had his letter printed in the September 1967 issue – and earned himself three guineas.

> I think it is time someone said something about the idea foreigners hold that all us British are stolid, dull and unemotional. Any of them who hold this view should go along to a League Soccer match. Let him take a look at the wild delight, the crazy explosion of pent-up excitement, the overwhelming joy when the winning goal is scored.
>
> Can this madman, leaping in the air, embracing his neighbours really be British? Yes, and thanks to Soccer for revealing the true character of the English!
>
> **SEBASTIAN C. FAULKS**
> **The Anglesey**
> **Wellington College**
> **Crowthorne, Berks.**
>
> *(This letter wins £3 3s for the prize letter of the month.)*

Who is *this* man of the world? The badge from his blazer is the clue

Men of the World all the World over..

prefer the Perfect Hairdressing

Yes, Brylcreem, with massage, aids the normal flow of sebum, the scalp's natural oil, thus relieving dandruff and dryness. Brylcreem's special emulsion grooms without greasing—and without stiffening the hair. Like world-famous sportsmen, use Brylcreem—it's *all* your hair needs for health and appearance. Tubs 1/10½, 2/10 and 5/-; handy tubes 2/10.

NOT MESSY
NOT GREASY

BRYLCREEM

for every style of hair

A MORAL DILEMMA FOR WAYNE
Part Five

When Wayne got home, he found his parents in a much better mood. His dad had seen all the game while his mother had been delayed but had managed to see the second half. They were both very pleased by Wayne's performance, but commiserated with him on losing.

'I've got a surprise for you,' said his mother, going into the kitchen.

'Spaghetti bolognese?' asked Wayne, but not with much enthusiasm. 'I don't actually feel very hungry, mum. In fact I feel a bit sick. Everything's going wrong. Not just getting beat. United won't have me now because I played for the school …'

'Who says they won't?' said his mother, reappearing from the kitchen, holding up an envelope.

'You didn't post it?' exclaimed Wayne. 'You said you did …'

'Your stupid dad didn't post it,' said his mother. 'All his fault. I left it for him to post that day when he woke up, as I was rushing for work. He went straight to the bookie and left it there …'

'Not my fault,' said Wayne's dad. 'Must have fallen out …'

'And I suspect he didn't want to post it anyway. He was hanging on for one of the scouts to make him some stupid offer, which I'm sure they wouldn't have done anyway. Pure greed, if you ask me.'

'No, no, I was only thinking of Wayne's good …'

'Pull the other,' said his mother. 'I had to grub around at the horrible bookie's before I found the envelope, lying behind a stool in a corner. Anyway,' continued his mother, 'it's just as well they haven't got your signed form yet. But it just means in future, from now on, you can't play for Brookpark …'

'The season's over anyway,' said Wayne's dad, a sudden thought striking him. 'You did sign the form before you played for the school. Let's hope they won't worry about that.'

'Right,' said his mother. 'Let's you and me go to the main post office now in Kentish Town. We'll post it together and they'll get it first thing tomorrow.

W ayne, accompanied by his father,
arrived for his first day of training
at United's training ground the following
Tuesday. Before he had got stripped off,
he was told he had to go and see
Mr Docherty, the Academy Director,
at once, in his office, along with
his father.

Neither of them had actually
seen Mr Docherty before and
wondered whether to call him
Gaffer or Boss, as they did on
the back pages of the newspapers, or perhaps Director.

'What took you so long, Wayne?'
asked Mr Docherty.

'Sorry,' said Wayne. 'My dad's car's
a bit beat up and he can't go very fast
in it …'

'I mean signing the form,' said Mr
Docherty. 'I was beginning to think a bit of
tapping-up might be going on, talking to
other scouts, after you had agreed to sign
for us.'

Wayne's father started to edge in his
chair and look decidedly uncomfortable but
said nothing.

'But I know the post is pretty dodgy
these days,' said Mr Docherty. 'So not to
worry. It got here in the end. The only thing

is, you haven't dated it. You must have
forgotten. Just put today's date on, that'll
keep things neat.'

Wayne signed the date, in his best
joined-up handwriting.

'I gather you were Man of the Match on
Saturday,' said Mr Docherty. 'Well done, but
shame about the score.'

'Was you there?' asked Wayne's dad.

'No, but our scout was – and a few
others, I gather. You do understand from

now on we don't allow Academy scholars to play for their school? And of course you aren't allowed to talk to other scouts.' (The latter remark appeared to be aimed at Wayne's father.)

'Oh, yes,' said Wayne and his father together.

'Now, go and get stripped off,' said Mr Docherty. 'You were Man of the Match on Saturday. Let's see if you can win the Yellow Bib.'

'Yes, sir,' said Wayne, not knowing what on earth the Yellow Bib could be.

In the corridor, on the way to the dressing rooms, Wayne asked his dad what the Yellow Bib was. ('How do I know,' replied his dad.)

On Thursday, at the end of his first week of training, Wayne found out what it meant. Each week, it was awarded by all the coaches to the person in each year they considered had tried hardest and done his best in training.

'Wayne, you've started as a winner,' said Mr Docherty. 'And you've also been very lucky.'

'Oh, yeah,' said Wayne, feeling slightly peeved. He considered he had worked very hard, trained all his life, always done his best, so he didn't quite see what luck had to do with it.

'You're lucky in that this Saturday, before the first team's home game against Man Utd, we're going to make a presentation to all the Academy boys who've won a Yellow Bib this week. They're trying to give the Academy a bit more publicity, and also of course encourage everyone to do their very best …'

'Oh, that's brilliant, Mr Docherty,' said Wayne.

'Now all you have to do is keep it up …'

Will Wayne succeed? In seven years' time, will he have made it through the ranks of United's Academy to become a professional? In eight years' time, will we see his name in United's first team? In 10 years, will he be playing for England? Remember, you read his name here first …

Index

Redknapp, Jamie 18
Revie, Don
  all-time win record 194
  first game 195
  first seven games 196
Robson, Bobby
  all-time win record 194
  first game 195
  first seven games 196
Rochdale, club mascot 155
Rooney, Wayne 74
  ball boy 23
  story of 14–18
Rous, Stanley 103
Rowley, Arthur, highest goal
  scorer 197
Roy of the Rovers 253
rules of football, quiz 150–1
Rush, Ian, famous quotation
  260

S
Savage, Robbie, quotation
  about 258
Schmeichel, Peter,
  superstitions 134, 137
Scholes, Paul, quotation
  by 263
Scottish Football Museum
  185
Scunthorpe, club mascot
  155
Seaman, David, quotation
  about 258
seat prices in Premiership
  63
Seeburg, Max, first German
  in English League 207
Shackleton, Len
  autobiography 254
  famous quotation about
    262
shamateurism 39
Shankly, Bill 25, 157, 159
  legend and quotations
    264–5
Sheffield Club rules 35
Sheffield FC, world's first
  football club 207
Sheffield United
  basic facts 59
  club mascot 154
  foreign players 204
  most expensive
    programme at auction 170
Sheffield Wednesday
  basic facts 59
  club mascot 154
Shilton, Peter, first to play

1,000 League games 207
shirts, players'
  collecting 176–7
  replica 176
soccer camps, in USA 21
soccer, origins of word 253
Southampton, basic facts 59
Southend United, club
  mascot 155
Southgate, Gareth,
  quotation about 259
Sprake, Gary, own goal 249
Springett, Ron, 1966 squad
  details 85
Spurs, *see* Tottenham
  Hotspur
stamps, collecting 177–8
Stein, Jock, first manager
  of the year 206
Stiles, Nobby, 1966 squad
  details 86
Stockport County, club
  mascot 155
Stoke City
  basic facts 62
  founding member of
    Football League 42
Subbuteo 178–9
Sunderland
  basic facts 62
  club mascot 154
superstitions 134–7
Swansea, club mascot 154
Swift, Frank, profile 217
Swindon Town, club mascot
  155

T
Taylor, Graham
  all-time win record 194
  first game 195
  first seven games 196
  inane quotation 261
Taylor-Fletcher, Gary, scorer
  of 500,000th League goal 197
televised game, first 206
Thames, short-lived League
  team 246
three halves, game of 246
tickets, collecting 176
Torquay United, club
  mascot 155
Tottenham Hotspur
  basic facts 62
  club mascot 155
  foreign players 204
  history of cockerel on
    roof 273
  most expensive

programme at auction 170
  on Arsenal's move
    north of river 271
  popularity among
    children 23
  programme cartoons
    232–3
Town, twelve teams called
  202
Townley, William, first
  hat-trick 206
toys, football 178
Tranmere Rovers, club
  mascot 155
transfers
  corruption in 275
  fees, records 199–201

U
United, thirteen teams
  called 202
Uruguay
  first commemorative
    stamps 177
  first World Cup winners
    97

V
Venables, Terry
  all-time win record 194
  first game 195
  first seven games 196
Volz, Moritz, scorer of
  Premiership's 15,000th
  goal 198

W
Waddle, Chris, 'musician'
  166
WAGs 121
Walsall, club mascot 155
Wanderers, three teams
  called 202
Watford
  basic facts 66
  club mascot 155
  foreign players 205
  museum 187
Welsh football collection, in
  Wrexham County Borough
  Museum 187
Wembley
  new stadium 113–6
  White Horse final 102–3
West Bromwich Albion
  basic facts 66
  club mascot 155

first 100-page
    programme 173
  founding member of
    Football League 42
West Ham United
  basic facts 66
  club mascot 155
  1923 Cup Final players,
    79–81
  club museum 186
  foreign players 205
  popularity among
    children 23
Wharton, Arthur, first black
  professional 206
whistles, first 41
Wigan Athletic
  basic facts 66
  club mascot 155
  foreign players 205
Wilson, George, profile 214
Wilson, Harold, famous
  quotation 262
Wilson, Ray, 1966 squad
  details 86
Winterbottom, Walter
  all-time win record 194
  first game 195
  first seven games 196
Wolverhampton Wanderers
  basic facts 66
  club mascot 155
  founding member
    of Football League 42
women, need for smaller
  hats 270
women's football 100–2
  FA ban on 102
World Cup
  best final (1970) 112
  England defeat Germany
    in 2001 qualifier 112
  England win 110, 112
  first 98–9
  leading goalscorers 99
  table of results 98
Wycombe Wanderers,
  club mascot 155

Y
yearbooks, collecting 180–1
Yeovil,
  club mascot 155
  sloping pitch 131

Z
Zidane, Zinedine, record
  transfer fee 201

Picture credits

The following images are from Hunter Davies' football memorabilia collection:
Pages 15, 16, 21, 24, 27, 28 (top and bottom), 29, 31, 34, 35 (top and bottom), 37, 38, 39, 40, 42, 43, 44, 48 (r/h image), 50, 51 (r/h image), 56, 58, 60, 62, 69, 70 (both), 71 (both), 72 (r/h image), 74, 76, 101, 102, 106, 107, 110, 111, 119 (top left), 129, 144, 150–51, 156, 157 (bottom left), 159, 163, 166 (both), 167, 168, 169, 170, 171, 172, 174, 175, 176, 177 (bottom right), 178 (both), 179, 180 (all), 181, 183, 184 (both), 186 (both), 187 (both images), 194 (both), 199, 202, 206, 211, 212, 213, 214, 215 (except heads), 217, 220, 230, 231, 232, 233, 234, 235, 236, 237, 238, 239, 240, 241, 244–45, 253, 254, 255, 269, 273, 274 (both), 275, 276, 279.

Images on the following pages are from agencies:
Pages 11, 12, 19, 22, 30, 51 (b/w image), 54, 55, 72 (top left), 73, 87, 98, 114/115, 123, 125, 133, 161, 201, 203, 222, 243, 259 © Corbis.

Pages 13, 20, 23, 41, 45, 46, 48 (Ferguson), 52/53, 59 (Clough), 61, 63, 64, 65, 68, 75, 77, 78, 79, 80, 83, 84, 88, 89, 95, 96, 99, 100, 104/105, 109, 113, 117, 118, 119 (bottom right), 120, 122, 124, 126, 128, 130, 135, 136, 137, 147 (all of top and bottom rows), 148, 149, 152, 153, 154, 157 (top right), 158, 160, 177 (top), 182, 185, 193, 195, 196, 197, 198, 200, 205, 207, 209, 215 (heads only), 216, 219, 223, 246, 247, 248, 249, 250, 252, 257, 258, 260, 262, 263, 264, 265, 266, 267, 268, 271, 272 © Getty.

Illustrations on pages 91, 92/93, 139, 140/141, 189, 190, 225, 226/227, 281, 282 © Juliet Breese.

In particular, thanks are due to the following for their kind permission in using the specified material:
Page 15: Wayne Rooney for use of the signed photo; Page 16: Wayne Rooney and HarperCollins, publishers of *Wayne Rooney, My Story So Far*, 2006; Page 218: *Sunday Times* and *My Life in Football*, by Hunter Davies, published by Mainstream 1990, for the George Best interview; Page 221: IPC Media and *Studs*, published by Ebury Press, 2006 for the Sam Allardyce interview from *Shoot* magazine; Page 222: Headline, publisher of *Gazza: My Story*, 2004, and Paul Gascoigne, for Gazza's list; Page 223: *FourFourTwo* magazine for the Peter Reid interview; Page 240: Cartoons from *Best of Charles Buchan's Football Monthly*, © copyright Football Monthly, Ltd

While every effort has been made to credit the source of materials used in this book and to discover any existing copyright holders, the author and publishers apologize if any have been missed.

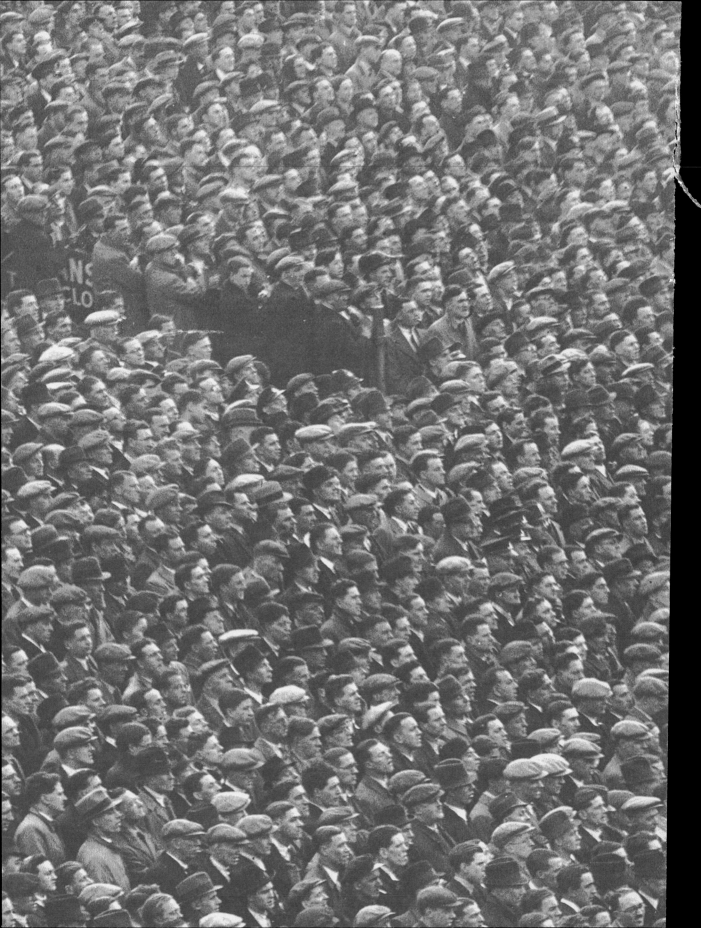